THE LONDON STAGE
1700-1729

A Critical Introduction

THE
LONDON STAGE

1700 - 1729

A Critical Introduction

BY

Emmett L. Avery

SOUTHERN ILLINOIS UNIVERSITY PRESS
CARBONDALE AND EDWARDSVILLE

FEFFER & SIMONS, INC.
LONDON AND AMSTERDAM

FOREWORD

THE LONDON STAGE, 1660–1800, now completed in eleven volumes, has resulted from a co-operative scholarly venture lasting for thirty-three years. The five authors have called upon aid from dozens of specialists in the field, and from the staffs of many a library to compile the day-by-day account of what went on upon the London stage, including the booths at fairs and the opera houses, for a hundred-and-forty-year period. Each has acknowledged his debt in the Preface to his own part.

The basic compilation provides the reader with factual and revisitable evidence in strict chronological order as to dates, plays, casts, facilities, scenes, costumes, theatrical management, specialty acts, music, dance, box receipts, and hundreds of illuminating items from contemporary comments in letters, journals, diaries, pamphlets, periodicals, and newspapers. The headnotes to each year tell of the composition of the acting companies, summarize forthcoming theatrical events, and suggest trends and novelties as well as the proportions of tragedy, comedy, history, and musicals to be presented.

Since the eleven-volume reference work may be too massive for individuals to possess, the authors now make available, in this series of five paperbacks, their Critical Introductions to each part. These are both factual and interpretive. Interpretations of identical basic material will, of course, vary as the years go on and as each up-coming stage historian brings to bear upon it his own predilections and interests. The authors, however, planned from the beginning to give the results of their own insights gained from searching out the details, organizing the facts, and living with the fragments of evidence for over a quarter of a century apiece.

Dr. Van Lennep, who undertook the difficult period embraced in Part 1, died before it was completed. The Critical Introduction for that period was prepared by professors Avery and Scouten, who were helping him with the calendar of events for the Restoration era.

The authors hope that these introductions will serve all readers interested in stage history. Each volume deals fully with theatrical events recorded in the blocks of time indicated. Together they tell the cumulative story of a flow of activities dominated by the manager-actor-dramatists who characterized each period—Davenant and Betterton, Cibber, Fielding and Rich, Garrick, and Sheridan and Kemble. All readers are referred for details to the full documentation presented in the complete calendar.

G. W. S., Jr.

New York University
21 April 1968

CONTENTS

INTRODUCTION

THE LONDON STAGE

1700-1729

I T HAS OFTEN been argued that the essence of history is a distillation of local history. Without a detailed account of what happened here, there, and anywhere, we cannot successfully trace to the full the larger scheme of events. So it is with theatrical annals. Without a detailed knowledge of daily performances in the London theatres, we can hardly arrive at proper judgments upon the broad trends of English drama, the reputation of individual plays and of authors, and the contribution of such other arts as dance and music to dramatic offerings.

Although the first thirty years of the eighteenth century are not the most extraordinary in the annals of London theatricals, they possess an excitement and importance of their own. They saw the introduction of Italian and ballad opera into English playhouses. They gave us the best works of George Frederic Handel; they gave us *The Beggar's Opera*. They witnessed a change from the practice of Restoration times, which generally offered a single play as the entertainment of the evening, to the typical programs of the 1720's involving a full-length drama, with *entr'acte* entertainments of song and dance, followed by an afterpiece, often a farce or pantomime or short ballad opera. These seasons also record the end, in 1714, of a theatrical monopoly by a single company; thereafter, London always had at least two theatres competing during the winter months. During these years the stage and its clerical opponents continued the engagement initiated by Jeremy Collier in 1698 by an assault upon the alleged profaneness of English drama; and a struggle between freedom of the stage and legal or moral controls persisted until Parliament enacted the Licensing Act in 1737.

This introductory essay is concerned, in part, with some of these developments in the London playhouses, but is much more concerned with the theatres as show business. Many previous studies have dealt with the nature of the drama written in this period, as well as with histories of the vogue and reception of plays, but far less attention has been paid to the management, finances, operations, and practices of the houses devoted to drama and opera. Since the following calendar is a record of what happened each day in the theatres, the present introduction attempts to give a general view of the operations of the playhouses as producers of entertainment. It will be useful first, however, to examine briefly some of the distinctive patterns which management and the public—sometimes with obvious design, often by the drift that characterizes many of man's efforts to entertain himself—created during these thirty years.

To a constant reader of early eighteenth-century theatrical advertisements, probably the most striking characteristic of these thirty years is the growing emphasis upon variety. The typical season had a formula that seldom varied: a playhouse opened with a daily change of play until a considerable number of stock plays had been presented once or twice, after which the management repeated, with variations, the cycle of the basic repertory but mingled with the old plays a number of new productions, whose authors hoped for a run of at least three performances (in order to secure a dramatist's benefit), preferably six or nine (for further benefits), and a somewhat larger number of newly revived plays which had been inactive for three, five, ten, or even twenty years.

Within this pattern the management more and more frequently offered the spectator a broadening range of entertainment. The typical evening had its own diversity. Before the curtain rose, the orchestra played three compositions (overtures, sonatas), commonly known as the First, Second, and Third Music. A player stepped forth to speak a Prologue. After the first act of a five-act play, a song, dance, or piece of music (or possibly all three) filled the interval, and between the successive acts other skits, songs, dances, and music, most of which bore no essential relation to the theme of the drama, entertained the spectators. For example, between the second and third acts of *Hamlet*, Francis Nivelon might offer one of his specialties, the "Running Footman's Dance." The play concluded with an Epilogue. The program might also include an afterpiece, perhaps with its own Prologue and Epilogue. If it had more than a single act, it might have its own *entr'acte* entertainments.

Within this framework, the legitimate houses gradually transformed their offerings from straight drama to a medley of entertainments. The basic pattern of an evening's program remained essentially the same year after year, but the total offerings had great variety. In a season a theatre presented forty to seventy-five different plays, some old, some new; the songs and dances ranged from serious to comic, satiric to sentimental, classical to contemporary; new prologues and epilogues joined the oft-repeated ones. The management often stressed the novelty of an actor, singer, or dancer "who never appeared upon any stage before." The new mingled with the old in a constant search for freshness, variety, and vitality.

A similar trend toward variety appeared in the range of entertainments offered everywhere in London. In the first decade, when Italian opera appeared, the managements tried operas sung wholly in Italian, others in which Italian and English singers sang in their respective languages, and still others wholly in English. In the 1720's Lincoln's Inn Fields reintroduced some of the more popular Italian operas in new English versions. The opera houses also added *entr'acte* entertainments to their programs. In the third decade several Italian and French companies appeared in London, sometimes in competition with the English companies, sometimes within the patent houses as part of their repertories. Occasionally the managements added processions or elaborate ceremonial scenes to old plays to give them a fresh appeal. In the 1720's pantomime became the rage, and choreographers searched mythology and *commedia dell'arte* themes for plots and themes for these spectacles. Late in the third decade ballad opera entered the repertory. To make both old and new appeal to the audience, the managers gave greater care to the design of new scenery, the invention of machinery and stage props for pantomime and spectacles, and the fashioning of new costumes in the staging of new plays and, frequently, the revival of inactive ones.

Implicit in the emphasis upon variety was a willingness to experiment. The repertory system of this period could easily have led to staleness, to the "same dull round of plays," as an occasional critic emphasized. The theatres did not, however, follow a rigid formula. In the opening years of the century, for example, the managers experimented broadly with various means of supplementing the main play of the evening. In the first decade, also, the theatres tried various means of most satisfactorily fitting Italian opera and English plays into the seasonal offerings. Sometimes both opera and plays appeared in a single theatre under the same management; at times they were given in different theatres under separate management; occasionally one playhouse offered both operas and plays while its competitor acted only drama.

In management and operational organization, as will be pointed out more fully later, the early decades tried several approaches. At the opening of the century, one house had an actor-manager, the other a patentee, as the head. Later, Drury Lane had a successful management under three actors with equal powers. After several experiments with the problems of opera, its supporters formed the Royal Academy of Music to administer its fiscal and artistic affairs. In other matters management experimented until it reached a satisfactory mode of operations. In the first decade, for example, it wavered as to the best curtain time: five o'clock, five-thirty, six? Eventually London decided that six o'clock best suited the wishes of the spectators, and for many years curtain time stayed at that hour. The production of such elaborate afterpieces as pantomime created a problem in admission charges. The managers insisted that the greater expense of these spectacles warranted higher fees; many spectators, however, resented the increase, especially those who considered pantomime an affront to good taste. How should these complaints be met? Finally, management solved the problem by announcing that anyone leaving before the overture to the pantomime could have a refund of the extra charge.

Occasionally a desire arose for freedom to experiment within the confines of the typical theatrical schedule. For example, a letter to *Mist's Weekly Journal*, 20 November 1725, proposed a system of subscriptions for new plays to make certain that both theatre and dramatist received ample rewards from an assured financial backing. The writer argued that surely four hundred individuals would subscribe a half guinea on condition that a fine new comedy or tragedy be acted in the following season. Each subscriber would receive a box ticket and a copy of the printed play; the drama would be acted at least three times. From the subscription the treasurer would receive four shillings, the dramatist the rest; thus, management would be certain of at least £30 in the boxes for three nights, and the poet would have a guaranteed return instead of relying upon the uncertainty of benefits.

During this period Aaron Hill planned the most elaborate experiment in the interests of good theatre, although circumstances prevented his carrying out his plans. The *Daily Journal*, 21 December 1721, announced his program. He would be sole manager and director of a company at the Haymarket. The scenes had been "contriv'd after a Fashion entirely new, the Habits ... all new; the principal Characters of the Men, and all the Womens Characters, will be play'd by Persons who never appear'd upon the Stage before." Hopefully, Hill announced that the "chief End and

Design of this Theatre is the regulation of the Stage, and the Benefit and Encouragement of Authors, whose Works very often, tho' good, are despis'd and set aside." Unforeseen difficulties in securing a lease of the theatre caused Hill to abandon these plans, but he and others occasionally sought means of staging better plays with more artistic success than, in their opinion, the commercial theatres offered.

Expansion, experimentation, and variety required more money, more emphasis on business operations, more careful fiscal planning. We do not know the financial status of the theatres at the beginning of the century, but in the 1720's Lincoln's Inn Fields required a budget of approximately £10,000 yearly. Occasionally the opera house expended more than that for a much shorter season. By 1734 operations had expanded to the point where, writing on 2 November to Henry Fox, Lord Hervey reported J. J. Heidegger's estimate that two opera houses, one for foreign comedians, and three English theatres called for a minimum of £76,000 yearly before the managers could expect to show a profit.[1]

If one makes a conservative estimate of £7,500 as the cost of operating one theatre before 1714, one might expect that theatrical business between 1700 and 1714 entailed expenditures of between £125,000 and £150,000. From 1714 to 1729 the combined operations of Drury Lane and Lincoln's Inn Fields came to more than £20,000 yearly, a total of £300,000. The Royal Academy of Music probably spent a minimum of £75,000 during the same years, and a modest estimate of £25,000 for the Haymarket and lesser theatrical enterprises would raise the total for the seasons from 1700–1701 through 1728–29 to between £525,000 and £600,000. And these figures would not include the amounts spent on such other forms of entertainments as the Fairs, concerts, and theatricals in Greenwich and Richmond.

[1] *Lord Hervey and his Friends*, ed. The Earl of Ilchester (London, 1950), p. 211.

The Playhouses: Location and Description

WITH the restoration of the monarchy in 1660 and the consequent relaxing of Commonwealth prohibitions against theatrical enterprises, London began a period of extensive building and remodeling of playhouses. Between 1660 and 1700 several new ones were constructed; some of these burned, and others proved unsatisfactory.[2] By 1700 only three theatres remained normally in use: Lincoln's Inn Fields, Dorset Garden, and Drury Lane. Within ten years, two of these were abandoned, leaving only Drury Lane actively engaged in dramatic presentations.

The first three decades of the new century witnessed the building of several new theatres. In 1705 John Vanbrugh completed the Queen's Theatre in the Haymarket, which first housed plays but later became more useful for opera. In 1714 John Rich opened a new Lincoln's Inn Fields on the site of the earlier one. Six years later John Potter constructed a small house in the Haymarket, sometimes known as the Little Haymarket or the French Theatre, to distinguish it from Vanbrugh's more imposing structure. Playhouses arose on the periphery of London; most of these, particularly playhouses in Greenwich, Hampton Court, and Richmond, for many years kept close links with the London companies.

This gradual increase in the number of theatres in operation contrasted greatly with the control which during the Restoration had limited London to two patent houses, sometimes to only one. The Little Haymarket became a center for amateur or foreign performers; the Queen's (known as the King's after George I came to the throne) specialized in opera; whereas Drury Lane and Lincoln's Inn Fields supported two companies devoted to repertories of old and new English drama. In addition, several "Great Rooms," booths, and temporary establishments provided stages for occasional performances of plays; and a host of rooms catered to the early century enthusiasm for concerts, in which vocalists and instrumentalists from the opera companies as well as from the regular theatres performed.

[2] For an account of Restoration playhouses, see Leslie Hotson, *The Commonwealth and Restoration Stage* (Cambridge, Mass., 1928), and Allardyce Nicoll, *Restoration Drama, 1660–1700*, 4th ed. (Cambridge, 1952).

In the pages immediately following, the history, capacity, legal problems, and accommodations of the early eighteenth-century theatres are discussed. They appear in the order of their construction or opening, some of the lesser ones being grouped together. In the subsequent calendar of daily performances, the locations and other identifying features of the less important halls are given when they first appear.

LINCOLN'S INN FIELDS I: 1661–1708

The first playhouse in Lincoln's Inn Fields, which had been opened in 1661 and which had passed into the hands of a series of companies in later years, was occupied by Thomas Betterton and his associates when the new century opened.[3] It was a relatively small theatre,[4] and, according to the advertisements in 1703–4, it had, to supplement the usual boxes and pit, only a single gallery, whereas most of the larger theatres constructed in the eighteenth century contained two galleries.

Betterton's company played there until John Vanbrugh had completed the Queen's Theatre in the Haymarket. Welcoming the opportunity to act in a larger house, the players in 1705 moved into this magnificent structure. Although Lincoln's Inn Fields was reopened in the summer of 1705 for a few performances, it was not used thereafter for theatrical offerings. In the *Daily Courant* 7 September 1708 the building was advertised to be let for a tennis court or for any other nontheatrical purpose. Not until 1714, when Christopher Rich planned a new theatre there, did the site again assume importance to London's actors and playgoers.

DORSET GARDEN: 1671–1709

The playhouse in Dorset Garden, which had opened in 1671 and which had come under the same management as that of Drury Lane, occasionally offered operas and concerts after the opening of the eighteenth century but rarely presented plays. In 1703, however, it gave promise of being reopened, for on 13 May 1703 the *Daily Courant* announced that it was

3 See Hotson, *Commonwealth and Restoration Stage*, pp. 120–26.
4 For discussions of the theatre's merits and inadequacies, see Colley Cibber, *Apology*, ed. R. W. Lowe (London, 1888), I, 314; and *A Comparison Between the Two Stages* [1702], ed. S. B. Wells (Princeton, 1942), p. 22.

being fitted with new scenes for a new opera; but nothing came immediately of this plan. On 27 November 1704 the same journal reported that, after being damaged by winds, Dorset Garden had been repaired and would open on 6 December 1704 with Cibber's new play, *The Careless Husband.* On that date, however, a brief announcement stated that, because of inclement weather, acting at Dorset Garden would be deferred.

It did not reopen until the summer of 1706, when it presented Italian operas (*Arsinoe* and *Camilla*). In the following autumn the Drury Lane company played there, offering both operas and plays; but in December 1706 the company returned to Drury Lane and thereafter Dorset Garden was rarely occupied. On 1 June 1709 the *Daily Courant* reported that the playhouse "at Dorset-Stairs is now pulling down."

DRURY LANE: 1674–

The theatre in Drury Lane which Londoners patronized at the opening of the eighteenth century was the second in the historic line bearing the most famous name in English theatrical annals. According to Cibber,[5] Drury Lane was a model theatre, a point he emphasized when he discussed the less satisfactory acoustics of the Queen's Haymarket, even though by 1700 the original excellence of Drury Lane had been modified by remodeling to increase the capacity of the pit and boxes. To make this change, Christopher Rich had shortened the forward portion of the stage, thus enlarging the pit, and had narrowed the stage by adding boxes at the sides. One result of these changes was that the actors were forced about ten feet farther back from the auditors in the pit.

Unfortunately, no detailed account remains which clarifies the capacity of Drury Lane after these alterations, although fragmentary evidence appears in the bills in the *Daily Courant*. According to an advertisement for 23 January 1703 the management for that night put the pit and boxes together and sold tickets, not to exceed 400, for the combined sections. The same figure appeared on 1 and 11 February 1703, except that on 11 February the announcement specified 100 tickets for the front boxes, 300 for pit and side boxes. An announcement of a subscription for *Rosamond* on 22 March 1707 referred to "the two Side Boxes," implying the existence of only two, and the Drury Lane expense vouchers (Folger Shakespeare Library) state that in November 1714 each of the "double boxes" held 20 persons. Drury

5 *Apology*, II, 80–81.

Lane, then, may possibly have held no more than 100 in the front boxes, 40 in the side boxes, and 260 in the pit.

If the pit and boxes accommodated 400 persons and if the galleries held no more than 263 spectators, the number present on 26 December 1677,[6] there would be a minimum capacity of 663 auditors. No doubt the maximum was greater, since the managers occasionally allowed spectators to sit or stand on the stage and, in all probability, the galleries held more than the 263 individuals present on a single night in 1677. In addition, the capacity of the pit could always be increased by crowding more persons onto the benches.

To these cold figures may be added a more colorful account of the interior of Drury Lane. Writing many years later, Thomas Davies drew a vignette of life backstage as he remembered it from earlier years:

There is a little open room, in Drury-lane theatre, called the settle; it is separated from the stage and the scene-room by a wainscot inclosure. It was formerly, before the great green room was built, a place for many of the actors to retire to, between the acts, during the time of action and rehearsal. From time out of mind, till about the year 1740, to this place a pretty large number of the comedians used to resort constantly after dinner, which, at that time, was generally over at two o'clock. Here they talked over the news and politics of the day, though, indeed, they were no great politicians; for players are generally king's men. Here they cracked their jokes, indulged in little sallies of pleasantry, and laughed, in good humour, at their mutual follies and adventures.—Kings, footmen, aldermen, cardinals, coblers, princes, judges, link-boys, and fine gentlemen, in short all characters, were mingled together; and, from this chaos of confusion, arose a harmony of mirth, which contributed not a little to reconcile them to their various situations in the theatre.[7]

Not a great deal is known concerning the physical beauties of the theatre, although the author of *A Critical Review of the Public Buildings* (1734) thought that Drury Lane did not have a frontage which would "require grandeur or magnificence." He added that its interior seemed "to be best calculated for the convenience of the speaker and hearer," with the exception that "the division in the middle" (referring, possibly, to the "middle gallery box") was an absurdity and that the "decorations on the stage" left something to be desired.

After Christopher Rich lost control of Drury Lane on 5 March 1707, when he was silenced by the Lord Chamberlain[8] for disobeying an order

6 See the *Theatrical Inquisitor and Monthly Mirror*, July 1816, pp. 25–26; and Montague Summers, *The Restoration Theatre* (New York, 1934), pp. 64–65.

7 *Dramatic Miscellanies* (Dublin, 1784), III, 273–74.

8 See Allardyce Nicoll, *Early Eighteenth-Century Drama*, 3rd ed. (Cambridge, 1952), p. 282.

not to let George Powell appear on his stage, the theatre passed through a series of managers during a period of rivalry between it and the Queen's and through some adjustments after Italian opera appeared on the London scene. Out of this turmoil eventually came a long and relatively stable administration by the actor-managers (in various combinations including Dogget, Cibber, Wilks, Booth, and Estcourt) which lasted, with general prosperity, into the 1730's.

QUEEN'S (KING'S) HAYMARKET: 1705–

The Queen's Theatre in the Haymarket (known as the King's after the accession of George I) was the first playhouse constructed in the eighteenth century. In its emphasis upon size and elaborate design, it set a pattern followed in the building of Covent Garden in the 1730's and the continued enlargement of Drury Lane throughout the century. Although intended for drama, its acoustics proved somewhat unsatisfactory for the voices of actors. Better suited to song, it eventually became the opera house.

The plan and construction were essentially the work of John Vanbrugh, who on 15 June 1703 wrote to Jacob Tonson that he had completed the purchases involved in his project, that the tenants would be out by Midsummer Day, and that he hoped to open the theatre by Christmas.[9] On 13 July 1703 he again wrote Tonson, reporting that the papers for the acquisition of the site had been completed and that work was to begin shortly.[10] The site, for which he paid £2,000, was "the second Stable Yard going up the Haymarket," a new district for theatres; the playhouse, he emphasized, was to be "very different from any Other House in being." The construction did not, however, proceed as rapidly as he had hoped, for the cornerstone was not laid until 18 April 1704. (Workmen removing some of the walls on 19 March 1825 found the cornerstone with coins in it and the inscription: "April 18th, 1704. This corner-stone of the Queen's Theatre was laid by his Grace Charles Duke of Somerset."[11]) According to the *Diverting Post*, 28 October 1704, the structure was then nearly completed; but it did not open until 9 April 1705, nearly two years after Vanbrugh had begun negotiations for the site.

9 *The Complete Works of Sir John Vanbrugh*, ed. Bonamy Dobrée (London, 1928), IV, 8.
10 *Ibid.*, IV, 9.
11 Percy Fitzgerald, *A New History of the English Stage* (London, 1882), I, 238n.

According to Cibber's detailed account of the theatre, Vanbrugh built it with a subscription of thirty stockholders' shares valued at £100, each subscriber during his own lifetime to have free entry to the playhouse upon all occasions.[12] In describing the structure, Cibber stated that the "vast Columns ... gilded Cornices ... immoderate high Roofs" made it difficult to hear distinctly one word in ten. The ceiling over the orchestra and pit was very high, "being one level Line from the highest back part of the upper Gallery to the Front of the Stage," with the front boxes a "continued Semicircle to the bare Walls of the House on each Side." So much empty space created "such an Undulation from the Voice of every Actor, that generally what they said sounded like the Gabbling of so many People in the lofty Isles in a Cathedral."[13]

These were not the only complaints. Cibber referred also to the Queen's being in an unpopulated area so that attendance incurred a higher cost of coach hire, a burden falling severely upon spectators in the pit and galleries.[14] A similar criticism appeared in *The Post Boy Robbed of his Mail* (Letter XLII), which ridiculed the building of a theatre at the "Fagg-End of the Town," where four out of five came at considerable expense. The anonymous writer also complained that the theatre was little better in construction than earlier ones, except the "Front, or Case," which was of little usefulness to play, audience, or actor. And the *Diverting Post*, 14 April 1705, amusingly commented upon the interior.

> *When I their Boxes, Pit and Stage, did see,*
> *Their Musick Rooms, and middle Gallery*
> *In Semi-Circles all of them to be;*
> *I well perceiv'd they took peculiar Care*
> *Nothing to make, or do, Upon the Square.*

All in all, the structure was disappointing, and within a short time was partially remodeled when the company with which Cibber was connected took it over in 1709–10. With only a brief period in which to alter the interior, the company could not make a wholly effective transformation. Nevertheless, the company contracted the width by three ranges of boxes on each side and lowered and flattened the oval ceiling above the orchestra to eliminate "those hollow Undulations of the Voice."[15] The implication throughout Cibber's critical discussion of the Queen's is his belief that the

---

[12] *Apology*, I, 319. Cibber may have been wrong concerning the worth of each share, for the Duke of Newcastle and John Hervey, first Earl of Bristol, paid one hundred guineas a share.

[13] *Apology*, I, 321.   [14] *Apology*, I, 322.   [15] *Apology*, II, 87.

Drury Lane structure created by Christopher Wren possessed the good, if not ideal, design.

No facts concerning its capacity exist for this period, but fragmentary data cast some light upon its size. In the advertisements in the *Daily Courant* during the first fifteen years of the Queen's existence, the house occasionally stated a limitation upon the number of tickets to be sold for the pit and boxes combined. For example, on 7 February 1708 no more than 400 persons were to be admitted there by ticket, the implication being that this number represented a comfortable capacity. For three performances in 1710–11 (22 November and 30 December 1710 and 3 January 1711) a manuscript in the British Museum lists the receipts by sections of the theatre and offers suggestions concerning the probable capacity.[16]

For example, on 22 November 1710 there seem to have been 178 spectators in the pit, approximately 140 in the boxes; on 30 December 1710, 164 and 121; on 3 January 1711, 217 and 129. If 400 spectators could be accommodated in the combined areas, at least 217 could sit in the pit, 140 in the boxes. For the first and second galleries on the three evenings attendance was: 206 and 20, 98 and 16, 109 and 17. (These figures, especially those for the upper gallery, corroborate Vanbrugh's statements that the galleries were not so well filled ordinarily as the managers had hoped.[17]) On these three nights 49, 6, and 9 spectators purchased places on the stage. To sum up, pit and boxes could hold in comfort at least 400 spectators, the first gallery at least 206, the second gallery 20, and the stage 49. (To these figures one should presumably add places for the 30 shareholders.) No doubt, the capacity of the second gallery was greater than 20—the upper gallery at Lincoln's Inn Fields held half as many persons as its first gallery—and since the managers skillfully crowded benches into the pit and on stage for special occasions, the capacity had a flexibility which makes difficult a determination of the highest potential figure.

Nevertheless, during the 1720's, when the Royal Academy of Music controlled the Haymarket, the directors usually announced a similar limitation on the number of tickets sold for the pit and boxes combined, the figure often being as low as 340 or 350. As was true earlier, it is not clear whether this number represented the maximum issued over and above those reserved for directors and subscribers, but it probably did. A report in the *Daily Advertiser*, 30 January 1736, concerning attendance at *Mithridates*

---

[16] Additional Manuscripts 38, 607. The compiler of the manuscript sometimes confuses the matter by using terms in one entry which he does not use in another.

[17] See Vanbrugh to the Duke of Manchester, 27 July 1708.—*Works*, IV, 24.

on 27 January 1736, supports this surmise: the house was very full, "above 440 Ladies and Gentlemen in the Pit and Boxes, besides the Subscribers."

Despite the lack of specific figures, the announced restrictions imply a larger capacity than was being utilized. The directors consciously limited the number of spectators, partly to achieve better decorum and partly to cater to a select clientele. These restrictions helped also to preserve in a large theatre a greater sense of intimacy, for these limitations probably held attendance at the Queen's to nine hundred patrons (excluding the footmen, who occupied the upper gallery).

GREENWICH THEATRE: 1709–1712

Among the outlying theatres of greater London, the playhouse in Greenwich was among the first in the eighteenth century to offer a season of any magnitude. Although strolling companies had presented plays there earlier, not until the spring of 1709, when William Penkethman, a talented show-man, thought of enticing Londoners down river on the long summer evenings did the town have an established theatre. In the *Tatler*, 16–19 April 1709, Penkethman announced that he had organized a company of comedians and that he hoped to offer there Tom D'Urfey's *The Modern Prophets* when it had concluded its London run. By 9 May 1709 he was reported to be acting daily, but only two performances are certainly known: *The Fine Lady's Airs* on 6 June 1709 and *Mithridates* on 20 June 1709.

Probably he had an encouraging season, for he returned in the summer of 1710 with a more ambitious program. In late May he announced a subscription and his intention of opening on 12 June following. His advertise-ments in the *Daily Courant* and *Tatler* differ slightly in the details; the former states that each subscriber would be entitled to twenty-four admissions, for himself or for friends; the latter refers to a paper or ticket with a silver medal on it, the ticket costing a guinea and providing for twenty-one admissions. Penkethman opened on 15 June 1710 with *Love Makes a Man* as a benefit for himself, with charges slightly below the current London rates: boxes 2s. 6d.; pit 1s. 6d.; gallery 1s. The curtain would rise at 5:30 P.M. so that Londoners could return home "before Night," Penkethman varying curtain time to suit the tides and moonlight. His advertisements possess touches of the master showman in tantalizing the public with a variety of plays and entertainments at some forty performances from June to September.

Penkethman reopened his playhouse in the following summer. On 21 July 1711 he announced that he would act three times weekly at the prices advertised in 1710; but he played only slightly more than half as many times as he had in the preceding summer. Probably attendance declined because Drury Lane also had a summer season in 1711. In addition, he advertised less colorfully and informatively; he rarely listed even the casts for the plays.

After three seasons Penkethman relinquished operation of the Greenwich Theatre. In 1712 there may have been a series of performances, but only three are certainly known: a concert on 19 May; *The Fatal Marriage* on 21 May; and *The Loves of Baldo and Media* on 19 July. The announcements do not mention Penkethman. No evidence of any further performances there in the early eighteenth century remains; Sybil Rosenfeld points out that the theatre probably was pulled down soon after 1712.[18] She has conjectured its location may have been in present Church Street west of the Hospital.

ST. MARTIN'S LANE: 1710–1712?

Among the minor London theatres, few had shorter careers than the playhouse in St. Martin's Lane. When it was erected is not known, but it was probably the building occupied in 1710–11 by Punch's Opera. In the spring of 1712 a company of young players, most of them sons and daughters of performers at Drury Lane or the Queen's, occupied it briefly. The first notice of their programs advertised *The Unhappy Favourite* for 21 May 1712, with a full cast, a new prologue, and Italian songs from the opera *Hydaspes*. Similar offerings occurred irregularly in June and July. This venture served as a theatrical nursery for several performers—Young Boman, William Mills, Henry Norris Jr, Miss Younger, and Miss Porter—who later became principals at Drury Lane or Lincoln's Inn Fields; but it seems not to have been occupied after the 1712 season.

Situated at the upper end of St. Martin's Lane near Litchfield Street, the playhouse was apparently of conventional design. It had boxes (admission at 2s. 6d.), pit (1s. 6d.), and gallery (1s.). Like other temporary theatres or booths, it may have been a building adapted to theatrical purposes, and it very obviously imitated the major houses by beginning at six o'clock, presenting plays "By Desire," having benefits, and offering prologues,

[18] *Strolling Players and Drama in the Provinces, 1660–1765* (Cambridge, 1939), p. 273.

epilogues, and singing, including the not uncommon songs "by a young Gentleman for his Diversion."

RICHMOND THEATRES: 1714–

Early in the eighteenth century Richmond Hill became a center of dramatic and musical entertainment. Apparently the first play given there was Benjamin Griffin's *Injured Virtue*, presented probably in the summer of 1714,[19] but nothing is known concerning the playhouse itself. Actually it was William Penkethman, who, after experimenting with a summer theatre in Greenwich from 1709 to 1711, selected Richmond as a likely site for a new theatrical venture. Before his death in 1725 he had managed at least two playhouses on the Hill.

He opened his first one in June 1718. According to the *Weekly Journal or British Gazetteer*, 31 May 1718, Penkethman was then building a "handsome Playhouse" to be opened after Whitsuntide. Connected to it was a room in which he would show his "musical Pictures . . . of the Royal Family," an entertainment which the *St. James's Evening Post*, 3 June 1718, described as a series of pictures of "the Royal Family . . . curiously painted by the first Master of the Age" and originally designed for the pleasure of the young Princesses. Plays began on 19 July 1718 with *The Spanish Fryar* and *The Stage Coach* supplemented by dances, songs, and a prologue by Penkethman. The theatre, whose site is not exactly known, contained boxes, pit, and gallery. Penkethman performed on Saturdays and Mondays through 1 September 1718, at least partially on a subscription basis, as had been his practice at Greenwich.

By the next summer he had built a new theatre, which he had converted from a stable for asses. He opened on 6 June 1719 with the Prince and Princess of Wales in the audience. He capitalized on the lowly origins of the site by speaking a prologue with his arm affectionately around the neck of an ass on the stage beside him, the prologue being printed in the *Weekly Journal or British Gazetteer*, 13 June 1719, and reprinted by Sybil Rosenfeld.[20] He did not advertise regularly during the summer, and we know only of plays given on 6 June, 6 July, 31 August, and 5 September 1719.

Possibly Richmond had theatricals in 1720 and 1721, but not until 1722 is there certain knowledge of Penkethman's again offering plays; then he apparently advertised only two performances: on 23 July 1722 *Richmond*

[19] *Ibid.*, p. 274.   [20] *Ibid.*, pp. 278–79.

Wells for the author's benefit, and on 20 August 1722 a dramatic entertainment, *The Distressed Beauty, or The London Prentice*, for his own benefit. In the summer of 1723 he again had a season, but we have only scanty information concerning a few performances in September; at one of these he again showed his pictures of the Royal Family to an audience of "Nobility, Gentry, and Ladies upward of 200."

In the summer of 1724 he had a full and successful season, highlighted by demonstrations of his loyalty to the Hanoverian regime. On 28 May 1724 he celebrated the King's birthday with an illumination of his house on the Hill, singing of a new birthday song by Mrs Hill, and treating gentlemen and ladies with wine and the "Commonalty" with a barrel of ale. Plays began on 22 June 1724, followed by another celebration on 1 August 1724, the anniversary of the Hanoverian succession. But the theatre apparently did not open in 1725, probably because of Penkethman's illness. His death on 20 September 1725 ended a colorful period in Richmond theatricals, which did not resume until the 1730's.

LINCOLN'S INN FIELDS II: 1714–

After Thomas Betterton withdrew his company from Lincoln's Inn Fields in 1705 to act at the Queen's, the old theatre remained vacant. Eventually Christopher Rich, who had been silenced at Drury Lane, acquired its lease and planned to rebuild the playhouse in Lincoln's Inn Fields. At the accession of George I, the ban against Rich was raised, but he died before he could make the renovated playhouse ready for occupancy.

John Rich, Christopher's older son, took over the enterprise, received a license, and prepared to act. On 4 December 1714 the *Weekly Packet* announced that the playhouse was finished; on 18 December it opened with *The Recruiting Officer*, receipts of £143 representing a substantial audience. There were, however, difficulties attendant upon Rich's rapid opening; he stood in danger of losing some of his newly engaged performers, for, according to the *Weekly Packet*, 18 December, some of the comedians whom Rich had lured from Drury Lane had been ordered to return to their former company "upon pain of not exercising their Lungs anywhere." The crisis melted away, however, without disaster to Rich.

The theatre was restored on conventional lines, with boxes, pit, and two galleries, including a "Middle Gallery Box," referred to in the theatre's announcement for 3 March 1720. According to Thomas Davies, "the stage was more extended than that of the rival theatre, superbly adorned with looking-glass on both sides of the stage."[21] According to the *British Journal*, 22 September 1722, over the stage was a painting of Apollo and the Muses; over the pit "a magnificent Piece of Architecture; where is seen a Group of Figures leaning over a long Gallery, viz. Shakespear, Johnson, &c. from the Originals. They seem in conference with Betterton, the most celebrated Tragedian, or English Rossius, of his Time. The Artists have given their Opinion, That this Performance excels any Thing of that Kind, both as to Design and Beauty." In the summer of 1723 Rich completely redecorated the house, and in the summer of 1725 he had the interior refinished, the *Daily Journal*, 27 September 1725, reporting that the "Gilding, Painting, Scenes, and Columns of Pier Glass, rais'd for the better illuminating the Stage and other Parts of the House" pleased spectators on the opening night of the season.

Far more information exists concerning the capacity of Lincoln's Inn Fields than for any other early eighteenth-century theatre, although interpretation of it involves some difficulties. The principal details come from a manuscript (an account book for 1726–28) in the Harvard Theatre Collection which lists the attendance and receipts for each section of the house during those years. As this period covers the sensational run of *The Beggar's Opera*, when more and more people crowded into the theatre, the figures not only demonstrate the probable capacity but illustrate the flexibility of theatrical accommodations achieved by increasing the number admitted onto the stage and by crowding more and more spectators onto benches elsewhere in the playhouse.

The Harvard manuscript records the income and sometimes the number of patrons reported by boxkeepers or doorkeepers under these headings: boxes, stage, balcony, pit, slips (the near-stage extensions of the upper galleries), first gallery, second gallery. During the first twenty nights of *The Beggar's Opera* attendance ranged as follows. In the boxes on one night sat 321 persons, but the number ranged between 250 and 300 as a rule. On one evening 81 persons had places on the stage, with 10 to 25 the normal figures. The pit ranged upward to 302, with 270 or 280 representing the customary high patronage. For the slips the highest number was 87, with 45 to 60 not uncommon. For the first gallery peak attendance came to 443, with the high figure usually between 380 and 400; and for the second gallery, a high of 199, with 185 to 195 the usual attendance.

An example of the distribution at a single well-attended performance is afforded by *The Beggar's Opera* for 5 February 1728, with receipts of

21 *Dramatic Miscellanies*, I, 139.

£189 11s.: boxes, probably 273; stage, probably 81; balcony, 1; pit, 282; slips, 60; first gallery, 432; second gallery, 187; a total of 1,316. As the popularity of this ballad opera grew, the officers of the theatre managed to squeeze in still more people, with a performance on 11 April 1728 showing an even more remarkable attendance: boxes, probably 254; stage, 124; pit, 295; slips, 75; first gallery, 433; second gallery, 200. The receipts came to £198 17s., plus orders to the value of £1 19s.; the attendance, 1,381.

In spite of the abundant statistical evidence, it is difficult to be certain of a maximum capacity for any unit of the theatre, let alone the entire house. One reason is that the Harvard manuscript for some sections lists only the receipts; one cannot be sure how many of the patrons paid full price, how many After-Money (half price or thereabouts). The common practice of "railing in" the boxes, stage, and pit makes it difficult to know the capacity of each one of these, particularly when the managers may have borrowed space from the stage to install temporary boxes. Occasionally the managers merged the boxes and pit, making it difficult to determine the borderline of each. Recently Paul Sawyer, making an assessment of figures from this manuscript, determined the capacity of Lincoln's Inn Fields to be: boxes, 378; pit, 302; slips, 65; first gallery, 458; upper gallery, 200; a total of 1,403.[22] In these calculations he apparently included attendance on stage with that for the boxes, and his figure for the first gallery represents a single extraordinary crowding in that area. In addition, the slips ran higher than the figure he gives, yet at times the counting of attendance for slips must have merged them, partially at least, into the galleries. Nevertheless, it seems probable that Lincoln's Inn Fields, by utilizing every inch of space, could entertain approximately 1,400 spectators at a time.

Rich occupied Lincoln's Inn Fields continuously until he built Covent Garden and moved there in the autumn of 1732, although for a short time early in his operation of Lincoln's Inn Fields he relinquished the management to some of his own actors. Between 1714 and 1732 Lincoln's Inn Fields and Drury Lane pretty well dominated offerings of old and new English dramas.

HAMPTON COURT: 1718–

Early in the eighteenth century occasional rumors implied that a playhouse was to be created in Hampton Court for the entertainment of royalty. For example, on 17 February 1702 the Lord Chamberlain issued an order

22 *Notes and Queries*, July, 1954, p. 290.

that the "old Guard Room" there should be floored, finished with a "plain Dale Wainscoat, without Mouldings," and provided with a door opening into the Great Hall, in all convenient speed to transform it into a theatre.[23] No performances for this period are known, however. Again, on 2 April 1715, according to the *Weekly Journal*, 9 April 1715, an order called for the removal of furniture and wardrobe from Windsor Castle to Hampton Court, where, among other alterations, a theatre would be built.

Three years later performances actually occurred, the newspapers implying, however, that not before August 1718 had a theatre actually been constructed within the palace. By command of His Majesty a short season of plays was given there, although the public was somewhat confused as to who would perform in them. The *Evening Post*, 30 August 1718, declared that Christopher Bullock, associated with John Rich in the management of Lincoln's Inn Fields, had been commanded to play several times in the "magnificent Theatre erecting for that Purpose." Actually, the Drury Lane company had the honor of acting before the King, the advance notices stating that it would be allowed £100 for each performance. The first apparently occurred on 23 September 1718, although the *Evening Post* for 2 September reported, apparently by mistake, that the players had "already perform'd several Times." The Drury Lane players acted seven times. The expenses came to £374 1s. 8d., a much higher average than the nightly expense at Drury Lane proper. To this sum King George added a gratuity of £200.[24] But regular performances at Hampton Court by the London companies did not follow upon this short series in the autumn of 1718.

THE HAYMARKET: 1720–

The second theatre in the Haymarket, commonly called the Little Haymarket to distinguish it from the more majestic King's Theatre nearby, was constructed in the late months of 1720.[25] According to the *Weekly Journal or British Gazetteer*, 3 December 1720, it was "just finished" and would

---

[23] Nicoll, *Early Eighteenth Century Drama*, p. 281.

[24] Cibber, *Apology*, II, 218–19.

[25] In a Petition to the House of Commons, 11 April 1735, John Potter stated that in 1720 he agreed to a lease of the King's Head Inn in St. James Haymarket, for sixty-one years, from John and Thomas Moor, paying "a Fine of near £200." In addition, he laid out at least £1,000 in the construction of the theatre, and approximately £500 in "Scenes, Machines, Cloaths, and other Decorations." In 1735 he estimated his investment as worth £1,700.—See *Journal of the House of Commons*, XXII (1735), 456.

open as soon as a company of comedians from Paris had arrived. On 29 December a French company duly appeared in *La Fille a la mode*.

Erected on a site "between Little Suffolk-street and James-street," the playhouse in its earlier advertisements called itself the "New Theatre over-against the Opera House in the Hay-Market." Apparently it had no license, although a note in the *London Journal*, 23 December 1721, stated that a patent for it had been "obtain'd in the late Reign for twenty Years, nine of which are already elapsed." If such a patent was issued around 1712, no confirmation of its existence has been found. Similarly, nothing specific is known of its capacity, although Aaron Hill, writing on 20 January 1722 to the Duke of Montagu, made clear that it was smaller than the King's Theatre; nevertheless, Hill offered to pay a rental of £270 for each of two seasons, a rather large figure for a small theatre.[26]

Without a patent or backing from an experienced theatrical producer, the Haymarket during the first decade of its existence never had a permanent resident company like those at Drury Lane or Lincoln's Inn Fields. It was, however, frequently occupied on a short-term basis (a few weeks to nearly a year) by French or Italian comedians and by English amateur or experimental groups. Nevertheless, it became a wedge to destroy the near monopoly of plays held by Drury Lane and Lincoln's Inn Fields, and its existence without a license or patent helped to make possible the later entry of the theatres in Goodman's Fields under similarly imprecise legal status.

THE FAIRS

Each of the principal Fairs in and about London offered entertainments as part of their attractions. At some booths proprietors presented puppet shows, pantomimes, exercises in dexterity, dancing, rope dancing, and singing; and at nearly every Fair patrons could see drolls, plays, ballad operas, farces, and adaptations of pieces seen in the London theatres. The Fairs also offered actors a means of earning rather good money when they were at liberty from their regular engagements. Among the many Fairs, the following constitute the principal ones which presented dramatic pieces.

MAY FAIR. From 1700 to 1709 May Fair, held around Whitsuntide, had booths for drolls and other entertainments, with Barnes, Finley, and Penkethman as the principal showmen. For a few years after 1700 the

[26] Historical Manuscripts Commission, *Duke of Buccleuch and Queensberry Manuscripts* (London, 1899), I, 369.

London theatres closed for this Fair, sometimes for a week or fortnight; but in 1709 an edict prohibited acting at May Fair, and the theatres thereafter usually played without pause in early May.

TOTTENHAM COURT FAIR. The Tottenham Court Road was the site of a Fair less traditional and substantial than May, Bartholomew, and Southwark Fairs. How early performances began there is not clear, but in August 1717 Leigh and Norris offered drolls in a booth on that site. On 26 February 1728 the *Daily Journal* reported that an unnamed dancing-master intended to secure a patent for an annual Fair, which would run fourteen days from 4 August (thus preceding Bartholomew Fair), at which he would have booths for drolls, music, and other diversions; rumor had it that the project might produce a yearly profit of £3,000. The Fair did not open, however, until 1730.

BARTHOLOMEW FAIR. One of the oldest in London, Bartholomew Fair has been chronicled by Henry Morley in *Memoirs of Bartholomew Fair*. At the opening of the eighteenth century the Fair flourished in spite of fairly constant agitation against the acting of plays and drolls. For example, on 28 June 1700 the Court of Common Council forbade acting in any booth, but the authorities enforced these restrictions sporadically, if at all. In 1708, however, the authorities limited the Fair to three days (23, 24, and 25 August) instead of the fortnight previously permitted.

In the next two decades from two to six theatrical booths operated whenever drolls and plays were permitted. Players from the London theatres ran most of them: William Penkethman, James Spiller, Thomas Dogget, William Bullock, Josias Miller, John Harper, John Hippisley, Tony Aston, Lacy Ryan, and Thomas Chapman. They usually chose the George Inn Yard and the area facing the Hospital Gate for their booths, and they advertised quite precisely the location of their performances. In August 1728, for example, the Fielding-Reynolds Booth stood in the George Inn Yard, that of Yeates in Smithfield Rounds facing Cow Lane, Lee-Harper-Spiller "over against" the Hospital Gate, Hall-Miller at the end of Hosier Lane. Usually these men returned to the same site year after year, with the result that a newcomer might advertise his booth as adjoining Penketh-man's, a familiar landmark.

Alert to the fads and varieties of theatrical fare, they quickly capitalized on a new trend in London, such as ballad opera, or skillfully combined a tragic or historical theme, such as the tale of Jane Shore, with farcical elements, such as the humorous adventures of Squire Noodle and His Man Doodle. The managers offered something for every taste, and nearly everybody went to this Fair at one time or another, the newspapers occasionally mentioning the presence of Persons of Quality or the Prince of Wales (incognito, as a rule) at the Fair.

SOUTHWARK FAIR. This Fair followed almost immediately upon the closing of Bartholomew Fair; as a result, many proprietors of booths took their shows directly from one to the other and put them in new booths on the Bowling Green. Again, they advertised their locations precisely. In September 1724, for example, the Norris-Chetwood-Orfeur booth stood next to Bullock's, which was in Bird Cage Alley. Penkethman's stood above Bird Cage Alley, over against St. George's Church; Lee's rose in the Queen's Arms' Tavern Yard next the Marshalsea Gate; and Lee-Harper chose the Green at the lower end of Blue Maid Alley. As a rule, Southwark Fair had essentially the same entertainments which had been shown a few days earlier at Bartholomew Fair.

OTHER ESTABLISHMENTS

London also possessed several concert rooms, halls, booths, and tennis courts at which plays as well as concerts were occasionally given. In the calendar of performances these are identified at their first mention, but a few are of sufficient importance to warrant brief attention here.

YORK BUILDINGS. Probably the most notable of these halls was the Great Room in York Buildings, Villers Street. From the opening of the century it was one of the most popular and became known by a variety of terms: Music Room, Great Room, Great Music Room, Concert Hall. As its control changed, it assumed the names of the men leasing it. In 1700 it was "Mr Reason's Musick Hall"; in 1711, Thomas Clayton's; in 1715, Richard Steele's, when it housed his *Censorium*, and as late as 1728 it was referred to as "Sir Richard Steel's Great Room"; in 1729, "Topham's Great Room." In the late 1720's more plays appeared there than had in the earlier years.

HICKFORD'S GREAT ROOM. Situated in James Street in the Haymarket, over against the Tennis Court, this room was a very popular concert hall; occasionally amateurs presented a play there.

SOUTHWARK. In addition to the Fair, entertainments at other times occurred in Southwark; evidence points to at least one booth—perhaps more—of a more permanent and elaborate structure. In September 1719, for example, Bullock at his booth in Bird Cage Alley gave *The Jew of Venice*, and from September through November 1720 a booth (or booths), sometimes called Bullock's, sometimes Hall's, gave several plays. These booths may, of course, have been put up for the Fair and not removed promptly at the close of festivities.

WINDMILL HILL. Although this site had both booths and a theatre, very little is known of either. In 1723 Rakestraw, a minor actor, lost his life by accident while acting in *Darius* in a booth on Windmill Hill, Moorfields. In 1724 Tony Aston presented his medley of characters at Lee's booth there, and on 19 July 1729 *Fog's Weekly Journal* reported that "Mr Miller, having left performing as usual, Mr Spencer intends to Entertain the Town with an antient Catalogue of Plays" to begin on 21 July 1729. Because these establishments rarely advertised in the London papers, few records exist to show the range of their offerings.

THE PLAYHOUSES: LEGAL PROBLEMS

The issuance of patents to Thomas Killigrew and William D'Avenant by Charles II had tremendous influence upon the legal situation of the early eighteenth-century playhouses.[27] These patents, issued in perpetuity, formed the basis of a monopoly (by two companies) and made the companies the servants of the Crown. In 1682 the two patents had, to all practical purposes, been consolidated by the formation of the United Company; in 1695, when Betterton and his associates formed a new company to act in Lincoln's Inn Fields, the situation was further complicated by the issuance of a license to the dissenting actors. This pattern—patent and license— repeated itself in the opening decades of the next century.

The legal status of theatrical establishments became more complex, in addition, as a result of the character of the relationship between the patentee, on the one hand, and the Lord Chamberlain and Master of the Revels, on the other. Following the issuance of Patents to Killigrew and D'Avenant, quarrels between these two heads of companies and Sir Henry Herbert, Master of the Revels, tested certain aspects of the legal responsibilities of the management to that officer.[28] For example, Herbert expected a fee for each new and each revived play,[29] and on 4 June 1662 Killigrew

---

[27] See Nicoll, *Restoration Drama*, p. 293.

[28] See Nicoll, *Restoration Drama*, pp. 316–18; A. F. White, "The Office of Revels and Dramatic Censorship during the Restoration Period," *Western Reserve University Bulletin*, XXXIV (1931), 7–11; and Hotson, *Commonwealth and Restoration Stage*, pp. 204–6, 210–13.

[29] Nicoll, *Restoration Drama*, p. 316.

and Herbert reached an agreement which provided such payments to the Revels. Another extension of the Lord Chamberlain's control lay in the theory, if not fact, that the players, as servants of the Crown, possessed immunity from arrest except by warrant from his office.[30] Yet there existed no perfectly clear settlement of the active and ultimate power of the Lord Chamberlain over the vast variety of details which comprise the functioning of a theatrical enterprise.

At the beginning of the eighteenth century both patent and license continued as the formal authorities for the operation of the two companies then exercising a theoretical monopoly of dramatic presentations. Christopher Rich at Drury Lane performed by virtue of the patents derived from Killigrew and D'Avenant through the United Company, whereas Betterton and his company at Lincoln's Inn Fields acted under the license granted that body of actors on 25 March 1695.

From 1695 to the opening of the new century the Lord Chamberlain had exercised a great deal of influence over the affairs of both companies, with little concern shown over possible differences in powers vested in a patent or a license. For example, on 16 April 1695 the Lord Chamberlain ruled that no player should quit either house without due process,[31] a principle which, with variations, was frequently restated, though never wholly enforced, in the next century. Similarly, the Lord Chamberlain intervened in the affairs of Lincoln's Inn Fields on 11 November 1700 to appoint Betterton sole manager of the company, an intrusion into internal operations which was followed by similar actions in later years. Of great importance also was his order of 24 January 1696 that every play should be fully licensed,[32] followed on 4 June 1697 by a corollary instruction that "Obsenityes & other Scandalous matters" be deleted by having all plays sent to the Master of the Revels for perusal and correction; these recurrent orders also suggest that similar rules issued earlier had not been satisfactorily followed.

Until 1737, when the Licensing Act stipulated precisely the number of theatres allowed to perform and instituted more drastic censorship, the loose relationships inherited from the seventeenth century remained in force, although variations in procedures occurred. For example, the patent which Christopher Rich had exercised lapsed by reason of nonuse when the Lord Chamberlain silenced Rich in the first decade for disobeying his directives. With the accession of George I in 1714, however, Rich, upon petition, obtained a removal of the silencing order and had his patent

[30] *Ibid.*, p. 318.   [31] *Ibid.*, p. 338.   [32] *Ibid.*, pp. 340–41.

declared a lawful grant. His assignee, John Rich, excercised it at Lincoln's Inn Fields and Covent Garden until his death in 1761. In addition, the Crown issued one new patent between 1700 and 1729, when Richard Steele sought and secured one on 19 January 1715 which gave him essentially the powers which Killigrew and D'Avenant had possessed.[33] One important difference between Steele's patent and those issued earlier was that his had validity only for his lifetime and three years thereafter.[34]

The issuance of licenses occurred, however, much more frequently in the first thirty years of the new century. On 14 December 1704 Congreve and Vanbrugh received a license to "form and establish" a company at the Queen's.[35] In addition, each change in the composition of the management of Drury Lane required new licenses for the managers,[36] grants which terminated at the death of the monarch who issued them. As a variation, the establishment of the Royal Academy of Music, structurally resembling a corporation more than a conventional theatrical company, came from a warrant issued by the Lord Chamberlain on 9 May 1719, which outlined the organization (Governor and Board of Directors) and which also gave the Lord Chamberlain (as the Governor of the Academy) a major share in its direction. On the other hand, as already indicated, some playhouses apparently functioned without either a patent or license; this seems to have been true of the Haymarket in 1720.

Inevitably opposition to the Lord Chamberlain's control reared itself; some of the conflict grew from uncertainty concerning the power of a patent in relation to the authority of the Lord Chamberlain's office. In the early years of the century such a conflict developed shortly after Steele received his patent for Drury Lane, when the managers refused the office the usual licensing fee for a new play. Cibber waited on the officer in charge, sought evidence for the authority over a patent company, and refused to pay the fee. For nearly five years Drury Lane neither submitted new plays for judgment nor paid the fees.[37]

Nevertheless, problems of this sort frequently arose. In the Preface to *The Perplex'd Lovers* (Drury Lane, 19 January 1712) Mrs Centlivre pointed out that the Epilogue intended for this play "wou'd not pass; therefore the Managers of the Theatre did not think it safe to speak it, without I cou'd get it License'd!" Because approval could not be secured before

33 John Loftis, *Steele at Drury Lane* (Berkeley and Los Angeles, 1952), p. 46.
34 *Ibid.*
35 The Lord Chamberlain Records in the Public Record Office, London, 5/154, p. 35.
36 Nicoll, *Early Eighteenth Century Drama*, pp. 275–76.
37 Cibber, *Apology*, I, 276–78; Loftis, *Steele at Drury Lane*, p. 49.

curtain time, the players faced resentment from the audience over lack
of an epilogue; but the next day the author "had the Honour to have the
Epilogue Licens'd by the Vice-Chamberlain," although by then rumors
labelled it "a notorious whiggish Epilogue." A vague statement in the
Weekly Packet, 11 July 1719, implied an effective kind of censorship against
an unnamed play: "It seems a very scandalous Interlude, or Play, has been
prepar'd for Action at . . . Lincoln's Inn Fields . . . but a proper Authority
has put a Stop to such Outrages against Common Decency and Manners."

A most positive example of the Lord Chamberlain's power to keep
a play from the stage occurred in 1729 when he refused a permit for Gay's
Polly. As a result, there was a good deal of public discussion of the problem
of censorship, and on 8 March 1729 the *Craftsman*, in a leading article on
the liberty of the stage, proposed a "Committee of learned Gentlemen"
who would maintain the freedom of the stage and would discourage those
who had it in their power to restrain or suppress the drama.

In addition to his ability to silence plays and companies, undoubtedly
his most powerful weapon, the Lord Chamberlain intervened in other ways
in the conduct of the playhouses. Some of his directives represented attempts
to systematize their operations. For example, a series of orders perpetuated
the seventeenth-century principle of preventing an actor from shifting from
one theatre to another without a proper discharge from his manager. On
9 January 1710 the Lord Chamberlain again ordered that no performer
be engaged without a proper discharge;[38] on 4 December 1721 he addressed
a similar notice to the managers of Drury Lane,[39] followed on 24 December
1721 by one to Rich at Lincoln's Inn Fields.[40] The Lord Chamberlain, perhaps
at the request of the theatres, also issued proclamations concerning behavior
within the playhouses, such as an order on 13 November 1711 forbidding
spectators to stand behind the scenes or come upon the stage,[41] a prohibition
so frequently stressed that it presumably represented a losing battle against
a privilege claimed by many young gentlemen.

Early in the century this office acted also as a clearing house for proposals
leading to better organization and management. Around 1710, for example,
it helped to formulate a series of rules for the directors of theatrical enterprises;[42] in the spring of 1709 it participated in a movement to arrive at

[38] Lord Chamberlain's Records, 5/155, p. 3; Nicoll, *Early Eighteenth Century Drama*, p. 279.
[39] Lord Chamberlain's Records, 5/158; Loftis, *Steele at Drury Lane*, p. 247.
[40] Lord Chamberlain's Records, 5/158; Loftis, *Steele at Drury Lane*, pp. 247–78.
[41] Lord Chamberlain's Records, 5/155, p. 125; Nicoll, *Early Eighteenth Century Drama*,
p. 282.
[42] Nicoll, *Early Eighteenth Century Drama*, pp. 279–80.

formal written agreements between the management and an actor, in which the salary, benefit privileges, and other terms of employment would be put on record.[43] In the first decade it also heard a number of complaints from Christopher Rich and his employees,[44] and it assisted Vanbrugh in his struggle in 1714–15 to obtain a settlement of his claim for payments for costumes used by Drury Lane.[45]

On the other hand, the Lord Chamberlain sometimes arbitrarily issued orders which the managers undoubtedly viewed as an unjustifiable encroachment upon their rights. On 2 February 1720, for example, he ordered Drury Lane to permit no benefit before those for Mrs Oldfield and Mrs Porter;[46] on 6 February 1720 he ordered that Gay's new pastoral tragedy (presumably *Dione*) be acted immediately after Hughes' *The Siege of Damascus*;[47] and on 29 January 1729 he directed the managers to send their advertisements to the publisher of the *Daily Courant*, who would print them free of charge.[48]

Like any regulatory agency, especially one dealing with such mercurial personalities as managers and actors, the Lord Chamberlain's office seems a maze of inconsistencies. It attempted at times arbitrarily to rule the companies; on other occasions the two groups appeared to co-operate toward mutually satisfactory ends; in other periods they remained strongly at odds. In 1737, with the passage of the Licensing Act, a fairly decisive settlement was made in some of the areas of conflict.

THE PLAYHOUSES:

ACCOMMODATIONS AND PRACTICES

Although the theatres, old and new, varied in capacity, decor, and details of accommodations, in structure they did not differ materially. Each had a pit, with rows of benches, facing the stage but sometimes separated from the acting area by space for the orchestra. Adjoining the stage on both left and right were boxes, and the space for acting could be contracted by placing benches or building boxes on it for special occasions. The tiers of side boxes extended into the front boxes, those more directly facing the stage. Above the pit and facing the stage rose the first gallery and—in the larger theatres—the second gallery, ordinarily about half as large as the lower one. At Lincoln's Inn Fields (and probably elsewhere) the slips (extensions of the galleries toward the stage) accommodated more than

---

43 *Ibid.*, pp. 286–87.   44 *Ibid.*, pp. 289–91.   45 *Ibid.*, pp. 284–85.
46 *Ibid.*, pp. 282–83.   47 *Ibid.*, p. 275.   48 *Ibid.*

fifty persons, but this area, with its awkward lines of vision, usually filled only when a very popular production brought a full house. An occasional theatre—Drury Lane, for example—had a "Middle Gallery Box," never clearly defined in the extant records, and Lincoln's Inn Fields had a "Balcony" (probably similar to Drury Lane's Gallery Box) so small as rarely to accommodate more than four or five spectators.

In 1714 John Macky published an interesting contrast between the interiors of the British playhouses and those on the Continent.49 He reminded his readers that in Venice, Paris, Brussels, Genoa, and elsewhere, the theatres contained "rows of small *Shut-Boxes*," three or four storeys of them, in a semi-circle with a parterre below. In England the parterre, "commonly called the *Pit*," catered to "the Gentlemen on Benches"; and in the first "Row of *Boxes* sit all the Ladies of Quality; in the Second the Citizens Wives and Daughters; and in the Third the Common People and Footmen," his second and third rows presumably denoting the first and second galleries. As a result, Macky observed, the spectator was as much diverted by the "Beauties of the Audience, as while they are with the Subject of the Play." Indeed, he asserted, the English do well to illuminate the whole house, "for no Nation in the World can shew such an Assembly of shining Beauties as here."

Much of Macky's account of the disposition of the spectators is borne out by allusions in prologue, epilogues, and plays. Generally speaking, gentlemen and the well-to-do citizens seated themselves in the Pit, where often gathered the more vocal critics, such as the young Templars. The Epilogue to Charles Johnson's *The Force of Friendship* (20 April 1710) refers to

> *You Gentlemen Impanell'd in the Pit,*
> *You Sovereign Judges both of Sense and Wit,*

and the Epilogue to Thomas Baker's *The Humours of the Age* (March 1701) commented upon the "Quibbles" in the Pit.

In the side boxes one could find the young men of fashion, the beaux, the wits. The Epilogue to Charles Gildon's *The Patriot* (1703) refers to "you side-Box Beaus"; a song in *The Island Princess* (1701) similarly alludes to "Side-Box Gallants." More caustically, the Epilogue to Thomas Baker's *The Humours of the Age* slaps at "Those Killing Side-Box Wiggs," and the Epilogue spoken by Mrs Oldfield to Cibber's *Perolla and Izadora* (3 December 1705) contrasts the lively young men of the side boxes with the soberer gentlemen of the pit.

49 *A Journey Through England*, pp. 109-10.

> *Of all the Sparks, that sigh and ogle here,*
> *(Hold! let me see) the Chief are There, and There.*
>   [Pointing to the Side Boxes]
> *But here, how many Husbands do I see* [The Pit].

In *The Theatre*, 5 January 1720, Steele selected a committee of "Auditors
of the Drama," on which he placed "Two Gentlemen of Wit and Pleasure
for the Side-Boxes."

By contrast, women of fashion more often occupied the front boxes,
where Steele placed "Three of the Fair Sex" on his committee. Many a
playwright complimented the "bright Circle" of the ladies and praised
their taste. In Scene I of Breval's *The Confederates* (1717) there is mention
of "th'Angelick Fair" ranged in each box. Many and many an epilogue
on a first night begged the "Fair Ladies" of the boxes to exercise their
moderating judgment by giving the dramatist a deserved applause.

In the galleries, generally, sat those of less wealth and, often, of less
delicate taste. The Epilogue to *The Humours of the Age* refers to "the Merry
Puns" in the gallery; the Prologue to Cibber's *Love Makes a Man* (9 December
1700) spells out the attractions to the galleries as the fooleries of "Dicky
[Norris] and Penkethman."

An occasional comment surveyed the whole range of taste and catalogued
nicely the division of the house. In a prologue intended for Mrs Manley's
Lucius (11 May 1717) Steele advocated for the ladies a scene "movingly"
written, for "the Heroes in the Pit—a Rape," for "the First Gallery a
Ghost," and for the Upper Gallery, though at a safe distance, "a good
Supper." Or, as the Epilogue to Mrs Centlivre's *The Perjur'd Husband* (1701)
put it:

> *Let Galleries no more for Judges sit,*
> *But leave to the bright Boxes, and the Pit,*
> *Their lawful Empire o'er immortal Wit.*

In *A Tale of a Tub* Swift made a panoramic sweep of the playhouse
scene.

First; the Pit is sunk below the Stage ... that whatever *weighty* Matter shall be
delivered thence (whether it be *Lead* or *Gold*) may fall plum into the Jaws of certain
Criticks (as I think they are called) which stand ready open to devour them. Then,
the Boxes are built round, and raised to a Level with the Scene, in deference to the
Ladies, because, That large Portion of Wit laid out in raising Pruriences and
Protuberances, is observ'd to run much upon a Line, and ever in a Circle. The
whining Passions, and little starved Conceits, are gently wafted up by their own
extreme Levity, to the middle Region, and there fix and are frozen by the frigid

Understandings of the Inhabitants. Bombastry and Buffoonry, by Nature lofty and light, soar highest of all, and would be lost in the Roof, if the prudent Architect had not with much Foresight contrived for them a fourth Place, called *the Twelve-Peny Gallery*, and there planted a suitable Colony, who greedily intercept them in their Passage.[50]

These basic accommodations were capable of considerable readjustment. It was not uncommon to have some or all of the benches in the pit railed into the boxes (at box prices) for a benefit or special performance. Similarly, a portion of the stage sometimes provided seats for spectators, a practice of mixed blessings. When a very popular play like *The Beggar's Opera* held the boards or a popular actor had a benefit or the friends of an author wished to boost his earnings on a third or sixth night, the management often constructed boxes on the stage, some being partially enclosed. Spectators also delighted in standing in the wings or behind the scenes in spite of warnings from the management that movement of scenes and machines exposed auditors on the stage to physical harm.

The managers were often quite specific in advertising variations in arrangements: pit and boxes "put together," perhaps only two rows of the pit benches "railed into the boxes," sometimes pit and front boxes unified.[51] But the disadvantages of these arrangements sometimes outweighed the gains. At Mrs Oldfield's benefit on 6 March 1729 at Drury Lane, when the stage was narrowed by improvised boxes, the *Universal Spectator*, 8 March 1729, reported the "greatest Appearance of Ladies of Quality . . . that ever was known; and the House so excessive full, Stage and all, that the Actors had scarce room to perform." Earlier, after Rich had paid the penalty of catering too frequently to the whims of spectators, he appended to his bill of 19 January 1720 a note intended to regulate, if not discourage, those who liked to appear on stage among the performers: "Whereas Liberty of Scenes has been abused by rioting and disturbances, none to be admitted but by Tickets at the Stage Door at half a guinea."

As has already been pointed out, both the playhouses and the opera, to keep proper decorum and to provide some assurance that all who came

[50] Ed. A. C. Guthlech and D. Nichol Smith (Oxford, 1920), p. 61.

[51] For example, at Drury Lane on 19 February 1730 the pit and boxes were "put together" for a benefit at the charge of five shillings, the usual price for boxes. On 21 March 1709 at Mills' benefit only two rows of the pit were "railed into" the boxes, this at the request of some Persons of Quality. On 25 January 1733 the pit and front boxes were" laid together." At *The Relapse* in Drury Lane on 11 March 1729 the announcements stated that "the Seats upon the Stage will be enclosed." For a concert, including *Marriage a la mode*, at Drury Lane on 11 February 1703, "the Boxes to be kept entire for the Ladies, as at a Play," and at Mrs Oldfield's benefit on 7 March 1728 "to prevent the Ladies taking Cold, all the Benches on the Stage will be enclosed."

might find places, had announced a limitation upon the number of tickets to be sold, primarily for the boxes and pit. These measures catered, of course, principally to ladies and gentlemen and Persons of Quality. For these patrons, the managers also devised means for keeping places, particularly on crowded nights, although the lack of individual chairs in the pit made this procedure difficult. If the stage was open to the public, servants could be sent to hold places, as Drury Lane announced on 22 March 1727, when part of the stage was formed into boxes. The ladies were advised to send their servants by three o'clock, the performance to begin at six. At Drury Lane on 12 February 1708 the management urged servants to be at the theatre at two o'clock with tickets in their hands. As a variation, at Mrs Oldfield's benefit on 7 March 1728 places were to be kept only for those with "Sealed Tickets" (i.e., those purchased from her and marked with a seal). At Lincoln's Inn Fields for the premiere of *Themistocles* on 10 February 1729 Rich announced: "All Persons that should want Places, are desired to send to the Stage Door of the Theatre, where Attendance will be kept, to prevent Mistakes."

But not all of these measures succeeded. It had long been customary for footmen to hold places in the boxes, but the extension of this practice to other areas of the house meant a crowd of servants, who often proved unruly. At Drury Lane, for example, on 14 February 1719 at the premiere of *Chit Chat* a footman, keeping a place, quarrelled with a gentleman and disturbed the audience. But from 1720 onward the managers made constant improvements (at least in the public announcements) in ways of assisting patrons to secure places and insure proper behavior. Sometimes the bills emphasized that tickets for boxes could be had at the box office in advance and that places could be spoken for. When *The Beggar's Opera* had its long run in 1728, London took advantage of this procedure, with the result that on the twelfth night nearly all the boxes through the twenty-fifth had been "spoken for." On the other hand, places in the gallery remained on a first come-first served basis.[52]

The managers also concerned themselves with the comfort and safety of their patrons, although they could not easily offset great heat or cold. When the weather was unseasonably warm, the closely packed audiences suffered from the heat. To avoid this discomfort, the managers advertised their intentions of keeping the house cool or of raising the curtain later

[52] Another variation occurred at the benefit of Mrs Porter (*The Way of the World*, 18 March 1718), when Drury Lane advertised that servants might keep places in the boxes only. All persons who did not have places kept should come to the Pit doors, "as the most easy way of Entrance," where tickets would be delivered, if desired.

than usual; sometimes they simply closed the theatre until the weather moderated. The management of Drury Lane on 18 June 1717 tried another device, for the bills stated that an exact computation of the capacity of pit and boxes had been made (unhappily, the management did not reveal this figure) to see how many could be accommodated "with ease" and added that no more than that number would be admitted; in addition, the play would not begin until nine, the doors remaining closed until eight, all "by reason of the Heat of the Weather." During the same season Lincoln's Inn Fields simply stopped playing "by Reason of the Heat of the Weather." A somewhat cryptic statement in the bills for the Queen's in the spring of 1711 implies that patrons were either actually or imaginatively cooled during hot days, for at performances of different operas in May, June, and July "by reason of the Hot Weather, the Waterfall will play the best part of the Opera" (16 May 1711) or "And by reason of the Hot Weather, the Water Scene will play the best part of the Opera."

Although the playhouses could be uncomfortably warm, patrons might also be justly fearful of the cold. Lord Hervey has written in amusingly caustic terms of a chilly night at the King's on 27 November 1731 when *Porus* was given before the King and Queen. Not feeling well, Hervey had nevertheless attended the opera, where he observed the King and Queen clothed in velvet lined with ermine from head to foot to avoid the suffering "we freezing plebeians shook under" and saw Lord Herbert and Lord Albemarle shivering without their waistcoats.[53] At Drury Lane on 6 March 1729 the benches on the stage were enclosed, apparently by improvised walls around them, to prevent the ladies taking cold.

The theatres also gave a good deal of attention and money to the illumination of their interiors. In 1714 John Macky emphasized the fine lighting and visibility of the English playhouses. Whereas on the Continent the boxes were usually somewhat closed—he called them *"Shut-Boxes"*—and apparently in shadow, in England the whole of the house was "illuminated to the greatest advantage" so that spectators could see the action on stage and, during the intervals, watch all who sat in the pit, boxes, and galleries. Congreve, writing of a particularly festive evening at Dorset Garden on 21 March 1701, emphasized the care taken to insure brightness: "It was all hung with sconces of wax-candles, besides the common branches of lights usual in the playhouses."[54]

53 *Lord Hervey and his Friends*, pp. 114-15.
54 *Works*, ed. Montague Summers (London, 1925), I, 72.

Not a great deal is known concerning the exact disposition of lights within the early eighteenth-century theatres. Generally speaking, chandeliers hanging over the stage were the main sources of light. In Garrick's day Drury Lane had a large chandelier suspended over the center of the auditorium, with six others (each containing twelve candles) above the stage,[55] and it is possible that these lighting arrangements existed before Garrick assumed the management. Since Congreve referred to "sconces of wax-candles" (i.e., a bracket candlestick or group of candlesticks hanging or projected from a wall, or possibly set on stands) and since Drury Lane's main lighting expenditures were for candles, the illumination there probably came chiefly from chandeliers and stands of candles, with oil lamps as supplementation. According to the incomplete Drury Lane expense vouchers for 1715–16 (in the Folger Shakespeare Library) the managers spent at least £225 in that season for candles, oil, wicks, and the cleaning of lamps as well as other similar supplies. By far the largest expenditures went for candles, purchased in weekly lots. For the week ending 27 November 1715, for example, the house bought 49 dozen candles at a cost of slightly more than 7s. a dozen. The frugality of the managers reduced the cost by returning tallow, in that week 70 pounds valued at 17s. 6d. The bills suggest that, one week with another, each acting day consumed about eight dozen candles; at that rate, the cost for 170 nights of a normal season would come to about £475.

Not much more is known about the lighting at Lincoln's Inn Fields, except that it had six chandeliers, "apparently iron rings hung on chains."[56] The account books for Lincoln's Inn Fields during 1724–25 and 1726–27 (British Museum, Egerton 2265–2266) offer very little specific information on this subject. There is a daily entry of two guineas to "Mr Lucas for Candles"; presumably, for this sum he kept the theatre in adequate supply. If this surmise is correct, the charge for candles on 170 acting nights would be about £360, somewhat less than the estimate for Drury Lane in 1715–16.

Lighting the house also created one of the serious threats to the comfort and calm of the audience—the danger of fire. Although there had been no major theatrical fire in London for some years, some auditors undoubtedly remembered the complete demolition by fire of the Theatre Royal in Bridges Street on 25 January 1672. The fear of fire revealed itself in an incident at Drury Lane on 26 October 1727, when, during a presentation of *Henry VIII*, with the "House being exceeding full," an alarm of fire

55 *The Oxford Companion to the Theatre*, ed. Phyllis Hartnoll (Oxford, 1951), p. 463.
56 *Ibid.*

spread through the packed theatre. According to the *Daily Journal*, 28 October 1727, a "Gentlewoman fancying she saw Smoke issue from under the Stage . . . and at the same time believing she smelt Fire," voiced her fears "so loud, and by her precipitate Endeavours to get out" raised such a turmoil that several persons were badly bruised and "one Woman big with Child [was] press'd to Death." According to the *Daily Journal*, 31 October 1727, Wilks, one of the three managers, told the audience later that the alarm had been "contrived by some malicious ill designing Persons," and Rich, manager of the competing Lincoln's Inn Fields, showed his concern by offering a reward of £20 for the detection of the "Author of that villainous Contrivance."

As a result of the incident, Drury Lane published in the *Craftsman*, 4 November 1727, a detailed account of the precautions constantly taken against fire. Each night the manager regularly posted several persons, with a "General Inspector" in charge, whose "proper Business" was to set all the lights and lamps in and about the playhouse "in large *Candlesticks* and on broad *Stands* made of Tin, in so safe a manner, that should any *Candle* swail and fall out of its Sockets, no danger would attend it." In addition, the theatre possessed "Large Cesterns of Water above Stairs and below, and *Hand-Engines* . . . always ready"; furthermore, the "*Carpenters, Scene-Men,* and *Servants*" were "employ'd in such Numbers . . . and disposed in such Order" that "upon the first Appearance of the least *Spark* of *Fire*, it cannot but be *instantly* seen and extinguished." Not only that, but every "Light in the whole *Theatre* being so plac'd, that it is in the View of some of the *Servants*," and if any "false Alarm" be uttered in any part of the theatre, the spectators should not "inconsiderately throw themselves into Disorder and Confusion, since the House cannot be subject to the least *Danger* from *Fire* on that Side where the Audience sit, as no Light is placed there, that can possibly occasion it." In addition, the "Walls are of such a thickness and such a space between, that no Fire could reach any part of the *Theatre* in several Hours." The report concluded with the point that a "Report of Fire within the House, can only proceed from Pickpockets, or some other ill-designing Persons."

Although we know less of Lincoln's Inn Fields' plans for coping with fires, an account book for 1724–25 (Egerton 2265) shows that Rich invested heavily in new equipment for firefighting. In that season he paid £15 18s. to Buck, a merchant, for fire buckets and similar utensils, and to Harrison £26 8s. for "a Water Engine and other Augmentations." Although these items loomed large in the year's budget, Rich had just had an object lesson in the hazards of flames, for in February 1725 Lord Cardigan's mansion, adjoining the theatre, had caught fire, and although Lincoln's Inn Fields was exposed to serious damage, a large crew of fire-fighters subdued the flames before they did more than make it necessary to suspend acting for one night.

Although Rich had little expense for renovating after the fire, he apparently sought to keep the good will of firefighters, who would be needed in a really serious conflagration; his records show that he spent a good deal of money in gratuities, for drinks, and for "assisting" on that night.57 The accounts show also that he could call upon engine companies from far and near, with many individuals, including men from Read's Printing House, taking their turns; all received liberal payment in money and drink, an investment in good will against that day when a fire might possibly threaten a crowded house.

In many other ways the theatres catered to the comfort and convenience of their spectators, but the details of many of these are hidden from us, probably because custom had long made them familiar to potential theatre-goers. For example, we know relatively little of the arrangements at the theatre for accommodating spectators as they arrived on foot or in carriages; details of toilet facilities, the chocolate or coffee rooms, ease of ingress and egress are not publicized. In one other matter—curtain time—the theatres made clear in their bills the gradual change to a more desireable hour for starting the performance. At the turn of the century, the bills usually specified five o'clock, but in 1702–3 curtain time occasionally was five o'clock (8 December 1702), sometimes five-thirty (10 April 1703). On 30 April 1703, Dorset Garden was quite specific about both opening and closing: to begin at five and end at nine. By 1704–5 five-thirty had become the more acceptable hour, yet spectators must have been confused by such announcements as that for Drury Lane on 26 August 1708: "To begin between 5 and 6 a Clock." Soon, except for the summer months, six o'clock became established as the best hour, and this time prevailed for many years. In the summer, however, the theatres frequently waited until seven, even later if the weather was unseasonably warm.

---

57 He spent approximately £40 for such charges as "to five Men of Sun Fire office watching all night & Expenses," £1 18s. 6d.; to J. Darby, who was continually at "ye Engine," 2s. 6d.; one bill "for Liquor" totalling £2 15s. 6d., two for "Beer Ale and Brandy" at the 3 Tuns Ale House," £7 11s.

Theatrical Finances

WITH very few exceptions, the early eighteenth-century playhouses, like the majority of companies the world over, were business enterprises operating to make a profit by entertaining the public. Few contemporaries, for example, doubted that John Rich, the proprietor of Lincoln's Inn Fields, deliberately put more and more stress upon pantomime and spectacle because they brought more money to the box office. Colley Cibber, contemplating the problems of Drury Lane, made the point that he and his fellow managers had to compete with Rich on his own ground (i.e., song and dance) or incur deficits. Since most of the managers—Rich, Cibber, Booth, Wilks, Dogget—had modest personal resources and depended upon the prosperity of their playhouses for their livelihood, they had to plan carefully within a limited budget and estimate shrewdly the probable response of the public. On the other hand, the directors of the opera companies usually had subsidies, subscriptions, or grants from the Crown with which to replenish their treasuries in lean periods.

The theatres, in fact, often made large profits. It is clear from lawsuits, particularly Thomas Dogget versus the actor-managers of Drury Lane or Richard Steele versus his creditors, that Drury Lane frequently had a large net income. In 1712–13, for example, it cleared £4,000 (according to Cibber); in 1713–14, £3,600; and in the four months between 21 September and 17 December 1714, £1,700.[58] In the early 1720's, to judge from Steele's accounts of his share in the Drury Lane profits, it may have cleared £3,000 to £3,600 yearly.[59] Rich had profitable seasons, also, if not sustained prosperity. The great success of *The Beggar's Opera* and the long runs of his most successful pantomimes, for example, brought capacity crowds and high receipts. In spite of occasional deficits in marginal seasons, Rich managed to stay in show business for forty-seven years.

True, some individuals emphasized art and experimentation more than Drury Lane and Lincoln's Inn Fields usually did. Aaron Hill, a man enormously interested in all phases of the theatre, sometimes managed

[58] See R. H. Barker, *Mr Cibber of Drury Lane* (New York, 1939), p. 99.
[59] Loftis, *Steele at Drury Lane*, p. 92.

dramatic enterprises (such as the Haymarket in 1722) or theorized about the stage (in the *Prompter*) in such fashion as to make acting, costumes, scenes, and drama his primary concern and financial gain a minor aim. The opera companies and the Royal Academy of Music spent enormous sums on salaries, costumes, music, and decor, incurring large deficits in the cause of good music and occasionally imperiling the future of opera. But these were the exceptions. The prevailing concept was that of the professional theatre with a growing emphasis upon providing popular and varied entertainment for a widening range of public taste.

How the theatres managed financially before 1730 can be known in detail for only scattered seasons, since very few account books have survived: the ledgers of Lincoln's Inn Fields for 1724–25 and 1726–27 (British Museum, Egerton 2265–2266) and a detailed account of the income for Lincoln's Inn Fields for 1726–28 (Harvard Theatre Collection). These obviously concern only a small fraction of the seasons between 1700 and 1729 and deal with Rich's theatre only; but they are supplemented by a large file of expense vouchers for Drury Lane between 1712 and 1716 (chiefly in the Folger Shakespeare Library, with a few in the Enthoven Collection and in Egerton 2159) and by much useful information in theatrical memoirs, contemporary newspapers, and prefaces to plays. From these sources can be ascertained the general nature of theatrical operations, the kinds of receipts and disbursements, and the types and numbers of personnel, both on and off stage. The limitations of these documents must be constantly kept in mind, however; being isolated records, they give no indication of the financial activities of any playhouse over any given number of consecutive seasons. In addition, even those few extant records are but parts of a complicated accounting system. The conclusion of the Lincoln's Inn Fields ledger for 1724–25 implies that the treasurer regularly kept as many as nine books for that season, in each of which he recorded a different phase of his bookkeeping.

FINANCING NEW ENTERPRISES

Very little is known of the methods of financing new theatres between 1700 and 1730. For example, no really specific information concerning the building of the Haymarket in 1720 has survived. Generally speaking, however, to raise funds for the construction of a new house, a proprietor usually sold shares to investors. This was Vanbrugh's method with the

Queen's, for he apparently disposed of thirty shares at either one hundred pounds or one hundred guineas apiece. Although the details of Rich's rebuilding of Lincoln's Inn Fields in 1714 are unknown, he listed payments to shareholders (commonly called renters) in his ledgers for 1724–25. In return for his purchase, each shareholder received free entrance to box, pit, or gallery for any performance. In some ventures, the shareholder also received a set return for each night of acting; if Rich in 1714 employed the principle he used later in building Covent Garden, this return was probably one shilling, perhaps two shillings, for each acting night. In the Lincoln's Inn Fields records, the disbursement to shareholders is nearly always the first item in the debit column, as though it might well be a first lien upon receipts, and is entered for every night the theatre gave a performance. In raising money for opera, the Royal Academy of Music in 1719 followed a somewhat similar principle. It enlisted subscribers who pledged a specific amount and who, in return, had free entry to any performance. These subscribers might theoretically expect dividends from profits, but probably most subscribers to it came to look upon their subscriptions as contributions to sustain opera.

THEATRICAL INCOME

The principal income of the theatres—actually the only really substantial source of money for the production of plays—came from paying patrons. Almost no theatre except the opera house could forecast any important revenue except from nightly receipts; as a result, the acting night became the center of a theatre's financial structure. If Lincoln's Inn Fields was dark, the records usually show no receipts or disbursements for that day, and the personnel normally received no pay for non-acting nights. The performers ordinarily could expect salaries for about 170 nights, as the theatres opened early in September, acted two or three times weekly until early October, then (with a few exceptions) daily until June. (In the summer the management frequently turned the house over to the young actors, who played two or three times weekly until the Fairs began.) This schedule was shortened to four days weekly in Lent; the theatres closed during Passion Week, and, if a member of the Royal Family died, they remained dark for six weeks. On these occasions receipts and salaries ceased.

During the first two-thirds of the season—roughly to the first of March—the treasurer received the full receipts from a night's performance.

After the first of March, when the benefits began, the theatre received for its own purposes only a portion of the income on a benefit night. As a result, the financial success of a season was roughly determined by what happened before Easter, because April or May rarely brought sufficiently large receipts to offset a deficit incurred earlier or brighten a ledger close to a break-even point. At a benefit the treasurer usually kept a sum equal only to the nightly charge of the house (a sufficient amount, around £40, to cover the cost of opening and operating the theatre for a night) or all the money taken in at the offices (the player keeping the income from tickets which he personally sold) or, in unusual circumstances, nothing at all, the whole of the receipts going to a player or charity. If a player was required to pay a specific charge (£40, for example) and the receipts at the office did not equal that sum, the performer usually had to make good the difference. The playhouse, then, rarely operated at a loss on benefit nights, and yet a long sequence of benefits made it difficult for the treasurer to acquire sufficient sums after March 1 to meet new and exceptional expenses.

In addition, the theatres acquired small sums from forfeits from players or from their issuance of passes. The account books show only vaguely the forfeit system at work before 1730, but an entry in Egerton 2320 lists a fine against Mrs Cibber, who had been posted for a week to act Ophelia at Drury Lane on 17 September 1737 but who at the last moment refused to act. As to passes, the Lincoln's Inn Fields accounts for 1726–28 (Harvard Theatre Collection) show that the bookkeeper entered the name of each actor who had issued free orders for that night. These payments, however, brought in only negligible sums.

More important, especially for the patent theatres and the opera house, was assistance from the royal household. In Restoration times, the theatres had been generously supported by Charles II, but in the early eighteenth century Queen Anne rarely attended the theatre although she commanded performances at Court. From 1714 onwards some of the playhouses could depend upon payments from royalty and their retinue. Royal attendance from the court of George I first favored Drury Lane, but Lincoln's Inn Fields later gained recognition, and George I's difficulties with the English language led him to patronize the performances by foreign comedians, especially the French, at the Haymarket. He also liberally supported opera, not only with a yearly grant of £1,000 for a considerable period but also with frequent attendance.

At Drury Lane during 1714–15 a voucher (Egerton 2159) shows that the treasurer charged the royal box at £4 nightly (it held twenty persons), and from November 1714 through April 1715 the royal household paid £116 for boxes and £49 11s. for attendant servants and guards and for copies of the plays acted. Royal attendance also brought larger crowds as a rule, particularly for boxes and pit, and the theatres often announced in advance, either in the bills or in the newspapers, the expected presence of royalty. Drury Lane also profited occasionally from special performances ordered by the King; at Hampton Court, as already noted, the company received £374 1s. 8d. for acting there in 1718.

Theoretically, the collection of all admission charges should have been a relatively simple matter, but it was not. Some of the difficulty arose from the practices prevalent among the upper classes in the reign of Charles II; the sparks and gallants had developed great skill in evading the fees and yet seeing part, even all, of a play. As Saunter in Cibber's *The Double Gallant* (1 November 1707) proudly exclaimed:

[I] go behind the Scenes, make Love in the Green-Room, take a Benefit Ticket, ferret the Boxes, straddle into the Pit; Green-Room again, do the same at both Houses, and stay at neither,

probably without paying a penny. And the Prologue to *Love Makes a Man* (9 December 1700) refers to those "Who for an Act or two are welcome gratis." Constantly the managers sought means to make sure that every one paid. On 26 October 1714 the King's, for example, appended to its bill a compromise between a firm statement and a plea: "It having been the Common Practice of several Persons to come into the Opera and stay a whole Act, and sometimes longer, without paying, to the great Prejudice of the Opera, therefore it is humbly desired for the future that no Person will take it ill that they are not admitted without Tickets." But the patron often defeated the treasurer. Between 1726 and 1728 the entries in the Lincoln's Inn Fields accounts (Harvard Theatre Collection) bear an occasional note by the boxkeeper to the effect that Lord So-and-So came into the boxes but simply "would not pay."

A principal means of making certain that the theatre received payment has already been mentioned: the issuance of tickets, either in advance or at the door. For example, at Drury Lane on 23 January 1703, the management advertised several days in advance *The Country House*, with an accompanying concert, the pit and boxes to be put together, "where none are to be admitted but by printed Tickets." Spectators could purchase them at White's Chocolate House, Tom's or Will's Coffee House. For benefits, when a player gained financially in proportion to the number of tickets he sold, an actor took the additional measure of issuing "Seal'd Tickets" (i.e., those with a daub of sealing wax marked with the beneficiary's initials or a mark to prevent counterfeiting). A benefit ticket preserved in the Folger Shakespeare Library reads:

LINCOLN'S-INN-FIELDS

Monday, May ye 4th 1730

THE BEGGARS OPERA

For the Benefit of

Mrs CANTRELL.

Pit   3s.
.
No. 119

The income of the theatre, as well as its collecting, was complicated by fluctuation in admission charges in the early years of the century. Around 1700 the common fees were: boxes 4s., pit 2s. 6d., first gallery 1s. 6d., upper gallery 1s. Sometimes the bills spelled out these charges; often they merely bore the statement "At Common Prices." Yet another scale of prices existed: 5s., 3s., 2s., 1s. In the first decade the theatres charged advanced prices chiefly for a new play, an old one newly revived with fresh costumes, or a performance which included many entertainments. A revival of *The Albion Queens* at Drury Lane on 6 March 1704 brought the higher fees, a notice explaining that the rise was due to "the extraordinary Charge in the Decoration of it." Occasionally a theatre attempted to raise the charges still higher; at a concert coupled with a play at Drury Lane on 11 February 1703 the front boxes were listed at 6s., the side boxes and pit at 4s. On 1 June 1703 at Lincoln's Inn Fields, Mrs Lee, for her benefit, first sold tickets at 6s. for the boxes, 4s. for the pit, and 2s. 6d. for the first gallery, but before the day of performance she reduced them to 5s., 3s., 2s.[60]

The rise in charges made some spectators hold more persistently to privileges which had developed in the days of Charles II: the custom of leaving before the curtain rose and having payment refunded, or of coming at the end of the third act and paying "After-Money" (half-price) to see only the fourth and fifth acts. Theophilus Cibber, writing in 1753 about problems of admission earlier in the century, pointed out as an extreme example a man who would come in on an order or frank if he could; if not, he paid, took a place in the pit, and, wishing to hear only the orchestra, listened to the First, Second, and Third Music; retiring just before the

[60] The Opera House, which had higher admission charges, will be discussed later.

curtain rose, he had his money returned at the door. With the development of the afterpiece, especially pantomime, as a fairly regular part of the program in the 1720's, the scale of 5s., 3s., 2s., 1s., became the prevalent one and produced a variation on the problem Cibber alluded to. Many spectators, grumbling at the higher charges and holding pantomime in contempt, were outraged at having to pay advanced prices for an evening's entertainment, only half of which they thought proper or enjoyable. Ultimately the managers solved this problem with a method which Theophilus Cibber, again writing in 1753, claimed as his own.[61] He recommended that a notice be inserted in the bills to the effect that "The Advance Money will be returned to those who chuse to go out before the Overture to the Entertainment." This scheme, he contended, silenced objections and did not, in his opinion, greatly lessen the receipts, "for I question if there was a Demand for the Return of twenty Pounds in ten Years."

Cibber implied that this change occurred around 1724, when pantomime rose to great popularity, but such notices did not appear frequently in the newspaper bills until later. It did, however, eventually become a common practice, and can be illustrated by a bill falling outside the period under study: Drury Lane's for 12 February 1733. On that night the managers advertised *Richard III* followed by a new pantomime, *The Judgment of Paris; or, The Triumph of Beauty*, the latter having new costumes, scenes, machines, and other decorations, and the admission being set at 5s., 3s., 2s., 1s. After stating that "No Money under the full Price [was] to be taken during the Time of Performance," thus preventing an individual from paying "Common Prices" and staying also for the afterpiece, the bill continued: "The additional Money to be return'd (if desir'd) to those who go out before the Overture of the Entertainment begins." Although these measures satisfied some objectors, they made the collection of admission charges more complex.

The procedure of collection within the theatre is partially outlined in the record of daily receipts at Lincoln's Inn Fields between 1726 and 1728 (Harvard Theatre Collection). The first entry, for 24 October 1726, with *The Mistake* and *Pan and Syrinx* on the bills, lists the receipts turned in to the treasurer by the boxkeepers, pit doorkeepers, and gallery doorkeepers. For the boxes five ticket takers—Wilmer, Redfern, Taylor, Lawrence, and Atkins—collected tickets worth £18 15s. 6d. and 17 orders. For the balcony, Mrs E. Rogers received 5s., three pages attending the Princess of Wales (who was in a box) being accommodated there. The pit

61 *The Lives and Characters of the most Eminent Actors and Actresses* (London, 1753), pp. 70-71.

had two doorkeepers, Gwin and Gallant, with 105 tickets and 19 orders entered on Gwin's side, 113 tickets and 1 order on Gallant's. Similarly, the slips had two collectors: Shafto, with 3 paying customers and 10 on orders (all of them the Princess's servants), and Tubman, with 8 paid tickets and 1 order. The same attendants had charge of the "Pidgeon Holes," in which were placed three Yeomen of the Guard. The first gallery had a single doorkeeper, Main, who received 161 paying customers and 7 on orders; and the upper gallery, with Aylett in charge, accommodated 101 paying spectators and none on orders. The receipts came to £76 10s., with the orders valued at an additional £9 17s.

The document also shows in detail the handling of orders. On 24 October 1726 they amounted to 17 box, 20 pit, 14 slips, and 7 first gallery. Each collector kept a record of orders received at his post, with the recipients listed alongside the receipts. For example in the boxes that night on orders were Sir George Skipwith, Major Smith, two by the signature of Christopher Rich, four by John Rich's order, the Princess of Wales and five with her. In the balcony were three pages of the Princess, in the slips ten of the servants, and in the "Pidgeon Holes" three guards. The players also issued orders. In the pit were "Mr Ryan 2 . . . Mrs Barbier's brother . . . Mr Quin 1 . . . Mr Milward from the Boxes 1. Mr Hippisley. Mr Walker. Mr Fairbank"; in the first gallery "Notes Mr Quin 2 Mr Ryan 2. Orders Mr Harrison Hosier Mr Ogden Mr Chapman." All in all, probably 570 persons paid to attend that evening, with 58 entering on orders. (Probably the Princess, her servants, and her guards were paid for later.)

The ledger also throws some light upon the taking of After-Money, which in Restoration times accrued, at least in part, to the actors themselves. During 1726–27 the management accepted After-Money occasionally for a play not followed by a pantomime. On 31 October 1726, for example, *Henry VIII* brought receipts of £41 18s. in the regular collection. Wilmer, a boxkeeper, took in as After-Money 2s. 6d. (half the regular 5s. box charge); Gwin, in the pit, took in 20s. and Gallant, at the other entrance to the pit, received £1 1s. The total, £3 8s. 6d., came to about 8 per cent of the regular receipts, and on nights of poor attendance After-Money was undoubtedly a welcome addition to the treasurer's accounts. After-Money was not, however, a factor when a ballad opera like *The Beggar's Opera* had a good run, but it reappeared when attendance fell off.

The theatres also collected some money by seasonal subscriptions, a practice frequently followed by the opera companies, but the practice never became common for dramas. In the first decade the theatres sometimes offered English musical plays in this fashion. Drury Lane on 29 December 1702 offered *The Judgment of Paris* by subscription for the pit and boxes only, with the galleries, balconies, and stage boxes by payment at the door. After Italian operas had been offered by subscription, the Queen's in 1706–7, producing both operas and plays, presented three dramas by subscription. According to Cibber, the house undertook a public subscription for "Reviving three Plays of the best Authors," each subscriber to have three tickets for the first day of each play upon payment of three guineas.[62] The project matured speedily, and the house gave *Julius Caesar*, *A King and No King*, and the comic scenes of *Marriage à la mode* followed by *The Maiden Queen*. The management announced the subscription as a means of putting plays on an equal footing with opera; the actors got an increase in salary, and the manager "stood a considerable Gainer." Rich also utilized this plan occasionally at Lincoln's Inn Fields, especially for musicals. On 22 March 1718 he offered *The Lady's Triumph*, a new dramatic opera, with the pit and boxes by subscribers' tickets, stage boxes at 15s., "Box in the Gallery" 5s., First Gallery 3s., Upper Gallery 1s. 6d. Given four times for the subscribers, it continued its run at lower prices. Rich made a similar offering of *The Island Princess* on 6 February 1720. In addition, several visits by French or Italian comedians were financed partly by subscriptions, particularly in 1719–20 and 1724–25. But this practice never became established as a customary means of carrying on a repertory of plays.

The opera companies, however, relied constantly on subscription or subsidy to supplement receipts. Unlike the playhouses, the Queen's almost never succeeded in operating within the money paid by listeners, which was often high but rarely sufficient. The most specific information concerning daily receipts is for 1707–8 (British Museum, Ad Ms 38607). One document gives the income for sixteen performances at the Queen's between 13 January and 6 March 1708: £2,243 13s. 6d., an average of about £140 nightly, much more than plays brought at that period. For 23 nights the receipts came to £2,943 1s. 6d., about £124 nightly. At this time the admission charges varied a great deal, with a new opera on 26 February 1708 charging for stage, boxes, and pit a half guinea, first gallery 5s., upper gallery 2s. 6d. On a less special occasion, 10 February 1708, pit and boxes cost 7s. 6d., stage boxes a half guinea, first gallery 3s., upper gallery 1s. 6d. For some time the common charge was 8s. for pit and boxes, the first gallery varying from 2s. to 4s. and the upper gallery from 1s. 6d. to 2s. Occasionally stage

[62] *Apology*, II, 4–5.

boxes cost 15s. After 1720 the opera charges became settled at a half guinea for boxes and pit and five shillings for the first gallery.

But even these charges could not sustain opera on a grand scale, and the management early turned to subscriptions, not only to increase its income but also to ascertain at the beginning of a season how much support it would have. In 1707–8 the management issued "Subscriber's Tickets" which admitted a patron to pit or boxes (usually put together on subscription nights) and often entitled him to a printed copy of the opera. Available in advance, these tickets had to be presented at the door, for at subscriptions the house accepted only tickets for entrance to pit and boxes. The management usually gave a new opera six nights for the subscribers, after which it continued its run at reduced charges. For the premiere of *Ernelinda* on 26 February 1713 the terms included a payment of ten guineas by a subscriber, for which he received three tickets nightly for six performances, no more than four hundred tickets to be given out for any evening.

In 1719 patrons of opera instituted a more elaborate project for its support: the Royal Academy of Music. Headed by the Duke of Newcastle, the association planned to have a guarantee of £50,000, towards which the King promised £1,000 annually, a sum paid for seven years. In principle, the Academy involved an investment by friends of opera, each member subject to assessment and, of course, eligible to receive dividends whenever finances permitted. In March 1720, Vanbrugh estimated that the fund stood at £20,000, a sum sufficient, he thought, to maintain opera "'till Musick takes such Root, as to Subsist with less aid."[63] Instead of less support, however, it constantly needed more, for, if the notices of assessment in the *Daily Courant* between 1720 and 1728 mean what they imply, each member was assessed 100.5 per cent of his pledge, less a single dividend of 7 per cent. This type of financing ended in 1728, when the Royal Academy of Music felt it could no longer sustain opera in this way; but in later years variations on this type of support were tried by J. J. Heidegger and G. F. Handel, the principal entrepreneurs in operatic enterprises.

In principle, then, opera relied very substantially upon subsidy, subscription, and relatively high admission charges. On the other hand, drama drew its principal support from the fluctuating receipts which a public might pass over the counter for tickets, with occasional but somewhat negligible support from subscriptions.[64] In examining the disbursements

[63] *Works*, IV, 125–26.

[64] The Academy on 21 October 1727 gave very precise directions concerning the handling of admissions: "The Directors have caused the Tickets and Method of receiving them to be altered for the future, the better to prevent Frauds,—therefore will be placed at the fore

of the managers, one can see how differing conceptions concerning salaries, costumes, scenery, and overhead accounted for some of the variations in profit and loss in the world of entertainment.

DISBURSEMENTS

Although the theatres collected their revenue from relatively few sources, they spent their receipts in many ways. In an effort to place theatrical operations on a proper budget, someone early in the century drew up a rather elaborate plan for the proper structure of a company in which the probable expenses were carefully outlined.[65] It called for twenty actors (with Betterton at the head) at £1,710 annually; eleven actresses at £800; and "Pentions & Young Actors" at £190, a total of £2,700. There were to be six singers (with Richard Leveridge in charge) at £150, with a supplemental £200 for vocalists not yet engaged; seven dancers (L'Abbe as the master) at £250, with another £250 if needed; twenty musicians (Eccles as the leader) at £1 each weekly, a total of approximately £800; Under Officers (two treasurers at £75 each; twelve doorkeepers at £20 apiece; wardrobe keeper and servants £60; four tiremen £80; four tire-women £100; four scenemen or carpenters £100). For the rent was allotted £600; for candles, wax, tallow, oil, £600; for three managers, £600. There remained £1,950 for scenes, clothes, printing, new plays, coals, musical compositions, and, almost as an afterthought, two candlemen £30, a prompter and clerk £60, two barbers £40, four bill carriers £40, and three "Necessary Women" £30. The total was nearly £10,000.

This was the theory. Not until 1724–25 and 1726–27 is it possible to examine in detail how a theatrical company actually spent its money. The account books for Lincoln's Inn Fields for these two seasons (Egerton 2265–2266) record the salaries and wages, rent, taxes, cost of scenes and machines, charges for properties, advertising, maintenance and repair, printing, and many related activities. Nearly all expenditures involving payments to regular personnel of the theatre were placed on a per-diem basis, for, as a general principle, the actors, musicians, dancers, guards,

---

and back Door leading into the Stone Passage, a Box into which the Gentlemen and Ladies are desired to drop their Tickets as they go into the House. The Subcribers will be admitted on producing their Silver Tickets only & not otherwise. The Gentlemen and others going into the Gallery are likewise desired to deliver their Tickets into the Box, to be placed at the Gallery Door, for that Purpose."

[65] Nicoll, *Early Eighteenth Century Drama*, pp. 276–77.

barber, lawyer, bill setters, and shareholders received payments for services rendered each acting night; if the playhouse was closed, they received no pay. The sum of these costs comprised the daily charge of approximately £40, the standard deduction at benefits. Let us look at some of these items in detail.

FIXED CHARGES. A basic entry was the payment (commonly called *rent*) to shareholders. In 1724–25 it was £3 12s. daily, approximately £600 for the 167 acting days in that season. In 1726–27 it was £4 12s. for 151 days and £5 for 3 days, approximately £700. The theatre also paid 8s. daily for the Chocolate Rooms, about £60 annually. As proprietor, John Rich received a daily payment of £1 13s. 6d. in 1724–25 and £3 6s. 8d. in 1726–27, about £278 in the first season, £510 in the second. (In each year—about £210 in 1724–25 and £445 in 1726–27—there were numerous other payments to Rich, which may have been repayments for sums he paid out of pocket.) His brother, Christopher M. Rich, who assisted in the management, drew 16s. 8d. nightly for 67 nights and 6s. 8d. for 100 nights in 1724–25, with additional sums bringing his total to about £140. In 1726–27 he received 16s. 8d. nightly as well as other sums. The treasurer also paid one Slater a guinea nightly for law fees and another guinea to "Mr Duel on Bond," neither charge being explained in detail.

The treasurer also put many operational costs on a daily basis. In 1724–25 the orchestral music was listed at £3 14s. 2d. daily for 157 days, £3 10s. 10d. for 4 days, and £3 6s. 8d. for 6 days. The barber received a daily 5s. Payments for "Side Drums" at 2s. and "Kettle Drums and Trumpets" at 15s. occurred frequently, though not each day. The bill setters received 9s. daily, and Mrs Lucas received two guineas nightly for candles and lighting. Just what determined whether the treasurer placed some wages (such as those for the barber) on the daily charge instead of the weekly payroll is not evident.

TAXES. Although the theatres paid a variety of taxes, the rates represented only a small fraction of the season's expenses. Generally, they were paid twice yearly, usually some time after the date due. Among the Drury Lane vouchers for 1712 to 1716 there seems to be only one which specifically concerns taxes. Dated March 1716 (Enthoven Collection), it covers the half year's "Land Tax" due at Lady Day 1716. According to it the yearly rates were: "The Theatre and Sceen Rooms" £16; the stock £3; "Mr Riches House adjoyning" £4; and "The Office" £1. In 1724–25 the principal taxes were also on a yearly basis: lamp tax £1; window tax £1 10s.; "poor's rate" £4 3s. 5d.; the watch £1; and a special assessment

"To Mr Cunningham for $\frac{1}{4}$ pt of a Horse in the Militia for the year 1724 due Lady Day last," with 16s. paid on 13 April 1725. In 1726–27 the payments were essentially the same, with a few variations: 10s. 2d. for highway repairs; a scavenger's charge of £1 9s. 2d. yearly; 6s. 4d. for repair of Chertsey Bridge; 2s. 6d. for "Trophy Money"; and, again, 16s. for a fourth of a horse in the Westminster Militia.

REPAIRS AND UPKEEP. The news columns of the early eighteenth-century newspapers give ample proof that the playhouses frequently made general repairs, such as repainting, laying a new floor, or remodeling a portion of the house. The account books also show that each theatre allotted systematically a large portion of its income for repairs, renovation, maintenance and improvement. Often the entries simply record the settlement of a bill to a plumber, glass man, or carpenter, without revealing the nature of the work.

For the years from 1712 to 1716 the Drury Lane expense vouchers indicate no major alterations. Many bills concern normal replacements: 4s. paid on 26 February 1714 for "6 pound of new Rope for the Scene frames in the Celer at 8d per pound"; 2s. on 18 March 1714 for repair of matting; 7s. on 14 February 1715 to Thomas Castle for plumbing and pipe work; 4s. on 25 November 1714 for painting "ye Side Box on ye Stage"; and £1 8s. on 23 February 1716 for tin and other materials for new candlesticks, including six for the music room. The patronage of royalty after the accession of George I brought more elaborate changes. On 4 November 1714 tin work, costing £2 4s., was done on the lights in the boxes, and by 23 December 1714 alterations in the Prince's box costing £4 3s. had been completed. The most detailed alterations appear in a bill for 14 October 1715 submitted by Thomas Arne for £4 17s. 6d.; the repair of four seats in the pit and three in the gallery over the Prince's box, with 52 yards of matting, 106 yards of "web," and nails and labor costing £2 5s.; covering the fronts of the "2 Stage Boxes" and one seat with "Green Bays" at £1 6s. 10d.; repairing and restuffing benches, putting more "Green Bays" on the side and seats of a "Side Box" and some binding in the Prince's box. The vouchers show constant payments to plumbers, glaziers, tinmen, carpenters, and bricklayers, not to mention the regular scouring of lamps, their reflectors, and the drip pans.

The Lincoln's Inn Fields accounts (1724–25 and 1726–27) contain items for repairs and maintenance amounting to about £340 for the first season, £240 for the second; but so many entries are simply final payments to glazier or bricklayer or plasterer that it is not clear whether they represent repairs or additions to properties, scenes, and machines. For example, in 1724–25 the treasurer paid Gibson, a glass man, £42; Hopkins, bricklayer, £20; Hunt, a smith, £16 4s. 8d.; Holt, plasterer, £30; Wooley, glazier, £13 18s. 11d. Dumont received £2 monthly for tuning the harpsichord; Cornwall painted the ceiling at a cost of £13 13s.; and £13 7s. went to "a Years Repairing the Pavement." There is no doubt that the managers gave constant attention to upkeep and improvement of the theatre and its accommodations.

STAGE PROPERTIES. The Drury Lane vouchers (1712–16) list property bills for over forty different plays, and they suggest that the managers made careful provision for properties. For example, the theatre rented sheets and pillowbiers for many plays, especially those with death scenes, and normally specified that they must be fresh and clean each night. For elaborate productions like *Apollo and Daphne* (24 January 1716) Drury Lane expended £3 1s. 5d. for boards, nails, cloth, screws, etc. and £7 for painting Apollo's chariot. The managers often advertised new scenes, habits, and decorations for plays, a superlative example being the revival of *All for Love* on 3 December 1718 for which, Cibber reported, the playhouse expended £600 on new habits, scenes, and decorations.

At Lincoln's Inn Fields between 1724 and 1727 the personnel concerned with scenes, properties, and supernumeraries presented bills daily or weekly. Dovey, in charge of supernumeraries (a very flexible term), tendered a bill almost every day, his charges for 1724–25 amounting to nearly £300. Powell, head sceneman and carpenter, submitted bills for nearly £700 in 1724–25. Harvey, scene painter, received nearly £375 for the season, including £54 for "work done in fall of Siam," a new tragedy. Clarkson, in charge of "Incidents," and Newhouse, a property man, had bills amounting to £100. Lincoln's Inn Fields possibly spent a tenth of its income in 1724–25 on scenes, machines, and properties.

WARDROBE. The stock of clothes and habits, one of the principal physical assets of a company, was often difficult to evaluate, as is evident from the long quarrel between Vanbrugh and the managers of Drury Lane concerning how much they owed Vanbrugh for the habits which had once belonged to him at the Queen's Haymarket.[66] And the wardrobe required constant augmentation and renovation. The Drury Lane vouchers (1712–16) show regular acquisitions of new cloth, costumes, wigs, hose, feathers,

---

[66] For a detailed account of a theatrical wardrobe, see Sybil Rosenfeld, "An Inventory of the Wardrobe of Christopher Rich Esqr Deceas'd," *Theatre Notebook*, V (Oct.–Dec., 1950), 16–17.

buttons, lace, and payments to the house tailor for refashioning and mending and weekly charges for washing and cleaning. The incomplete set of vouchers for 1715–16 show at least £175 paid out for the purchase, renovation, cleaning, and making of costumes.

In the Lincoln's Inn Fields accounts for 1724–25 the sums which most clearly pertain to wardrobe total nearly £925. Because the bills are normally unitemized, it is uncertain just what they covered. There were, for example: "Mr Lafoss Staymaker," £17 16s. 6d.; "Mr Lovick for Hatts," £11 13s.; "Mr Paxton Laceman," £100; "Mr Sirr Mercer," £3 18s.; "Mr Taylor Laceman," £141 12s. 11d.; "Mr Tildon Woolen Draper," £27 1s.; "Mrs White Mantua Maker," £75 17s.; and similar ones for furs, hair, hose, suits, gowns, and wigs.

PRINTING. The playhouses paid several kinds of printing charges: the Great Bills to be posted around London, tickets for boxes and pit (occasionally other portions of the house), newspaper advertisements, and copies of plays (sometimes given gratis at the door). Of these the Great Bills were the most costly, the total for Lincoln's Inn Fields in 1724–25 being almost £150 in addition to the wages of the bill setters, usually 9s. daily. Printed admission tickets normally cost 2s. 6d. a hundred, and in 1724–25 Rich at Lincoln's Inn Fields purchased many thousands. In that season he also advertised in the *Daily Courant* and *Daily Post*, the charge for insertions being 4s. 6d. daily.

As a convenience to patrons the theatres sometimes gave free or offered for sale at the door copies of plays, operas, songs, prologues, or epilogues. On 14 December 1708 the Queen's at the premiere of *Pyrrhus and Demetrius* furnished auditors with "Printed Books of the Opera" and repeated the practice at the premiere of *Antiochus* on 12 December 1711; on 23 October 1714, however, it offered for sale at 1s. copies of *Arminius*. Similar practices existed at the playhouses. At Drury Lane on 12 March 1715, when *Venus and Adonis* was given, the house advertised: "A Printed Book of the Masque will be given each Person that pays in the Pit or Boxes." At Lincoln's Inn Fields James Spiller for his benefit on 13 April 1717 spoke a new "Comi-Tragi-Mechanical Prologue," which he had printed and distributed at the theatre. On 22 November 1723, when Lincoln's Inn Fields produced *The Union of the Three Sister Arts*, a musical interlude, it offered copies at the premiere for 6d. each. The foreign comedians assisted English auditors not well versed in other languages with a synopsis of the action as well; for example, the Italians at the King's on 21 October 1726, offering *The Enchanted Island of Arcadia* announced: "For the better

Information of those who do not thoroughly understand the Italian Language, a Book with the Argument and Explanations in English, of what is transacted in every Scene" will be sold at the door at 6*d*.

WEEKLY PAYROLL. By all odds the weekly salary list formed the major theatrical expenditure. For Lincoln's Inn Fields during 1724–25 salaries and wages came to approximately £4,200, not quite half the income for the season. At that time Rich had on his roll twenty-eight men whose primary vocation was acting. Nearly all received a set sum for each acting day: Anthony Boheme at 16*s*. 8*d*., William Bullock at 13*s*. 4*d*., John Hall at 6*s*. 8*d*., down to Young Clark at 1*s*. Of the sixteen actresses, the principal one, Mrs Bullock, ranked fourth on the acting list, but whereas four actors received more than £100 yearly (exclusive of benefits), she was the only woman to earn that much. There were eight individuals whose principal talent was singing, the best ones receiving good salaries: Richard Leveridge, about £150; Mrs Barbier, specializing in Italian, £200 by contract; Mrs Chambers, about £180. The salaries for the eight came to about £580. The vogue of pantomime and *entr'acte* song and dance made dancing a profitable vocation, and in this season Lincoln's Inn Fields engaged some fifteen dancers, the men earning about £740, the women about £165. Francis Nivelon, whose heels delighted London, led the list in salaries.

The basic charge for the music came to a nightly £3 14*s*. 2*d*., with occasional variations, for a total of about £610. The management paid extra for kettle or side drums, and some individuals—Pepusch, Galliard, and Hudson—received special payments. Galliard, for example, was paid fifteen guineas for composing the music for *Harlequin Doctor Faustus*, one of Rich's most successful pantomimes. The treasurer had a host of other personnel on the weekly schedule: charwomen, number unspecified, 5*s*. nightly; women dressers, under Mrs Carter, 13*s*. 2*d*. nightly; Stede, the prompter, 5*s*. 6*d*., with additional sums for copying out parts; Wood, the treasurer, 6*s*. 8*d*. Other categories included pit doorkeeper, gallery, stage, box, and lobby doorkeepers, sweepers, lampman, candlewoman, porter, washer, house tailor.

No definite indication exists, however, as to the exact number of persons associated with the entire operations of Lincoln's Inn Fields, as far too many groups like charwomen and dressers appear without a specific statement of the number of individuals in each group. In 1735, however, when legislation to restrain the playhouses appeared in Parliament, *The Case of the Comedians . . . in Goodman's Fields* stated that over three hundred persons depended upon that theatre for their livelihood. Although that figure may well have included both employees and their dependents, a comparable figure for Lincoln's Inn Fields would probably be somewhat higher, as it was a larger house than Goodman's Fields.

RECEIPTS *vs.* EXPENDITURES.   Because the account books, even the relatively complete ones for Lincoln's Inn Fields in the 1720's, represent only one out of several ledgers kept each season, it is difficult to determine whether the theatre made a profit. Taking the 1724–25 records as an example, the total income of Lincoln's Inn Fields was about £10,500, the disbursements about £10,700. But among the payments are some (the nightly deduction and extras) paid to John Rich, the proprietor, totalling about £500, a sum sufficient to turn an apparent deficit into a net balance. At the close of the ledger there is a settlement of the season's finances, signed by John Rich and Thomas Wood, the treasurer, which states that the sum of £336 10s. 9d. was due "from the said John Rich Esqr to Thomas Wood." This amount is sufficient to alter the apparent deficit into a slight profit.

In fact, scrutiny of the books suggests that the company overcame a deficit by midseason. In November 1724 the house was not meeting expenses, and Rich paid only partial salaries due each Saturday; but toward the end of the month a profitable run of *The Prophetess* enabled the treasurer to reduce the arrears. As receipts increased in December, he settled some old bills, on 10 December 1724, for example, paying Paxton £50 and Hudelston £100 on account as well as sums owing the theatrical staff. The house apparently prospered, slightly at least, in January, February, and March, but the start of benefits brought a decline. The treasurer often got only £40 (the basic charge), not enough to pay all the back bills. In late spring the house cut expenses sharply, but the margin between profit and loss became narrower. At the end there was a technical deficit, the proprietor having overdrawn his account; even without Rich's withdrawals, the theatre seems always to have been on the delicate edge between gain and loss.

EXPENSES OF THE OPERA COMPANY.   Just as the opera enterprises had admission charges and income different from those of the playhouses, so their disbursements, though similar in kind, involved a higher proportion of salaries to other expenses. In addition, the budget for the opera house, even though it performed less than half as many nights as the theatres offering drama, was much greater. For the early years the most specific information concerning actual expenditures and estimates of probable costs appears chiefly in British Museum Ad Ms 38,607,

Nicoll, *Early Eighteenth-Century Drama*, pp. 276–81, 284–86, and the newspapers.

One set of documents concerns the season of 1707–8, when Italian opera still bore an air of novelty. A prospectus (*ca.* March 1708) estimates the expense of a season as £7,320, with costs for materials and operations as follows: house rent £800; wax candles and oil £320; printers' bills £60; and attendants £640, an overhead of approximately £1,760. In other documents (8 March and 7 April 1708) these costs were reduced to a nightly basis: candles £3; wax £3; oil £1; office keepers and attendants £9 19s. 2d.; printer £2 5s.; manager £3 (7 April 1708) or managers £8 5s. (8 March 1708); rent and use of stock £15; incidentals ("one night with the other") £6 7s. 10d.; and small bills £10. These amounted to £53 13s. or £58 18s., contrasting with about £40 at a playhouse.

Although the operational costs were high by playhouse standards, salaries for singers, dancers, and musicians were even higher. The document for March 1708 names six women singers at salaries from £80 to £400, the total being £1,370; five men from £40 to £430, a total of £1,030. (It was the rare actor who could command a salary of £200.) The instrumental music fell into two categories: "Chief Basses" at £70 each, and others at £750, a total of £1,080; on a nightly basis these averaged £17 2s. or £17 12s. Salaries and costumes for eight dancers required £800, the nightly charge for all singers and dancers being set at £44 17s. The list provided £1,275 for two new operas, including costumes and scenery, or £20 nightly.

For part of 1707–8 these estimates can be checked against actual expenditures. Between 13 January and 6 March 1708 the company presented sixteen operas; at a nightly charge of £120 17s. 6d., they cost £1,774 8s. A new opera (*Love's Triumph*) cost £250, with £42 paid for its "practice" and £20 for new scenes. By 7 April 1708, twenty-three nights of opera had cost £2,672 15s. 8d., plus bills for habits and scenes amounting to £815 12s. By then the cost of *Love's Triumph* had reached £334 10s., with the inevitable entry, "Extraordinary Allowances," £107 10s. The costs for twenty-three nights, all in all, stood at £4,090 7s. 8d., approximately £177 nightly, offset partially by receipts of £2,943 1s. 6d.

For no other season before 1740 does this kind of information exist concerning the expense of opera, but the newspapers and other records made clear that expenses steadily rose. For example, the *London Journal*, 3 July 1725, cited the cost of opera at £16,000 yearly, whereas Lincoln's Inn Fields at this same time, performing more than twice as often, had a budget of slightly below £11,000. Salaries for imported singers constantly rose and inflated the budget for opera. For example, on 27 November 1719 the Court of Directors of the Royal Academy of Music instructed Handel to treat with Durastante at £500 for three months commencing 1 March 1720 and at £1,100 for the following year. In December 1720, the engagement of Nicolini prompted *Applebee's Weekly Journal*, 31 December, to report that he would receive 2,000 guineas for the year. Such extraordinary salaries made the expenses of opera skyrocket, and it is not surprising that between 1720 and 1728 the Academy required a subsidy, apparently, of nearly £50,000 to close the gap between income and outgo. In fact, such salaries and other expenditures make unprofitable a comparison between the finances of the opera companies and the legitimate houses; more and more their operations moved in different realms.

THEATRE ROYAL, HAYMARKET

From an engraving by Hixon before the theatre was demolished in 1821. It was constructed by John Potter in 1720, largely as a remodelling of the King's Head Inn between Little Suffolk Street and James Street. Known first as the "New Theatre" it was later called "The Little Theatre" to distinguish it from the larger King's Theatre, Haymarket.

THE DUKE'S THEATRE, DORSET GARDEN

Reproduced from an old print among a collection of prints in the *Folger Shakespeare Library*. It was opened by the Duke of York's company under Betterton's management 9 November 1671, and demolished in 1709. It stood a little eastward of the Dorset stairs on the Thames waterfront.

For the Benefit of
Mr. GRIFFIN
Theatre Royal in Drury Lane
Tuesday April 22 1729
The Provok'd Wife
and the
What d'ye call it
PIT 3s

ELABORATE BENEFIT TICKET for a seat in the Pit, reproduced from *Garrick and his Contemporaries* (a collection of documents and prints illustrating the 18th-century theatre) p. 126. *Folger Shakespeare Library.*

By His Majesty's Company of Comedians,

AT the Theatre-Royal in Drury-Lane, this present Tuesday being the 31st Day of December, will be presented, a Comedy called, *The Relapse: Or, Virtue in Danger.* The Part of Lord Foppington by Mr. Cibber; Loveless, Mr. Wilks; Worthy, Mr. Mills; Young Fashion, Mr. Wilks, jun. Sir Tunbelly Clumsey, Mr. Shepard; Coupler, Mr. Johnson; Lory, Mr. Penkethman; Seringe, Mr. Norris; Shoemaker, Mr. Miller; Berinthia, Mrs. Oldfield; Amanda, Mrs. Porter; Miss Hoyden, Mrs. Younger. With Entertainments of Dancing by Mr. Thurmond, Mr. Boval, Mrs. Topham, Mrs. Booth, Mrs. Bullock, and Miss Tenoe; particularly the Dance of Lads and Lasses.

By the Company of Comedians,

AT the Theatre Royal in Lincoln's-Inn-Field, this present Tuesday being the 31st Day of December, will be presented, the Tragedy of *Julius Cæsar*; with the Death of Brutus and Cassius. Written by Shakespear. The Part of Brutus by Mr. Quin; Cassius by Mr. Boheme; Cæsar by Mr. Leigh; Anthony by Mr. Walker; Calphurnia by Mrs. ... The Comic-Parts, by Mr. Bullock, Mr. Hall, Mr. Morgan, and Mr. H. B...

By the New Compa...

AT the New Theat...
Opera House in the Hay Mark... 31st Day of December, will be presen... *The Female Fop*; Or, *The False One*... ments of Singing and Dancing. Bo...

At the earnest Desire of seve...
TONY ASTO...
(*This present Tuesday being the 31...
Vine Tavern in C...*
The best Parts of his ... Lorenzo, and Elvira, in the S... truction, and Peg, in the Tami... Fondlewife, and Lætitia, in the ... Hillaria, and Squib, in the Ye... Æsop; Sir Toby and Philosoph... With Songs and Drunken Man.
Beginning at S...
N. B. He performs on Frida... next, Engler's Rents in Holborn...

At the particular Desire of several Ladies of Quality.
By His Majesty's Company of Comedians,

AT the Theatre Royal in Drury-Lane, present Tuesday being the 1st Day of November, will be seated, A Comedy call'd, *The* PROVOK'D WIFE. Revis'd by the thor. The Part of Sir John Brute, by Mr. Cibber; Constant, Mr. W... Heartfree, Mr. W. Mills; Lord Rake, Mr. Bridgewater; Colonel ... Mr. Harper; Justice, Mr. Shepard; Rasor, Mr. Miller; Taylor, ... Griffin; Lady Brute, Mrs. Oldfield; Lady Fancyful, Mrs. Cibber; ... da, Mrs. Booth; Madamoiselle, Mrs. Brett. With a new Epilogue add... to the Ladies, in Favour of the English Stage, and Entertainments of ... cing. And To-morrow will be presented LOVE's LAST SHIFT ... The Fool in Fashion, with Apollo and Daphne.
N. B. The Company will continue to Act every Day.

By the Company of Comedians,

AT the Theatre-Royal in Lincoln's-Inn-Fi... To-morrow being Wednesday the 2d Day of November, will be ... sented, A Comedy call'd The PILGRIM. The Part of the Pilgri... Mr. Ryan; Roderigo, Mr. Quin; Alphonso, Mr. Hippisley; Mad En... man, Mr. Spiller; Mad Scholar, Mr. Boheme; Mad Taylor, Mr. ... Alinda, Mrs. Bullock; Juletta, Mrs. Younger. With several Ente... ments of Dancing; particularly, The Humours of Bedlam. Mad So... Mons. Nivelon; Mad Dancing-Master, Mr. Glover; Mad Gamester, ... Helling; Mad Taylor, Mr. Newhouse; Mad Astrologer, Mr. Lan... Mad Lady, Mrs. Legar.
To which will be added, A Masque of Musick, call'd, Pan and Sy... Pan, by Mr. Leveridge; Syrinx, Mrs. Barbier; Diana, Mrs. Cham... a Sylvan, Mr. Legar; a Nymph, Mr. Salway. With proper Dances, ... perform'd by Mon. Nivelon, Mon. Salle, Mon. Dupre, Mr. Lally, Mr. ... house, Mr. Pelling, Mr. Lanyon, Mon. Dupre, jun. Mrs. Legar, ... Bullock, Mrs. Pelling, and Mrs. Ogden.
N. B. None to be admitted into the Boxes, but by printed Tickets, ... will be deliver'd at the Theatre, at 5 s. each. Pit 3 s. First Gall. 2 s... Gall. 1 s. 6 d.

By PERMISSION.

AT the Crown Tavern in West-Smithfield ... Dock-Lane, this Evening at Seven o' Clock will be perf... an Entertainment by Mr. Clench of Barnet, who imitates the ... Huntsman, Pack of Hounds, the Sham-Doctor, old Woman, ... ken Man and the Bells, the Flute, Double Courtel, the Organ with ... Voices; all Instruments are perform'd with his Natural Voice, a... Essex Song by Mr. Clench, after which Manner none but himself can ... form. Price one Shilling.

PLAYBILLS FROM THE LONDON NEWSPAPERS. Above from the *Daily Post*, 31 December 1723. Below from the *Daily Post*, 1 November 1726.

A Bill for Printing

		£	s	d
Mar: 6 } 17 13/14	Venice Preserv'd, 1 day—	00	09	00
8	The Careless Husband— —	00	09	00
9	Love makes a Man, &c —	00	09	00
10 } 11	Love for Love 2 dayes—	00	18	00
12	Philaster — — — — —	00	09	00
		02	14	00
The Courant 6 dayes —		01	01	00
		3	15	0

Three pound fifteen shill

Allen

Rob Wilks

B Booth

ADVERTISING COSTS for inserting play notices in the *Daily Courant*, 1714, reproduced from *MS. Collection of Wardrobe and Property Bills, Drury Lane* now in the *Folger Shakespeare Library*.

Tuesday
~~~~~ Gallant,   pd the Hire of A Monkey . . . . 0 : 2 :
                    The Use of A Tea Canister . . . . 0 : 0 :

Thursday   pd for yͤ Use of A Fine Holland pr ⎫
Othello   of Sheets, & Three pillowbiers . . . ⎬ 0 : 1 :
                    pd for yͤ Use of Two White Blankets . 0 : 1 :
                    A Fine Wrought Hand kercheif . . . . 0 : 1 :
                    Pumatum for Mr Booth, 3 Ounces . . 0 : 0 :

Fryday   pd for yͤ Use of Six case of Pistolls . 0 : 3 :
The Pilgrim   A Drum for Mr Bignall . . . . . 0 : 0 :
                    pd for A Truss of Straw . . . . . 0 : 1 :
                    Pumatum, & Vermilion for Mr ~~~~ 0 : 0 :
                    pd for Two Fine Baskets of Flowers 0 : 1 :
                    A Leake for Mr Norris . . . . . 0 : 0 :

                                                    1 : 4 :

                    one pound four . . .
                    ~~~~~~~~~
                    ~~~~~~~
                    Cibber

this is a property bill.

COSTS FOR RENTING STAGE PROPERTIES [c. 1715], reproduced from *MS. Collection of Wardrobe and Property Bills, Drury Lane* now in the *Folger Shakespeare Library*. The hand in the lower left is that of James Winston.

Left to Pay a Bill Amounting to — 3 - 7 - 0

Feb: ye 25th Mithridates

Wash: a white Plume m^r Wilks — — 0 - 7 - 6
Ditto m^r Mills — — — — 0 - 7 - 6
Wash: & Mending a white feather ⎱ 0 - 5 - 0
m^{rs} Santlow — — — ⎰

ye 28th

Wash: a white Spanish feather ⎱ — 0 - 2 - 6
m^{rs} Younger — — ⎰

March ye 3^d Henry ye 4th

for a Beard for m^r Mills — — 0 - 10 - 0
for Wash: 2 white toors — 0 - 3 - 0
for Wash: a Bonnet feather — 0 - 1 - 6
3 - ✳ -

Three pound
Clither.
D Doth
Robt Wilks

COSTS FOR CLEANING AND MENDING feathers and costumes, reproduced from
MS. Collection of Wardrobe and Property Bills, Drury Lane now in the *Folger
Shakespeare Library*.

A: Bill ffor work done by
Tho: Arne Octob: 14: 1715

	£	s	d

ffor 52 y.ds of woll to cover 4 seats in the
pitt and 8 in the Gallery over the princes box at 4d   — 17 : 4

ffor 106 y.ds of wirb woll for Ditto ab 2d p.y   — 17 : 8

Nails and work to cover the seats —   10 :

ffor 3 y.ds of Green Bays to cover the fronts
of the 2 stage boxes and 1 seat in Ditto ats 3d   12 : 4

ffill cotton and 600 hundred of Brass nails
used for D.o and mending the front boxes   8 :

ffor work to cover the fronts of the stage
boxes and one seat in Ditto and mend
the front boxes   6 : 6

yds of binding Lace to add to the princes box —   — : 8

ffor 7 y.ds of Green Bays to line 1 side and
for the seats in one of the side boxes —   15 : 9

Oldham and Toe, to stuffe the seats —   4 :

tape Lace and setting the seats covering
covering one side of the box   5 : —

£   4 : 17 : 3

Four pound ~~Clibber~~

R: Wilks

B Booth

COSTS FOR REFURBISHING AND REDECORATING Seats and Boxes of Drury
Lane Theatre, 1715, reproduced from *MS. Collection of Wardrobe and Property
Bills, Drury Lane* now in the *Folger Shakespeare Library*.

Administration and Management

THE LONDON PLAYHOUSES during the early eighteenth century offer interesting problems in the theory and practice of the management of both legitimate and operatic companies. Inheriting both an actor-manager system—for example, the Betterton management of Lincoln's Inn Fields following its opening in 1695—and the proprietor-manager structure—Christopher Rich at Drury Lane—the new century continued both types, coped with the problem of how to run an opera company, tried mixing opera and drama under the same roof, saw a successful venture of a triumvirate of actor-managers, and witnessed the trial of a consolidated management of operas in the Royal Academy of Music. The complexity of the problem prompts a discussion under two headings: the opera companies and the legitimate playhouses.

THE MANAGEMENT OF OPERA

Italian opera made its formal appearance in London in 1705 as part of the repertory of a company primarily devoted to drama. From this beginning the producers of opera faced problems which differed from those of the managers of plays and which persistently confronted them for the next twenty-five years as well as later: high costs for salaries and operations; the necessity of finding large sums with which to produce opera on the grand scale; the recruitment of foreign performers, whose financial expectations and temperaments created endless perplexities; the securing of a proper decorum within the Opera House and among the directors and performers; and the formation of an administrative organization which could solve these complex difficulties. From 1705 to 1728, when the Royal Academy of Music ended its first sponsorship of opera, London experimented with a variety of administrative and fiscal plans for its support.

The advent of opera occurred, in a sense, when Drury Lane on 16 January 1705, under the direction of Christopher Rich, presented *Arsinoe, Queen of Cyprus*, the joint work of Peter Anthony Motteux, Thomas Clayton,

Nicolino Haym, and Charles Dieupart. Sung in English, it was, however, at first given only once a week, English plays being presented on the other five evenings. It did not present heavy administrative or financial problems, for all the singers had been attached to the London theatres in recent years.

More important in the development of opera was the opening on 9 April 1705 of the Queen's Theatre in the Haymarket, with a new Italian opera, *The Loves of Ergasto*. It was sung by a set of performers from Italy, who temporarily became rivals to the native English vocalists at Drury Lane. Nevertheless, the basic plan at the Queen's resembled that at Drury Lane: performances of opera intermingled with offerings of English plays.

Essentially the same situation prevailed during 1705–6, with Betterton's company at the Queen's offering operatic pieces, such as *The Temple of Love* on 7 March 1706, as an occasional part of its repertory, and Rich at Drury Lane countering with *Camilla* on 30 March 1706 as a supplement to his dramatic fare. In 1706–7 a similar combination of operas-and-plays prevailed, but in the middle of the next season, on 12 January 1708, Drury Lane assumed sole responsibility for plays, acting six nights weekly, and the Queen's gave only operas, acting on two evenings only.

In theory, this division had much to recommend it; in fact, Colley Cibber, who had played in companies which presented operas and plays conjointly as well as in purely dramatic units, thought joint operation an unsatisfactory practice.[67] Nevertheless, the separation did not work to the advantage of opera in 1707–8, as Vanbrugh makes clear in a letter to the Earl of Manchester on 17 July 1708. Explaining that the season had not been financially satisfactory, Vanbrugh blamed the deficit on the fact that performances did not begin until the season was half over; that the town, supposing the venture inherently profitable, did not enter freely into subscriptions; and that, although attendance in pit and boxes had been good, the gallery patrons, who previously had attended out of curiosity, now stayed away. In addition, the opera company, cut off from the acting units, lacked a good stock of costumes and scenes, and because there was barely enough income to pay the singers and normal daily charges, the other costs fell heavily upon Vanbrugh and other backers of opera.[68]

As a result of this financial debacle, London in 1709–10 returned to the earlier system of plays and operas jointly given in each of two competing theatres; but in 1710–11 a new division occurred, with opera farmed out to Aaron Hill, and in 1711–12, as Cibber put it,[69] opera was thrust upon

---

[67] *Apology*, II, 87.   [68] *Works*, IV, 24.   [69] *Apology*, II, 107.

Owen Swiny, who in mid-January 1713 created a crisis by taking the receipts after the second performance of *Theseus* and departing the country. He left the singers and many tradesmen's bills unpaid, but the performers, who naturally were in "some Confusion" rallied and instituted a co-operative company, installing John Jacob Heidegger as manager. When the company had £162 19*s*. in clear balance, the Lord Chamberlain ordered the money to be shared among the performers.[70] Although this co-operative enterprise marked the emergence of Heidegger as an operatic impresario, a role he played for some years, this type of loose organization failed to prosper and was unsuited to cope with the problems of opera. The financial disaster of 1711–12 had continuing repercussions; the immense success of *Cato* in 1712–13 cut attendance at operas; and the tense political situation in 1715–16 made the Court and King hesitate to mingle in "such Crowds these troublesome times," as Colman's Opera Register, July 1715 noted. And thus the first series of experiments in operatic management ended when operas ceased in 1716–17, not to resume until 1719–20.

The first really comprehensive attempt to develop opera magnificently as an institution separate from the legitimate theater came in 1719 with the creation of the Royal Academy of Music. This corporation, whose Letters Patent are dated 9 May 1719, was established for twenty-one years, and it was to receive a royal subsidy of £1,000 yearly. Shortly after its legal inception, it had sixty-two names on the list of original subscribers, most of whom guaranteed £200 of the stock of the company. At that time the original proposals for £10,000 were overpledged by £5,600.[71]

From the beginning the Lord Chamberlain, by virtue of his office, was the Governor of the Royal Academy. The subscribers held a yearly meeting at which they elected a Deputy Governor and Board of Directors, the meeting legally occurring on 22 November or within fourteen days thereafter.[72] The Directors were empowered to hold a General Court every three months or oftener. The Lord Chamberlain, as Governor, exercised in effect a veto power, for no order was valid without his signature. The

[70] Nicoll, *Early Eighteenth Century Drama*, p. 285.

[71] A good deal of confusion exists concerning the amount of the basic subscription. John Mainwaring, *Memoirs of the Life of the Late G. F. Handel* (London, 1760), p. 97, gives it as £40,000; Charles Burney, *A General History of Music* (4 vols.; London, 1776–89) and others raised it to £50,000; but no documentation for these specific sums is known. Nevertheless, the initial subscription was certainly £15,600; in 1719 some additional subscribers joined (Burney, apparently, had a list including 73 subscribers), who may have added another £2,200; Vanbrugh on 18 February 1720 says that £20,000 had been subscribed; and the King's bounty totalled £7,000 by 1729. The sums imply a basic subsidy of approximately £25,000.

[72] See the *London Gazette*, 3 December 1728.

Directors could issue calls for payments by the subscribers and could manage the operas; the Academy had a "Common Seal" and the power to make bylaws. In the deliberations each share worth £200 had one vote; a £600 share, two votes; a £1,000 share, three votes; but no individual was permitted more than three votes. At its origin the Academy apparently had three subscribers at £1,000 each; fifty-eight at £200; one at £400; and one at £600.

By October 1719 the Academy had begun to function as a corporate body. It held a General Court on 6 October 1719, chose directors on 18 November and a Deputy Governor on 25 November. By 2 April 1720 it had twenty Directors.[73] In its early years, it designated a corps of specialists. Besides the Governor, Deputy Governor, and Directors, it named James Bruce as treasurer, John Kipling as a Deputy Governor, John Jacob Heidegger as manager, Paolo Antonio Rolli as Italian secretary and librettist, Roberto Clerici as decorator and machinist, and G. F. Handel the Master of the Orchestra. In due time it named as composers Ariosti, Handel, and Bononcini, and as designers of scenes Peter Tillemans and Joseph Goupy.[74]

To judge from the very few extant records of their early meetings, the Directors set about enthusiastically and systematically to organize an operatic company and open a first season in 1719-20. At the first meeting in late 1719 the Court assigned duties: Heidegger to enter into negotiations with Attilio and Senesino, and to propose to Signora Galerati a contract for £250 from 1 March 1720 to 1 June 1720 and £400 for 1 November 1720 to June 1721. Dr Arbuthnot was to request Mrs Anastasia Robinson to submit to the Directors her proposals for singing with the company. James Bruce, treasurer, should ask L'Abbe to submit a plan for operatic dancers. Alexander Pope was to be asked to prepare a seal with suitable motto. (He apparently did not agree to do so.) The proposals also intimated that the subscribers might expect to be gainers from their investment. Vanbrugh, in fact, expected the season of 1720 to be a "very good one," 1720-21 "a better one," for the Academy had engaged the "best Singers in Italy" at—it seems hardly necessary, in view of later developments, to mention— "a great Price."[75]

On 2 April 1720 the Academy opened a short season which ran until 25 June 1720, approximately twenty-two performances. During the next season its offerings were presented twice weekly from 19 November 1720

73 See the Dedication to *Numitore* (London, 1720), dated 2 April 1720.

74 Otto Erich Deutsch, *Handel: A Documentary Biography* (New York, n.d.), p. 176.

75 *Works*, IV, 125-26.

to 1 July 1721, a total of some fifty-eight performances. By that time it
had drawn upon the subscribers for a total of at least 24 per cent of the
initial subscription. In addition, the King contributed £500. Thus, the
Academy had by June 1721 accumulated possibly £5,000 over and beyond
the box-office receipts from nonsubscribing patrons, a sum difficult to
estimate.

At the beginning of 1721–22 the Academy changed its procedures
by instituting a system of annual subscribers, an action which suggests
that, although the Directors had had a good deal of money at their disposal
in the first two years, they needed a more certain knowledge of the probable
receipts. The new scheme, advertised in the *London Gazette*, 25 November
1721, offered a season ticket for twenty guineas, payable in installments,
with a guarantee of fifty operatic performances or a reduction if fewer
were given. (As the company gave fifty-nine performances, it more than
met its agreement.) On 9 December 1721, when *Floridante* had its premiere,
the announcement stated that because of an increase in the number of
subscribers no more than 350 tickets would be sold for that performance,
a contrast to the usual figure of 400 in previous notices. Possibly, then,
fifty annual subscriptions had been sold, bringing £1,050 in certain income;
and the King paid £1,000 to the Academy.

This system of annual subscribers continued at least through 1726–27.
For one season, 1725–26, an estimate exists of 133 annual subscribers, but
no source or authority is known for this figure.[76] At one time the Academy
had sufficient financial security to pay a dividend. As early as 27 October
1722, the *London Journal* stated that the Directors would distribute some
of the profits, and the same journal reported on 16 February 1723 that a
dividend of 7 per cent had been declared. For the rest of its career, however,
the Academy continued to make calls upon its members until by 1727–28
each had apparently paid 99.5 per cent or 100.5 per cent of his pledge, less
a dividend of 7 per cent.

In spite of support of members of the Academy, the King, annual
subscribers, and other patrons, the Academy had difficulty living within
its income (including assessments), let alone building a surplus with which
to make new plans; further evidence of its financial difficulties appears in
the fact that although the initial subscriptions presumably were to cover
the expected twenty-one years of the corporate life of the Academy, they
were exhausted in seven years. In addition, in 1725–26 the Directors had
to rent the opera house during part of the season to a company of Italian

[76] See Deutsch, *Handel*, p. 188.

comedians as a means of supplementing their income. Furthermore, the Directors as well as the principals, both singers and composers, augmented their troubles by quarrels, the most damaging controversy being the notorious feud between the supporters of Signora Cuzzoni and the adherents of Signora Faustina, which culminated in a public brawl at a performance of *Astyanax* on 6 June 1727 in the presence of the Princess of Wales. The first venture of the Royal Academy of Music in sponsorship of opera ended at the close of the season of 1727–28.

Nevertheless, this management, unsatisfactory in many ways, gave London nine seasons of opera with an average of around fifty performances yearly. It imported most of the finest singers in Europe, investing large sums in scenes and habits as well as engaging the most eminent composers of the day. Actually it spared no cost to bring to London patrons the best in opera which it could achieve; but it did not overcome many of the administrative and financial problems inherent in an organization composed of elected Directors, salaried managers and other personnel, and talented but temperamental performers.

These financial and administrative problems were not the only ones which the development of opera had to solve. There were problems relating to the theory of opera itself. During the years following the introduction of opera to London, operatic performances took a variety of forms. As has previously been mentioned, *Arsinoe* (16 January 1705), though based on an Italian work, was sung entirely in English. Shortly thereafter, on 9 April 1705, *The Loves of Ergasto* was performed in Italian by singers from Italy. In contrast, *Thomyris* (1 April 1707) was sung in two languages, as was *Clotilda* (2 March 1709). The vogue of opera stimulated Addison to attempt an original English one, *Rosamond* (4 March 1707), but fashionable London, not deterred by satiric comment upon the folly of listening to a musical drama whose words almost no one in the audience understood, soon came to accept Italian lyrics only, and by the advent of the Royal Academy the Haymarket produced operas almost exclusively in Italian.

From its inception the Academy faced dilemmas concerning the nature or theory of the libretto. For example, P. A. Rolli, writing to Giuseppe Riva on 18 October 1720, pointed out that the opera *Amore e Maesta* could not be produced in London as it was in Florence, "because it would then have so much endless recitative and so few arias, that Senesino would have only four in all."[77] As a result, the Directors instructed Rolli to adapt it to the needs of the Academy. In addition, the policy of engaging the finest

[77] See Deutsch, *Handel*, p. 114.

singers in Europe had by 1725 somewhat limited the kinds of operas it could most advantageously produce. The clearest statement of the needs and restriction appears in a letter from Riva, writing from Hanover on 7 September 1725, to Ludovico Antonio Muratori, who apparently had inquired concerning a friend who wished to submit an opera to the Academy.

In England, according to Riva, the requirements included few recitatives, some thirty arias, and at least one duet, all of these to be distributed throughout three acts. The subject matter should be tender and heroic, preferably Roman or Greek, but not Gothic. Because of the composition of the company, there must be equal parts for the two leading women, Cuzzoni and Faustina; they should have the duet, which must come at the end of Act II. As Senesino was the principal castrato, his part must be heroic, and the other three castrati must sing one aria apiece in each act. It was possible to have a third female role.[78] Although Riva did not specifically make the point, operas at this time, generally speaking, had only six to eight roles. A year later, on 3 October 1726, Riva, again writing to Muratori, confirmed this analysis: "Few verses of recitative and many arias is what they want over here."[79]

To secure operas, especially the two, three, or four new ones desired for each season, the Academy tried a variety of methods, not with entire success. At first it commissioned Rolli to be its librettist, but difficulties with the management resulted in his removal and the substitution of Haym, a less talented man. Riva, writing in retrospect on 7 September 1725, was caustic on Haym's deficiencies: "a Roman and a violoncellist, who is a complete idiot as far as Letters are concerned. Boldly passing from the orchestra to the heights of Parnassus, he has, for the last three years, been adapting—or rather making worse—the old librettos which are already bad enough in their original form."[80] With the music the Academy was more successful, although disagreements disturbed the scene. Among its early minutes (30 November 1719) is a resolution that Bononcini be approached to know his terms for composing as well as performing in the orchestra. In 1720 both Bononcini and Attilio Ariosti composed for the Academy, and on 27 April 1720 Handel presented his own composition, *Radamistus*. Jealousies arose among the composers and their friends, and in 1721 it was decided to commission an opera by three men jointly. It was *Mutius Scaevola* (15 April 1721), for which Filippo Amadei set the first act, Bononcini the second, and Handel the third. The superiority of Handel's

[78] *Ibid.*, p. 186.   [79] *Ibid.*, p. 197.   [80] *Ibid.*, p. 186.

portion did not ease the tension, but the Academy managed to keep the services of a small number of composers.

Throughout the twenty-five years of opera under consideration, producers were also concerned with spectacle, decorations, and supplemental attractions. In these respects they were affected, as were the playhouses, by the growing taste for *entr'acte* entertainment, lavish scenes, intricate machinery, expensive habits, and song and dance. The bills occasionally advertised supplemental dance and music which did not necessarily have an integral relation to the opera proper. For example, at *Amadis* on 21 March 1717 de Mirail's Scholar and Mlle Crail, both from Paris, danced; and at a performance on 11 April 1717 Glover and Mlle Crail did a Spanish dance. On 5 June 1717 danced the exceedingly popular young brother-sister act of M and Mlle Salle. On 20 June 1716 at a performance of *Amadis* the bills stressed "Two New Symphonies" and for the same opera on 30 April 1717 "Two Pieces of Musick between the Acts."

The case for lavish embellishment of opera was made by Aaron Hill in the preface to the word-book of *Rinaldo*, dated 24 February 1711. There he emphasized that one of the deficiencies of Italian operas as presented in England was their "wanting the Machines and Decorations, which bestow so great a Beauty on their Appearance, they have been heard and seen to very considerable Disadvantage." He hoped in this production to "fill the Eye with more delightful Prospects, so at once to give Two Senses equal Pleasure." Some means of accomplishing these ends may be seen in the stage directions for *Rinaldo*. In Act I Armida was to be transported in the air in a "Chariot drawn by two huge Dragons, out of whose Mouths issue Fire and Smoke" and there was to be a "black Cloud" descending, "all fill'd with dreadful Monsters spitting Fire and Smoke on every Side." As a variation, in Act II two mermaids were to dance and sing in the water, and in Act III there were to be "Waterfalls" and "Thunder, Lightning, and amazing Noises."

The somewhat gentle spoofing of these embellishments in the *Spectator* for 16 March 1711 suggests that it was easier to plan these spectacles than to produce them. The dragons did not fulfill expectations; there was "a very short Allowance of Thunder and Lightning," though the spitting of fire and smoke from the dragons was exceedingly generous; and the sparrows and chaffinches, who had received attention previously in the *Spectator* for 6 March, "fly as yet very irregularly over the Stage."

Nevertheless, the production of opera continued to be attended with great care for scenes and machines. In January 1713 the *Colman Opera Register* mentioned that in the plans for a new opera were intentions of having "all ye Habits new & richer than ye former with 4 New Scenes, & other Decorations & Machines." A performance of *Theseus* on 24 January 1713 was advertised as being presented "in its Perfection, that is to say with all the Scenes, Decorations, Flights, and Machines," with an apology that something less than perfection had been achieved at the previous offering of the opera. A revival of *Rinaldo* on 6 May 1713 carried the notice, "With all the proper Scenes and Machines," and the bill for *Amadis* on 20 June 1713 emphasized "Particularly, the Fountain-Scene."

There can be little doubt of the zeal with which the Academy held to its goal of providing the best in opera created by the best composers and sung by the ablest performers, improving the tone of audience and theatre, and providing new scenes and habits as constantly as possible. In many of these aims it succeeded. *A Letter to my Lord on the Present Diversions of the Town* (1725) gave the Academy high praise: "Our *Opera's* indeed are in perfection: we have a Composer or two, and two Singers that cannot be excell'd, if rivall'd by any in the Universe" (p. 7). In the same year the author of *Letters Describing the Characters and Customs of the English and French Nations* thought the music "to be but indifferent" but the machines nearly as good as those at Paris and the decorations "fine," especially those of "Sattin [which are] extraordinary Magnificent." Although the English did not dance so well as the French, they danced "less frequently, and perhaps more to the Purpose. The same thing may be said of their singing; they sing only the Airs, and rehearse the rest. There's something uncommon and agreeable in these Airs, and in my Opinion is more suitable to the Taste of melancholy Persons than others" (p. 32).

The Academy, of course, had many other problems. For example, in the early 1720's it began a series of public rehearsals of new operas, usually charging a guinea for attendance. This means of giving patrons a preview of an opera and of raising more money did not always work out happily; according to *Mist's Weekly Journal*, 18 January 1724, a public practice of *Vespasian* a few days earlier had occasioned a "civil Broil among the Subscribers." Maintaining proper decorum within the organization as well as in the opera house was not an easy matter. The engagement of Mrs Cuzzoni precipitated, according to the *Daily Journal*, 23 January 1723, "very great Debates, and warm Speeches" among the Directors, who at the same time had to threaten to close the Footmen's Gallery if noise and disorders there did not cease.

By 1726–27 the difficulties of the Academy had become acute. In June 1727 the most notorious of the internal squabbles came into the open: the quarrel between Signora Cuzzoni and Signora Faustina over precedence in the company. The town took sides, the Directors split over their allegiances to these singers, and in the opera house on 6 June 1727 "the Contention at first was only carried on by Hissing on one Side, and Clapping on the other; but proceeded at length to Catcalls, and other great Indecencies" (*British Journal*, 10 June). An effort by Senesino to act as moderator only increased the tension. By the following autumn conditions had worsened; on 25 November 1727 Mrs Delany wrote that there had been many divisions among the Directors; in addition, the subscription had expired and "nobody will renew it."[81] All of these tensions, coupled with financial problems, brought an end late in 1728 to the performance of operas. The formal organization of the Academy continued and had a share in the revival of opera after a hiatus, but the next approach to opera management was a considerably different one from that employed between 1720 and 1728.

MANAGEMENT OF PLAYS

At the opening of the century Drury Lane and Lincoln's Inn Fields competed under differing types of management. The company at Lincoln's Inn Fields was headed by Thomas Betterton, the foremost living actor, who, with other major performers, had in 1695 opened that theatre as a partially co-operative venture. By 1700 the strength of the company had lessened, leaving the theatre with a diminished reputation. A glimpse of conditions within the playhouse appears in the preface to David Crauford's *Courtship à la mode*, a comedy which he had submitted, unsuccessfully, to Betterton. Crauford's view is, of course, that of an author who has just had a play rejected, but he had quite specific complaints concerning the functioning of Lincoln's Inn Fields. Crauford had given his manuscript to Betterton, who "did me all the Justice I cou'd indeed reasonably hope for." But Betterton's example had not inspired his fellow actors, especially John Bowman, whom Crauford selected as an example of the failure of the management. Bowman had had the principal part in his hands for six weeks, "and then cou'd hardly read six lines on't." In addition, those "who valu'd their reputations more" attended rehearsals, but six or seven

<hr />

[81] Mary Delany, *The Autobiography and Correspondence of Mary Granville, Mrs Delany*, ed. Lady Llanover (London, 1861–62), I, 149.

actors could "not perform what was design'd for fifteen," and Crauford emphasized "how far that way of management makes of late for the Interest and Honour of that House, is easie to be judg'd." Not long afterward, on 11 November 1700, the Lord Chamberlain ordered that Betterton was to have sole management of Lincoln's Inn Fields in order to rectify the disorders resulting from a lack of sufficient central authority to keep the actors at their duties. The sharers, however, continued to possess power, for all money for clothes, scenes, etc. could be spent only by consent of a majority of the sharers, with the exception that Betterton could lay out a sum not exceeding 40*s.* if absolutely necessary. Lincoln's Inn Fields, then, represented a company of sharing actors which had gradually moved toward greater executive authority in the hands of one player.

At Drury Lane, Christopher Rich, who was not an actor himself, managed affairs as a patentee and proprietor. Whereas some of the players at Lincoln's Inn Fields were sharers, Rich at Drury Lane, according to Cibber,[82] took two shillings from each pound of the day's receipts for himself, Cibber alleging that Rich took his tithe first and made other payments only when he had sufficient money. But by contrast with the disorganization he found at Lincoln's Inn Fields, Crauford, trying to get *Courtship à la mode* produced, thought that Rich ran Drury Lane capably and efficiently. After withdrawing his comedy from Betterton's hands, Crauford took it to Drury Lane, "where 'twas immediately cast to the best advantage and Plaid in no less than twenty days." Rich's company, however, considered him a parsimonious man, and he and his actors had constant difficulty, the differences eventually culminating in a dispute over Rich's making deductions from actors' benefits. He and Drury Lane were silenced on 5 March 1707.

From 1705 onward, when Vanbrugh opened the Queen's, London witnessed an almost yearly reorganization of theatrical companies until players and managers could secure a more orderly policy. The new theatre gave Betterton and his company a fresh start, but Betterton, past his prime, did not maintain masterful control. At the same time the entry of Italian opera into the repertory created new problems for management. Patentees, actors, and members of Parliament juggled companies in a confusion of theatrical enterprises. In the midst of these shifts, around 1707, an elaborate plan for the proper organization of a company was drawn up.[83] As already indicated, this proposal envisioned twenty actors, eleven actresses, an

---

[82] *Apology*, I, 263.
[83] Nicoll, *Early Eighteenth Century Drama*, pp. 276–78.

unspecified number of pensioners and young actors, six singers, seven dancers, twenty musicians, and at least forty-five servants, all for a proposed outlay of £9,000 to £10,000 yearly. This plan, with an emphasis upon three managers, foreshadowed the formation in 1710, with the approval of the Lord Chamberlain, of a system which lasted nearly thirty years: the actor-managers of Drury Lane. Although the composition of the group changed occasionally, Colley Cibber and Robert Wilks from 1710 onward dominated the management. In November 1710 they, with Owen Swiney and Thomas Dogget, received a license to play at Drury Lane, the comedians to pay William Collier, who controlled the company legally, a flat sum each year. Within a short time Drury Lane entered upon one of its most prosperous eras, an achievement which, though for a short time aided by a virtual monopoly of plays, Cibber attributed to excellent acting and skilful management.

This type of management began with a careful delineation of managerial duties and operational methods. In 1710 (probably) the Lord Chamberlain issued a series of directives setting forth the principles by which the company should be conducted.[84] First of all, the directors, especially those with salaries (Cibber, Wilks, and Dogget), should have regular meeting days, with two comprising a quorum; they should prepare bylaws (to be approved by the "Honorary Directors"), make a list of all plays "fit to be acted," revising them to be certain they were free from indecencies, and keep in their office a copy of each new play "for their justification." In addition, the directors were to assign plays and parts and purchase all things necessary "for ye well performing," but they must not undertake an expensive entertainment without consent of the Honorary Directors. A further provision was evidently never enforced: that there "be no poets night, but yt ye board agree for new plays at certain rates" for both printing and acting, with prologues, epilogues, and songs to be published by order of the directors. Another recommendation also failed to become effective: that no benefits be allowed or tickets given to any person. As to rehearsals, one actor-manager should be present at each practice and should see that the young actors have three sessions weekly in which to learn to dance and sing. In financial operations, the actor-managers at each meeting should inspect the receipts, give directions for paying salaries once each week and for settling all bills and other charges by the first of each month. (These accounts should be inspected every three months by the Honorary Directors.) As a check on the managers, it was ordered that they could not raise salaries, take in new players, or make an addition to the "constant charge" of the

84 *Ibid.*, pp. 279–81.

house without approval of the Honorary Directors and confirmation by the Lord Chamberlain. Furthermore, the managers should have written agreements with every person in the company, these to include a penalty for anyone, except the musicians, who might perform in any other place without permission; if the company should be commanded by the Court to forbear acting for six weeks, the usual period of mourning on the death of royalty, or even longer during the winter, the company should be allowed only half salaries.

The second directive simplified some of these matters: 1] The actor-managers should meet weekly (more often, if any two require it). 2] All orders should be entered into a book for the use of the treasurer, such orders not to be revoked or contradicted except by all three men and nothing must be construed an order which does not bear the three signatures, except the purchase for not more than twenty shillings of "any little Necessarys." 3] If any manager refuses or neglects to attend meetings, the other managers present shall have full power. 4] No new or revived play should be scheduled without the consent of all three and the parts should be assigned by approval of the three by evidence of their signatures. 5] No actor or servant should be changed in status without consent of all three. 6] All tradesmen's bills must be signed by all the managers and paid weekly if there be sufficient money, and no money is to be shared until all debts are discharged. 7] The treasurer must neither pay nor refuse to pay any money contrary to his directives on penalty of discharge.

This systematization aimed to provide an orderly, co-operative management, in which all the managers agreed upon every major decision, with a provision permitting continued operations if one proved neglectful. (The wisdom of this provision became evident when Dogget fell at odds with the other managers.) How these procedures worked out has been indicated by Cibber. In general operations, Dogget, an economical man, kept expenses and accounts well-regulated; Wilks, however, wanted to spend more freely; Cibber, a mediator, tried to keep on good terms with both and to hold disagreements to a minimum. The three agreed that no creditor should have occasion to ask twice for payment of his bill, and each Monday morning they discharged all demands upon them before each took a sum for his private use. Contrary to the directive of 1710, they did not require written agreements with members of the company; instead, they entered the terms and salary for each person on the daily payroll. That, in effect, became the actor's contract.[85]

[85] Cibber, *Apology*, I, 311, reporting a gift to Mrs Oldfield after her fine performance in

In arriving at a decision concerning contracts, the managers could look back upon a variety of previous arrangements. The principal documents concerning a player's relations with his manager in the first decade come from appeals to the Lord Chamberlain, such petitions presumably representing the last stage in the negotiations. For example, among those summarized by Nicoll is a complaint by Anne Oldfield on 4 March 1709 stating that she had returned to Rich's company under an agreement which, she thought, gave her the same terms she had had at the Queen's; to this Rich filed a reply setting forth his understanding of the matter.[86] A manager's complaint appears in Rich's representation to the Lord Chamberlain concerning Mrs Hooke [Harcourt], who, Rich asserted, had been lured away from his company by Vanbrugh and Congreve at the Queen's in spite of her articles with Rich.

Possibly as a result of similar disagreements there may have been an attempt around 1708–9 to regularize articles; the contracts summarized in Nicoll may reflect a new policy or may simply be renewals of previous engagements. At any rate, they are formal agreements stating expressly the terms of employment. For example, the one concerning John Mills dated 30 March 1709 is for five years from 1 July 1709 at £100 yearly, with a benefit in March and charges of £40 to be deducted from the receipts on that evening. Some contracts include additional clauses: Mrs Oldfield was to be free from the tenth of June to the tenth of September each year and to have her salary in nine installments; and her articles were to run for the unusually long period of thirteen years. The contracts also stipulate varying deductions at benefits: Mills, Johnson, and Penkethman got the receipts over £40, William Bullock, Benjamin Husband, Mary Porter, and William Bowen those over £50.

The actor managers, however, preferred a less formal contract, and Cibber makes it clear that the managers did not require an actor to sign an agreement.[87] An example of an order to enter a player's name has been reproduced by Alwin Thaler; in it, over the signatures of Cibber, Wilks, and Booth, the treasurer was authorized to enter Mrs Willis at 40s. weekly from Saturday 28 November 1719 and to reduce Mrs Hunt to 40s. weekly.[88] A similar document (Folger Shakespeare Library) on 11 July 1720 directed Castelman, the treasurer, to enter Mrs Robinson at 40s.; one dated

The Provoked Husband in 1728, states that she received fifty guineas over "her Agreement, which never was more than a Verbal one."

[86] *Early Eighteenth Century Drama*, pp. 286–92.

[87] *Apology*, II, 113.

[88] *Shakspere to Sheridan* (Cambridge, Mass., 1922), facing p. 64.

22 September 1722 ordered him to add 20s. to Shaw's salary. On 9 September 1726 the managers authorized striking the names of Ray, Roberts, Savage, and Mrs Roberts from "the Company Charges," reducing Dupar to 6s. 8d. nightly, the "two Willis's" to 5s., the constable to 2s., and entering Clark at 13s. 4d.

This type of procedure, beyond doubt, proved satisfactory to management, which held considerable power simply because few opportunities for actors existed outside the patent house. In addition, the Lord Chamberlain had frequently issued orders forbidding a theatre to engage a player who did not have a specific discharge from his previous employer. Although such restrictions, of course, prevented management from raiding another company, they sharply curtailed the freedom of actors, who could look to few openings. For example, an order by the Lord Chamberlain dated 9 January 1710 named the players, singers, and musicians currently engaged at the Queen's and declared "that they shall not have leave upon any Terms whatsoever to be Entertain'd in any other Company" without a written discharge.[89] Nevertheless, when Lincoln's Inn Fields opened in December 1714, Steele noted that some actors from Drury Lane went to the new house, others got increases in salaries "at the very moment when they were going to act," and that Drury Lane needed restrictions against these practices.[90] Later, Drury Lane and Lincoln's Inn Fields exchanged lists of performers as a means of preventing unauthorized changes.

Having established its working principles, the Drury Lane management did not alter greatly until 1713–14. By then the demands of Barton Booth for a share in the control had won him a place, but settling the terms of the new partnership brought disagreement, particularly over what title Booth should have in the stock of clothes and scenes. When the Lord Chamberlain suggested that the managers settle the matter among themselves, Wilks wished to set "a good round Value" on the stock but Dogget refused to name a price or dispose of any of his share. In this crisis Wilks and Cibber agreed that Booth should become a partner and pay them £600 for his share in the property; piqued, Dogget refused to act, manage or sell, yet insisted on his full share of the profits. Eventually a suit in Chancery settled the matter; Dogget received payment and withdrew. For many years thereafter, the triumvirate of Cibber, Wilks, and Booth managed Drury Lane, although not without differences of opinion. According

---

[89] Nicoll, *Early Eighteenth Century Drama*, pp. 278–79.
[90] G. A. Aitken, *The Life of Sir Richard Steele* (London, 1889), II, 51. See also Loftis, *Steele at Drury Lane*, p. 43.

THE LONDON STAGE, 1700–1729

to Thomas Davies, Booth could not be troubled with the management of the stage and Wilks confided in Cibber, with the result that Cibber appeared to the outer world to be the principal manager and received the brunt of all complaints.[91] Nevertheless, according to Theophilus Cibber, the managers met regularly, settled their weekly expenses, paid bills, fixed the order of new and revived plays and entertainments, heard the grievances and gave rewards through increased salaries, and never failed to be conscious of the improvement or good services of any performer. Had not the opening of Lincoln's Inn Fields in 1714 provided fresh competition, the managers probably could have kept the great prosperity of Drury Lane unimpaired but might easily have slipped into lethargy.

Other important problems had faced the actor-managers even before the quarrel with Dogget. Early in the century they had conducted their affairs with little interference by Owen Swiney or William Collier, who might well have been considered "honorary directors." At the death of Queen Anne and the subsequent termination of the Drury Lane license, Cibber and his fellow managers agreed that, since it was likely that there would always be a man of influence at Court who would receive the fees currently allotted to Collier and that there might always be complications in the relationship between the playhouse and the Lord Chamberlain, they might as well choose as titular head of the company a man of influence. They invited Richard Steele to join them, and he accepted. What share, then, should Steele, an influential man of letters and a politician but not an actor, have in the practical matters of management? The evidence is inconclusive, partly because the substance of the negotiations is known principally from a lawsuit of 1725, some time after the arrangement was initiated.[92] Although disagreeing in 1725 on some matters, the two sides acknowledged that one of Steele's functions was to write for the theatre and support it by his influence. They disagreed as to whether Steele was expected to attend the managers' meetings and to instruct young actors, a profession for which he had no technical experience.

In 1714–15, then, the management entered a new phase: a trio of actor-managers in partnership with a fourth who had theatrical experience only as a dramatist but who possessed influence at Court. At the outset the new license made no distinction between Steele and the others concerning their powers, although Steele for awhile continued to receive the sum which had previously been paid to Collier; but competition with Lincoln's

91 *Memoirs of the Life of David Garrick, Esq.* (London, 1780), II, 378.
92 See Loftis, *Steele at Drury Lane*, p. 36.

Inn Fields and a decline in the profits of Drury Lane brought an agreement
that Steele would forego the fixed sum and accept a share. Soon Steele
received a patent, assigned to him alone but with an understanding that
the managers would share in it. Steele outlined more fully his theory of
the relationship of a patentee and managers in *Theatre* No. 7. In his opinion,
a company needed at its head men who by experience knew the problems
of a playhouse, for in such matters as producing plays, assigning parts,
determining salaries, and handling the economy of the theatre only experience
and training afforded the basis for sound operation. A patentee like himself,
then, shared in the management only with respect to the expense and
general morality. From the available evidence, it seems likely that Steele
did not concern himself with financial details, rehearsals, or staging of
plays; the Drury Lane vouchers for 1715–16 show the signatures of the
three actor-managers only, and one or another of them supervised rehearsals.

But this arrangement did not work out successfully. Probably the
failure resulted not so much from defects in the scheme as from Steele's
personal problems, financial obligations, political involvements, and ill
health. Up to January 1720, when Steele was suspended by the Lord
Chamberlain, he shared in management and profits; after that, only in the
profits. At some time between 1720 and 1723 the actor-managers agreed
that since they ruled in all matters it was only reasonable to allow each
one the sum of £1 13s. 4d. each acting day "in Consideration of our Constant
Attendance, Management & Acting."[93] In his *Apology*[94] Cibber justified
this deduction by explaining in detail the many duties of the three men.
They had under their charge about 140 persons "in constant daily Pay,"
some of them "unskilful, idle, and sometimes untractable; all which Tempers
are to be led, or driven, watch'd, and restrain'd by the continual Skill,
Care, and Patience of the Menagers." In turn each manager attended two
or three hours or morning rehearsals; one or more had to attend each
public performance whether or not any of them had parts in the play.
In addition, a manager had to be present at the reading of every new play,
and since hardly one in twenty submitted was worthy of production,
"upon such Occasions the Attendance must be allow'd to be as painfully
tedious as the getting rid of the Authors of such Plays must be disagreeable
and difficult." Among other arduous duties, a manager had to order all
new habits, assist in their "Fancy and Propriety," limit the expenditures,
and withstand the "unreasonable Importunities of some that are apt to
think themselves injur'd if they are not finer than their Fellows." As if

93 *Ibid.*, pp. 56, 214–15.   94 II, 203–4.

these tasks were not sufficient, the managers must direct and oversee painters, machinists, musicians, singers, dancers, and such under-servants as doorkeepers and officers. Cibber did not mention that each of the three had a full career as an actor, each performing night after night, year after year. Examining this multitude of responsibilities, the actor-managers felt justified not only in sharing the profits but also in deducting £5 daily as managerial pay.[95]

These men dominated Drury Lane from 1710 to the 1730's, when illness, death, and retirement brought a dissolution of the partnership. Although their regime had many quarrelsome moments and litigation and suffered severe criticism from the enemies of one or another (especially of Cibber), Drury Lane usually presented more polished performances than its rivals and, by contrast with Lincoln's Inn Fields, concentrated more seriously upon legitimate drama. Cibber's recital of the duties and tribulations of the management might easily lead one to agree with Charles Johnson who, in the preface to *The Successful Pyrate* (7 November 1712), gave a tribute to Wilks which might well extend to his associates:

No Body who has not immediate Opportunity to know it, will imagine the Oeconomy that is requisite in the Management of a Theatre. This of Mr Wilks gives both Life and Being to, and adds to the best Capacity an Unweary'd Application to his Business.[96]

95 In addition, each manager took for himself twelve sealed tickets weekly to give to friends and agreed that no written note from them or from any other person would allow free admission. (See a document dated 22 September 1722 in the Folger Shakespeare Library.) Although this was an additional perquisite of the office of manager, probably the main point of the new policy was to protect each manager from the countless importunities of acquaintances by having only a fixed number of passes available each week.

96 If one thinks of the theatre as business, in the monetary sense of the word, it is apparent that, in addition to a daily payment for being a manager, another for being an actor, and other financial values of the office, the three managers of Drury Lane were also partners in an enterprise which had worth as an investment. An indication of this phase of the manager's status appears in the settlement to be made at Drury Lane after Steele's death. Wilks, Booth, and Cibber agreed to pay £1,200 for Steele's share in the patent, costumes, scenes, and good will; the worth of Drury Lane at the time this agreement was drawn (19 September 1721) was presumably £4,800, exclusive of the playhouse proper. In addition, Steele shared in the profits.—See Loftis, *Steele at Drury Lane*, p. 229.

Advertising

TO INFORM the town and attract spectators, the London playhouses used a variety of advertising media. Part of this was oral, part printed. The managers inserted their bills in the daily papers and posted them in the centers of London traffic; they grew steadily more proficient at persuading editors to print short items concerning forthcoming plays, benefits, special attractions, and the attendance of royalty and celebrities. In the absence of systematic reviewing, however, both managers and spectators relied considerably upon word of mouth for the evaluation of new plays, criticism of actors, both established and new, and gossip about fascinating life backstage and among players.

After a premiere, therefore, patrons often gathered at coffee houses to damn or defend the play and to chat about playwrights, actors, and managers. On 28 February 1729, for example, John Byrom wrote that he and some friends went to the Bedford Coffee House to "hear what Wilks, Cibber, should say about the disturbances that were last night at the old play house about the Village Opera, which had been hissed, and such noise and mobbing as was very extraordinary." Following the opening night of Samuel Johnson's strange play, *Hurlothrumbo*, acted on 29 March 1729, all London fell to talking about it, and Byrom stated that it became "one of the chief topics of talk" and that Dick's Coffee House resounded "Hurlothrumbo from one end to the other."[97] But when a patron wished to know what was scheduled for the evening's program at a playhouse, he had three sources of information: the announcement of the next day's offerings at the close of a performance, when the manager or a principal player "gave out" the intended play; the playbills posted in the center of London; and notices in newspapers.

Of these three media, two had been in vogue since the reopening of the theatres in 1660: the oral announcement and the playbill. Until 1702 the posted bill was the more important means of informing Londoners of theatrical offerings; for decades—Pepys is a well-known example—Londoners

97 Richard Parkinson, ed., *Remains of John Byrom*, Chetham Society, XXXIV (Manchester, 1855), pp. 335, 349.

had been accustomed to walking out or sending a servant to see what the Great Bills announced in large black or red letters. In 1702 the managers augmented these bills by inserting, at first quite irregularly, somewhat similar notices of their offerings in the newspapers. Because there was no daily journal in London before 1702, managers had not found it profitable to advertise regularly in periodicals which appeared only two or three times a week; but the founding of the *Daily Courant* early in 1702 offered a medium of advertising which the theatres soon adopted and never discarded.

The format of the Great Bills influenced that of the newspapers announcements, but since playbills are the kind of ephemera which few people collected or preserved in the late seventeenth and early eighteenth centuries, we have only a few extant bills by which to determine their form and variety. A surviving bill for 19 May 1703 (British Museum, 11795 g 19) shows the detail available to a potential spectator.

> At the Desire of several Persons of Quality
> At the THEATRE ROYAL in Drury-Lane, tomorrow being
> *Wensday* the 19th day of May, will be Reviv'd
> That Celebrated Comedy call'd
> VOLPONE, Or, The FOX.
> Written by the Famous *Ben. Johnson*
> The parts in general will be perform'd to the best Advantage.
> With several Entertainments of Vocal and Instrumental
> Musick, as will be exprest in the Great Bills tomorrow.
> And Dancing by the Famous Monsieur Du Ruel, Mrs.
> Campion, and others; particularly a Sabotier by him,
> never perform'd before.
> The Part of Corbaccio perform'd by BEN JOHNSON,
> For his own Benefit.
> To begin exactly at half an Hour after Five.
> No Money to be return'd after the Curtain is drawn
> up. By Her Majesty's Servants.   *Vivat Regina.*

Two examples from the *Daily Courant* for the same year show the variations in announcements inserted there.

> For the Benefit of Mr. *Pinkeman.*
> AT the Theatre Royal in DRURY-LANE, this present Friday, being the 12th of *February* will be presented the last new Comedy, call'd TUNBRIDGE WALKS, *or,*

THE YEOMAN OF KENT. With a piece of Instrumental Musick to be perform'd on the Stage. Also Singing by Mr. *Laroon* and Mr. *Hughs;* particularly a Two-part Song, compos'd by the late Mr. *Henry Purcell.* And the *Devonshire Girl* will perform several Dances, particularly the *Country Farmer's Daughter*, and the *Highland Lilt.* With an Irish Humour, call'd, *The Whip of* Dunbyn, by Mr. *Claxton* her Master. Also a new Entry perform'd by Mrs. *Campion* and others. With the Scotch Dance by Mrs. *Bicknell.* And a Dance between a Scaramouch Man and a Scaramouch Woman, by Mr. *Laferry* and Mrs. *Lucas,* both entirely new, and never perform'd before. And to conclude all, *Will Pinkeman* speaks a Joking Epilogue. No Money to be return'd after the Curtain is drawn up.

At the Theatre Royal in *Drury-Lane*, this present Thursday being the 11th of March will be acted a New Comedy written by Mr. *Tho. Durfey*, call'd, *The Old Mode and the New, or Country Miss with her Fourbelow.*

Of these types of advertising, the posted bill for some years apparently represented the more authentic notice, for it could be prepared and posted some time after copy for the newspaper had gone to a printing office and, if a last-minute change in the program occurred, new bills could be quickly prepared and posted in place of the old. The playbills were often more complete, also, for quite commonly in the first decade the newspaper notice stated that further details would "be express'd in the large Bills" (see Drury Lane, 1 February 1704 or 14 September 1704).

Just how many bills the managers posted daily is unknown, but they appeared in two colors: red and black, the former being referred to in the Prologue to *The Governour of Cypress* (January 1703) as follows:

> *Wide Folio Bills on ev'ry Post we place*
> *And huge* RED LETTERS *stare you in the Face.*

The Drury Lane expense vouchers for 1712–16 (Folger Shakespeare Library) show that during these years black bills cost 10*s*. daily; red, 15*s*. There is no positive indication as to what determined which bills should be red and which black, but the red occasionally seem to have been used to advertise a specialty. For example, the Epilogue to *The Temple of Love* (Queen's, 7 March 1706) stated:

> *Put out Red-Letter'd Bills, and raise your Price,*
> *You'll Lure a select Audience in a Trice.*

Even so, the more expensive red ones were printed during all parts of a season and for old as well as new or revived plays. During 1715–16, for example, vouchers for printing bills for 92 performances contain payments for 37 red, 55 black. At this proportion, the printers' charges for playbills for a season of 180 performances would be approximately £100. The frugal managers of Drury Lane watched these expenses as carefully as they did all others, and once—the voucher for the week ending 21 January 1716—deducted 5s. from the payment to the printer because of misspelling on one day's posters.

Important as the Great Bills were because of tradition, size, color, and location, the newspapers eventually became equally important. In 1704 the *Daily Courant* had a circulation of nearly eight hundred copies daily,[98] and every issue had many readers in the coffee houses. Although Lincoln's Inn Fields was slower than Drury Lane to make full use of the *Daily Courant*, by 1706–7 each theatre regularly inserted notices, with more and more details added until the advertisement assumed a format which prevailed for decades. The fact that newspaper notices were cheaper than playbills also stimulated increased use of that type of announcement. The Drury Lane vouchers for 1712–16 show that insertion in the *Courant* cost 3s. 6d. daily, approximately £31 for a season of 180 performances; and the account books for Lincoln's Inn Fields for 1724–25 and 1726–27 indicate that in fifteen years the cost had not risen markedly, for John Rich, the manager, then paid 4s. 6d. daily for joint insertions in the *Daily Courant* and *Daily Post*. And so anxious were the newspapers to have the useful prestige of printing theatrical notices that in 1729 Edward Owen, printer of the *Daily Courant*, which was losing ground to the *Daily Post* and *Daily Journal*, persuaded the Lord Chamberlain to direct the managers of all the theatres to send their announcements to Owen, "who will insert them gratis."[99] In spite of the greater expense of printing Great Bills, Rich in 1724–25 paid printers' bills of £150 for playbills, to which was added a daily wage of 9s. for the bill setter, whose

> Business was at Tavern Doors
> And City Gates the Play-House Bills to fix.[100]

These notices, though varying in details, contained a great deal of information. The heading usually included the name of the theatre, date,

98 James R. Sutherland, "The Circulation of Newspapers and Literary Periodicals, 1700–1730," *The Library*, New Series, XV (June 1934), 111.

99 Lord Chamberlain's Records, 5/160, p. 104, in Nicoll, *Early Eighteenth Century Drama*, p. 275. The order is dated 29 January 1729.

100 *Weekly Journal or British Gazetteer*, 12 February 1732.

and sometimes a formalized statement such as "By His Majesty's Company of Comedians," "By a Select Company of Comedians from both Theatres." In addition, notices of requests often appeared, such as "By Desire," "At the particular Request of several Ladies of Quality," "By His Majesty's Command," and, for benefits, the names of the players participating in the receipts. The body of the notice specified the play (often listing the cast), special prologues and epilogues, the afterpiece (possibly with its cast), and the *entr'acte* entertainments of music, singing, and dancing. The bills usually listed the male roles first, then the women's, but sometimes a leading actress (such as Mrs Oldfield in the 1720's) or a new performer or a player having a benefit received first mention. Usually, however, there was little star billing; very rarely did a performer see his name in capitals or noticeably accented; and rarely did an individual monopolize first place in the listing, although at Drury Lane the names of Cibber, Wilks, and Booth, the managers, quite often appeared among the first four or five in the bills. At the bottom of the notice there usually appeared the charges (perhaps in detail, such as boxes 5s., pit 3s., first gallery 2s., upper gallery 1s. or in such general terms as "At Common Prices," the time of performance, and admonitory, prohibitory, or restrictive orders, such as "No Money to be Return'd after the Curtain is drawn up," "By His Majesty's Command, No Persons are to be allow'd on the Stage," or "Servants may be sent to hold Places in the Boxes." Occasionally notices of forthcoming performances appeared, especially for benefits or new plays, and announcements of postponements or substitutions, such as "Owing to the Indisposition of a Principal Performer . . . is deferr'd Indefinitely." In fact, the notices informed the prospective spectator of nearly everything except the quality of the performance or the merit of the play, matters which he must learn from other playgoers.

In due time there also appeared the puff. As theatrical advertising became more important to the finances and prestige of the daily papers, their news columns contained more and more theatrical gossip and information: that *The Fall of Saguntum* was now in rehearsal and would be acted shortly; that Anthony Boheme had changed allegiance from Lincoln's Inn Fields to Drury Lane (later to be denied); that Mrs Oldfield would have a benefit next week; that His Majesty or other members of the royal family might be expected at a performance or had recently attended one. Quite often a newspaper stated that a new play had been received "with universal Applause by a large [or crowded] Audience," a statement which, sometimes appearing identically in several journals, smacked of the manager's rather than the editor's sentiment. In preparation for a premiere, a manager might hope to see, as did Rich at Lincoln's Inn Fields, an advance judgment like the notice in the *Daily Journal* for 12 February 1722 concerning the forthcoming play, *Hibernia Freed:* "the Play for Diction, and fine Sentiments is not inferiour to any Dramatick Piece that has appear'd on either Stage these 20 Years."

In time more extended puffs appeared. For example, on 25 March 1725, during Passion Week, when *The Rise and Fall of Massaniello* was advertised for 29 March 1725 as a benefit for Thomas Walker, the *Daily Journal* printed a long letter by J. Friendly, who pointed out the historical events forming the background of the play, gave a summary of its plot, and extolled Walker's merit.

The play it self is considerably improved. The original Song, new set, in praise of Fishing, is to be performed by Mr Leveridge. A New Comic Dance has been composed by an ingenious Master, proper to the Occasion. There is a Piece of Machinery, entirely new, part of which will be the Statue and Description of Massaniello; and a Composition of solemn Musick, vocal and instrumental, on the Confirmation of the Neapolitan Charter, admirably set, will be a singular Advantage to the Entertainment.

. . . It is to be exhibited for the Benefit of a very ingenious Young Actor.

Even more effective devices were employed by some managers and actors, especially for their benefits. William Penkethman, a lively clown and shrewd showman, advertised offerings at his Richmond theatre in a sprightly fashion, and his benefit notices usually contained a humorous solicitation. Richard Leveridge, who sang and acted for decades, amused London with short poems or epigrammatic appeals for full attendance at his benefits. And Tony Aston, whether announcing one of his frequent "Medleys" of characters by himself, his wife, and his son, or calling attention to his benefit, made a casual, often charming appeal to his followers. On 20 March 1724 he advertised his wares in the *Daily Post* with this stanza:

> *Three, more Diversion can show*
> *Than 20 that do little know;*
> *We shift the Dress, and change the Theme,*
> *We skim the Milk, and take the Cream.*

Although some of the comment in the papers was colorless in its objectivity, some of the news was partisan, vigorously defending or violently attacking. For example, in the late 1720's *Mist's Weekly Journal* had a constitutional aversion to Cibber as actor, manager, or playwright, and its vehemence spread to remarks about all the affairs of Drury Lane. After 1714 when Lincoln's Inn Fields opened and renewed competition between two playhouses became the established order, more and more comment appeared in the journals. This led to invigorating discussion, such as the controversy over the merits of Steele's *The Conscious Lovers*. Gradually, then, advertising spread from the impersonal bill through the puff and studied comment to lively discussion, often biting, frequently laudatory, but always keeping the public conscious that the theatre existed and that a world of varied entertainment was to be seen there.

The Benefit

ANOTHER problem of management which was of extreme importance to the actor was the benefit, which had its rise in the late seventeenth century. According to Cibber, the first indulgence of a benefit was given to Mrs Barry in the reign of James II, and for some years she alone possessed this privilege.[101] But in the troubled financial circumstances of the late seventeenth century when payments to actors fell into arrears, the practice developed of an actor's taking a chance on recovering these arrears by a benefit performance. In due time benefits became so valuable that they loomed large in the agreements between performers and management, a point amply illustrated in the agreements summarized by Nicoll.[102] What had begun as a means of securing back pay from the audience, not from the manager, became in a few years a bonus. Mrs Barry's original honor turned into an occasion which often brought the best crowds of the year and which passed beyond the players to doorkeepers, treasurer, prompter, and many lesser servants.

By 1703–4 the practice had grown almost chaotic, with benefits both early and late in the season to the detriment of the theatre's finances. During October 1703, for example, Drury Lane had a half-dozen, chiefly for major performers (Wilks, Mills, William Bullock, Norris, Cibber); in mid-season they occurred rarely, but in February 1704 they resumed and from mid-May to mid-July hardly a performance there or at Lincoln's Inn Fields was a nonbenefit. Some actors had two benefits; more than half were for one performer only; most of the others were for two jointly. At the close of the first decade a modification of the confusion set the pattern for many years thereafter. A feeble gesture toward banishing the actor's benefit appeared in the proposed regulations for a company in a rule stating "that no benefit plays be allowed."[103] This proposal failed. A more realistic directive of 17 April 1712 provided that no actors' benefits occur before the first of March, and that became the practice.[104] As a result, from a third to a half of the performances from March through June were set aside for actors and other employees.

[101] *Apology*, II, 67–71.
[103] *Ibid.*, p. 279.
[102] Nicoll, *Early Eighteenth Century Drama*, pp. 286–87.
[104] *Ibid.*, p. 281.

By the 1710's three characteristic types prevailed: actor, author, and charity. The actor's benefit was, naturally, the most frequent. The author's night was principally restricted to the production of a new play, the receipts (after charges) for the third, sixth and (possibly) ninth nights providing him a form of royalty. Somewhat rare early in the century, the charitable benefit gradually broadened into assistance to bankrupt merchants, individuals in debt or prison, indigent widows and children, and religious or patriotic causes. The financial arrangements became more settled. The most desirable, but also the rarest, was the clear benefit by which the beneficiary received all the receipts. The more common form, however, involved the deduction of a sum sufficient to meet the house charges. Lesser personnel were often permitted as benefits half the value of the tickets which they personally sold. On these occasions the beneficiaries advertised their nights well in advance and solicited friends and acquaintances to purchase tickets.

The sum required to meet the house charges grew steadily decade by decade. According to a statement by the patentees on 10 December 1694 the basic expense came to £30 nightly.[105] In *A Comparison between the Two Stages* (1702)[106] the "Ordinary Charge" was computed at £34. During the run of *The Tender Husband* in April 1705 it had risen to £38 15s. 10d. On 22 October 1707 Mary Porter stated that the deduction at her benefit came to £40,[107] and there it apparently remained for some time. In 1707–8, Rich, however, made an attempt to alter the sum. Noticing the large bonuses garnered by the players at crowded benefits, he decided to take a third of the proceeds above the house charges as a payment "for the proper Use and Behoof of the Patent." On 3 March 1709 at Mrs Oldfield's benefit *The Stratagem* brought £134 3s. The treasurer claimed the basic charge of £40, and Rich assessed her an additional £31 7s. 8d. Mrs Oldfield protested, and the Lord Chamberlain sustained her appeal by forbidding any subtraction for the use of the patent. Rich, however, persisted in the practice until the Lord Chamberlain silenced him.[108] With these fundamental procedures in mind, let us look at examples of benefits for actors, house servants, charity, and authors.

ACTORS' BENEFITS. As we have seen, the actor's benefit gradually became restricted to the spring. As the winter months, when London was crowded, were the best times for the theatres, March, on the edge of the social season, became the most profitable time for actors' benefits. The principals, therefore, sought by seniority or influence to get places

[105] Nicoll, *Restoration Drama*, p. 375.   [106] P. 8.
[107] Nicoll, *Early Eighteenth Century Drama*, p. 291.   [108] *Ibid.*, p. 282.

early in the sequence of benefits. In 1708–9 Mrs Oldfield had as part of her agreement a benefit in February; Penkethman one in March; Husband, Johnson, and Mills in April.[109] In 1716–17 at Drury Lane the sequence was as follows: John Mills, Mrs Oldfield, Colley Cibber, Mrs Porter, Dupre (a dancer), Mrs Santlow, Norris, and Booth in March; Mrs Bicknell, Penkethman, Johnson, Weaver (a contriver of pantomimes), Mrs Mountfort, the lesser actors and house servants in April. On 2 February 1720 Mrs Oldfield and Mrs Porter secured an order prohibiting any one else from having a benefit before theirs.

The theatres also varied the sums which the house took from the receipts. Occasionally a player was permitted to keep the money for all the tickets he sold *if* income at the door equalled the nightly house charges; the treasurer then kept the door receipts. If the box office receipts were insufficient, the player had to make up the deficit, and sometimes the treasurer, taking no chances, required an actor to deposit in advance £40. The Lincoln's Inn Fields account books for 1726–27 show the system at work. On 11 March 1727 Mrs Younger had the first benefit, receipts at the door totalling £42 9s., tickets sold amounting to £123 5s., all subject to a deduction of £40. In succession, Ryan, Mrs Barbier, Nivelon, and Quin paid the same sum for their benefits, money at the door always exceeding that sum. On 6 April Mlle Salle's benefit brought: money, £44 1s.; tickets, £48 11s.; yet on 8 April 1727 her father paid the treasurer £35 19s. "the deficiency of £80 on his Daughters Benefit." Deductions for others varied from £50 for Salle Jr, Mrs Berriman, and Mrs Fletcher to £60 for Rochetti and Glover.

To make his benefit profitable, an actor, knowing his night well in advance, took tickets, usually for boxes and pit, and solicited his acquaintances. Perhaps he could persuade an editor to insert a squib on his behalf, as happened in the days of the *Tatler* and *Spectator*.[110] In addition, he advertised his benefit some days in advance, and in March and April the newspapers occasionally had five to ten notices of forthcoming benefits. These often indicated where tickets could be bought, the player giving his home address or a coffee house as a source of tickets, and many an actor, ill or bedridden

109 *Ibid.*, pp. 286–87.

110 Benjamin Griffin, in the *Weekly Journal or Saturday's Post*, 1 April 1721, relied on Londoners' memories of this practice in seeking a good word for his benefit that evening at *The Pilgrim*: "Mr Estcourt had a good Word for having been the Squire's Apothecary, and Bickerstaff for his Name's-Sake; Dogget for his Humour, and somebody (forgot who that was) is recommended for Modesty. Bullock's elegant eating Fowle and Asparagus was enough, and Penkethman's Dexterity in creeping under a Table. What will you say of me, I can't tell?"

or otherwise incapacitated, begged his friends to forgive his inability to call on them personally. The receipts show how well these practices paid. In 1726–27 Mrs Younger sold tickets worth three times the receipts at the door; Quin, a leading actor, brought in £51 9s. 6d. at the office, £106 13s. in tickets. Hippisley and Mrs Egleton, in a joint benefit, attracted only £10 8s. 6d. in money but persuaded their friends to purchase tickets worth £93 11s. If an actor was a very popular performer, he might well expect other gifts on this occasion.

HOUSE SERVANTS' BENEFITS. In general, the major officers—prompter or treasurer—had individual benefits similar to those for actors, but their nights usually came after the principal actors had had theirs. The lesser employees frequently had group benefits, perhaps one for all the pit doorkeepers, another for the boxkeepers, but sometimes minor actors and servants had joint ones; the number might vary from three to as many as ten. These performances, supplementing rather meager wages, resembled a bonus for faithful services. For example, in 1726–27 Wood, the treasurer, had a full benefit on 3 May 1727, with door receipts of £12 18s. and tickets costing £152. On 15 May three lesser performers—Mrs Bullock, Houghton, and Montigny—shared in a performance of Hamlet, with office receipts of £17 5s. 6d. and tickets worth £134 17s. On 17 May four individuals—Gwin, Cook, Mrs Warren, Mrs Atkins, a mingling of actors and servants—participated in a performance of The Country Wife, the receipts comprising £11 3s. 6d. at the door and £186 6s. in tickets. On 18 May two boxkeepers, Wilmer and Redfern, shared in the receipts from The Fall of Saguntum: money £15 12s. 6d. and tickets £94 2s.

CHARITABLE BENEFITS. As a matter of public relations, the playhouses frequently supported causes. Some might be very far removed from their immediate interests, such as those at Drury Lane and Lincoln's Inn Fields on 28 June 1700 to raise money for the redemption of Englishmen held in slavery at Machanisso in Barbary. Closer home geographically was one at Drury Lane on 18 June 1706 "Towards the defraying the Charge of Repairing and fitting up the Chappel in Russel Court."III Of still more immediate concern was a benefit at Drury Lane on 26 April 1708 for the orphan children of Verbruggen, a respected actor. Benefits for "distressed" individuals occurred frequently. Often the beneficiary was not named, out

---

III Dr. James G. McManaway of the Folger Shakespeare Library has called my attention to a slip attached to Matthew Henry's A Sermon Preach'd Upon the Occasion of the Funeral of the Reverend Mr Daniel Burgess (2nd ed. [London, 1713]), which relates how Burgess, scandalizing those who thought the clergy and stage existed in incompatible worlds, persuaded the actors at Drury Lane to assist in raising £700 for the repair of the Chapel.

of deference to his sensibilities; for example, at Drury Lane on 6 July 1722 *The Feigned Innocence* assisted "A Person distressed by Losses in Trade." On the other hand, at Lincoln's Inn Fields on 8 May 1721 the management offered *The Spanish Fryar* for Samuel Smith, who had suffered misfortune by fire.

In not quite the came category but reflecting a charitable inclination on the part of managers were payments for the illness, imprisonment, indebtedness, or burial of players or their families. The most voluminous detail of this kind appears in the Drury Lane vouchers concerning mourning for George Powell, who died in December 1714 and "who had for many Years distinguished himself in his rare Accomplishments in the Theatre Royal [and who] came nearer to the Perfections of Hart and Betterton, whether we consider his Performance in the Tragic Strain, or his unaffected Gestures in the Comick."[112] One bill (Folger Shakespeare Library) records payments for coffin, shroud, and hats and clothes for the mourners; the other outlines the expense of the service given him by his superiors and fellow actors: "The 3d Bell," sixpence; "The Great Vault," £2; "The Beste palle," 10s.; the minister, 6s. 8d.; the clerk, 2s. 6d.; sexton, 1s. 6d.; gravediggers, 1s. 6d.; bearers, 6s.; lights in the church, 7s. 6d. and in the vault, 6d.; drink (five quarts of white port and five of red, £1; four quarts of sack, 11s. 3d.), and food, £3.

AUTHORS' BENEFITS. The author's nights, which with sales of printed copies constituted his principal expectations of financial returns, had a fairly consistent pattern in the early years of the century. In principle, a dramatist received the receipts above the house charges on the third and sixth nights, frequently those of the ninth. It was obviously to his advantage to keep the play on the boards to the third night, and if that goal was attained, to nurse it to the sixth. Six performances in an initial run constituted a success, warming the dramatist's heart and lining his pockets. Through negotiations he might secure an additional benefit on the ninth night or later in the season. Under unusual circumstances, he might achieve even greater rewards; for example, Elijah Fenton's very successful *Mariamne* at Lincoln's Inn Fields in 1722-23 brought him benefits on the third, sixth, ninth, and twelfth nights.[113]

---

112 *Weekly Packet*, 18 December 1714.

113 In the preface to *The Mod.rn Prophets* (London, 1709), dated 3 May 1709, Thomas D'Urfey states that Rich did him the kindness of "letting me be the first to raise the Prizes for my Benefit." As the admission charges on his third night were not advertised in the newspapers, just what increase was allowed is not known; but later it became common to put the pit and boxes together at five shillings on an author's night.

Under this system negotiations between author and manager could become quite complicated. On 29 October 1698 the contract for Cibber's *Woman's Wit* stated that Cibber would have all of the receipts after charges for the third day but that if the income on the fourth night came to £55 he would have the charges refunded.[114] If the receipts on the fourth night were £40 or better, Cibber would see it acted a fifth time, and if the receipts then came to £40 or more, he would on the sixth night receive the receipts above the charges but would have to make up the difference if the box office did not bring in at least £40. Once more, if receipts measured £40 or greater on the sixth night, the comedy would be offered a seventh time, and if the returns on that night amounted to at least £50, he would be reimbursed the charges for the sixth performance. The agreement specified that he must not publish the play before a month after the premiere.

This outline of theory can be related to the history of a new play at Lincoln's Inn Fields in 1727. On 16 January Rich produced Philip Frowde's tragedy, *The Fall of Saguntum*. Through careful scrutiny of the receipts and Frowde's willingness to make occasional sacrifices in the hope of having three benefits, Frowde managed to net £114 2s. 6d. for his first night, £60 1s. for his second benefit, and £14 16s. for the third, nearly £200 for the run of the tragedy.[115]

Some dramatists made a great deal from their benefits. John Gay's *The Beggar's Opera* was a shining example to his contemporaries and successors. According to Cibber, Steele secured about £300 as author (plus an equal sum as joint-sharer from the profits) from *The Conscious Lovers*.[116] And, according to the *British Journal*, 3 March 1723, Elijah Fenton was expected to make at least £1,000 from *Mariamne*. Many playwrights, however,

---

[114] Nicoll, *Restoration Drama*, pp. 381–82.

[115] In detail, the financial history of the initial run was as follows. There were receipts of £148 3s. at the premiere, but a falling off to £56 5s. 6d. occurred on the second night. For the first benefit, money at the door came to £81 6s. 6d. and from tickets to £82 16s., Frowde paying £50 to cover the charges. On the fourth night receipts dropped to £46 8s. 6d. and two days later Frowde paid £3 11s. 6d. to raise the total to £50. On the fifth evening the receipts were £50 6s. 6d., sufficient to meet the apparent terms of his contract (the receipts must equal £50 on the fourth and fifth nights to warrant a sixth, or he must make up the deficiency). At his second benefit the receipts were: money £77 1s. 6d.; tickets £36 11s., Frowde again paying £50 for the charges. As a result of this showing, the play had a seventh night (£50 8s.) and an eighth (£42 9s. 6d.). By agreement he had a ninth night: money £45 3s.; tickets £27 4s. On that night Frowde paid the treasurer £45 3s. in money received and added £12 8s. to cover the deficiency on the eighth night and the difference between door money and charges on the ninth. Although it appeared on a tenth evening, receipts of £45 17s. 6d. apparently convinced both author and manager that it could not easily be sustained to a twelfth performance, and the run ended there.

[116] *Apology*, II, 206.

realized almost nothing and suffered the further indignity of damnation
by noisy hissess and catcalls. Occasionally a play thus treated was acted
a second night so that the author might harvest whatever the generosity
of his friends in purchasing tickets would permit him.

The benefit system, obviously, had many defects. It created strife
among the players over priorities and variations in house charges, even
between the manager and actor over a choice of play. For example, Mrs
Barbier, noticing the great vogue of *The Beggar's Opera* (in which she did
not appear), chose it for her benefit and advertised it late in February for
her night, 16 March 1728. Rich, the manager, promptly announced in the
Daily Journal, 28 February 1728, that "the same will not be allowed of,"
and Mrs Barbier, in the same newspaper, 5 March 1728, waived her choice
"in Compliance to the Town" and substituted *Hamlet*. Sometimes quarrels
over the financial arrangements disrupted the schedule; at Lincoln's Inn
Fields on 16 April 1716 *Hamlet*, though advertised, had to be dismissed:
"No Play by reason Mr Thurmond [for whom it was to be a benefit] did
not lay down 20 Guineas in the office for his Benefit." Patrons, in turn,
wearied of the constant solicitation from actors and dramatists to purchase
tickets for benefits.

Nevertheless, when the *Universal Journal* received a complaint from a
correspondent that he was constantly pestered to buy tickets, the editor
on 6 May 1724 defended the practice, pointing out the £2,000 given to
an Italian singer and justifying aid therefore to English actors. Benefits,
he argued, justly rewarded older performers for their long services. In
addition, he thought, the system encouraged youthful actors to perfect
themselves so that they might also be rewarded in a similar fashion. Finally,
it served as an aid to young gentlewomen in distress, a point quite possibly
made with tongue in check. Certainly, no serious effort was made to
abandon the benefit; the established actor would not desire to see it go,
especially one reading a report of Mrs Oldfield's benefit at *Sir Courtly Nice*
on 6 March 1729. The *Universal Spectator*, 8 March 1729, calculated that
spectators paying about £240 attended, but the benefit is reckoned at
£500, "several Persons of Quality, &c. giving five, ten, and twenty Guineas
each." A worthy actor could double his yearly salary at a single benefit,
and the lesser personnel of a playhouse would have great difficulty in
visualizing an adequate substitute if they were deprived of participation
in the system.

Costumes, Scenes, and Machines

ANOTHER CONCERN of management was the need constantly to replenish the wardrobe, create new scenes, and, especially in the 1720's, as pantomime grew in popularity, to invent new and spectacular machines and illusions. Having gone to the expense of creating these embellishments, the theatres frequently advertised them. For example, Drury Lane on 5 November 1716 revived *Tamerlane* with "All the Habits being Intirely New" and Lincoln's Inn Fields on 5 October 1717 announced *Cymbeline*, "The whole Play being new dress'd." The same house revived *Circe* on 11 April 1719 "With New Scenes." In 1717–18 Lincoln's Inn Fields advertised new costumes (commonly called "Habits" in the bills) for five plays, Drury Lane for two; in 1718–19, Lincoln's Inn Fields had new apparel for two plays, Drury Lane for four.[117] Because Rich had to recruit a new company and stock his theatre in 1714, he of necessity had to fashion new costumes, and he quite regularly advertised new habits at premieres, but Drury Lane, by then a well-established company, gave equally great attention to the wardrobe, scenes, and machines. Because the repertory of both houses involved the frequent repetition of familiar plays, the managers attempted to give freshness to their offerings by change of decorations, costumes, and props.

THE WARDROBE. In 1700 two principal wardrobes existed: at Drury Lane under Christopher Rich and at Lincoln's Inn Fields under Thomas Betterton. Betterton's company later moved to the Queen's Haymarket and, after several changes of playhouse and management, that stock came under the control of Cibber, Wilks, and Dogget at Drury Lane. For the years from 1712 to 1716 the Drury Lane vouchers (Folger Shakespeare Library) offer an illuminating though incomplete glimpse into the functioning of the wardrobe and the acquisition of new materials, with records for the purchase of cloth, costumes, wigs, hose, feathers, buttons, lace; outgo to

---

117 John Dennis, in the midst of his attacks upon *The Conscious Lovers*, charged the managers of using "scandalous Methods, to make the most absurb and insipid Entertainments . . . pass for the very best," one method being to raise the admission charges for plays which had new scenes and costumes; this increase, he calculated, made the receipts a third larger, a disproportion to the expense of the new adornments.—See *The Works of John Dennis*, ed. E. N. Hooker (Baltimore, 1939–43), II, 254.

the house tailor for making, altering, and mending habits; and weekly sums for washing and cleaning. The latter, presented by Mrs Norris, normally ranged from 12s. to 15s. weekly; during 1715–16, the season for which the accounts are most nearly complete, they amounted to nearly £20. Often the bill specified the work: "Washing a White feather Mrs Porter" for *Cato* 19 March 1716, 4s.; "Washing & Mounting a Roman Feather Mr Booth" in *Julius Caesar* 22 March 1716, 10s.

The tailor usually presented detailed bills for his department, but in 1715–16 these amounted to only £14 3s. 11d., probably only a fraction of the season's outlay. A lengthy bill for November 1715 illustrates his work: altering "a velvet Shape" for Booth; a "Roman Shape" for *Timon of Athens* altered with the assistance of four men during three days; a remodeling of Wilks' velvet coat with "flannell," three dozen buttons and breast buttons, four ounces of silver thread, and labor costing £2 17s. 6d.

Materials purchased bulk larger and cost more. For 1715–16 the incomplete bills total £138 18s. 1d. and abound in detail: 8 December 1715, making a petticoat for Mrs Oldfield, one guinea; 12 January 1716, a new "Holland Shirt" for Booth, 11s.; 4 January 1716, altering a dress for Mrs Oldfield in *The Unhappy Favourite*, 8s.; 14 April 1716, wigs for Young Norris and others, 5s. The managers also invested heavily in materials: 5 November 1715, £1 13s. 6d. for cloth; 12 October 1715, £12 for gold and silver lace; 26 December 1715, £20 9s. for satin and white satin; 22 November 1715, £3 for silk hose; 14 April 1716, 9s. for "3 yards of Muslin for the Night Scene" (a dance); 5 January 1716, 3s. for a "Pearl for ye Crown" in *The Unhappy Favourite*; 17 January 1716, 2s. 6d. for two and one-half yards of ribbon for Mrs Santlow in *Othello*; 3 March 1716, 10s. for a beard for Mills in *I Henry IV*; and 16 March 1716, 2s. 6d. for "A Long Wigg for Penkethman" in *The Jubilee*. Occasionally the bills suggest details of a particular performance. For *The Unhappy Favourite* on 5 January 1716 Wilks (Essex) wore a white plume and Mrs Porter (Queen Elizabeth) was adorned with a newly designed crown with a new pearl inset and a black feather.

The Lincoln's Inn Fields account books for 1724–25 and 1726–27 show that the wardrobe involved a large share of the manager's budget. Although the summary nature of many entries makes allocation to habits or stage properties somewhat difficult, in 1724–25 Rich laid out nearly £900 (out of a budget approximating £10,000) on the wardrobe. He made payments to sword cutlers, lace makers, glovers, staymakers, shoemakers, furriers, hair and wig suppliers, hosiers, mercers, linen and woolen drapers. The theatre bought many expensive habits: "an Indian Gown and Pettycoat"

for Mrs Bullock, £10 10s.; a suit of "White Damask," £6 6s.; two pair of
"black Silk Stockings," £3 3s.; a "Brocade Suit of Cloaths for Mrs Chambers,"
£12 12s.; "a pair of Morocco Shoes" for Duplessy, a dancer, 6s.; "a Brocade
Mantua and Pettycoat Silver upon a Velvet Ground," £31 10s.; "Witches
Cloaths for Sorcerer," £5 2s. 6½d.; "a Gown & Pettycoat Brocade, used
for Mr Quins Dioclesian Cloaths," £15 15s.

Out of a budget of similar dimensions in 1726–27 Lincoln's Inn Fields
spent even more on the wardrobe. Because Rich had begun producing in
English many operas previously given in Italian, he had to outfit these
to a considerable extent. For newly costuming *Camilla* the treasurer paid
£1 10s. for a pair of stays for Mrs Barbier, who sang a leading role; £1 10s.
for "2 Shifts Wastcoats and Drawers for a Comic Dance" in it by Nivelon;
7s. for a pair of shoes for Leveridge, who sang; £21 for "caps and Feathers
for Camilla." The rage for pantomime involved large sums for outfitting
the performers: in *The Rape of Proserpine* clothes for Mrs Younger, £5 19s. 4d.;
"a childs Coat," 13s. 6d.; silver cloth for Mrs Chambers, £6 16s.; and masks,
£8. As was true in 1724–25, there were charges for luxurious habits:
"Embroidering a black Velvet Coat and Breaches for Mr Quin," £14;
"a blue Velvet Suit of Cloaths trim'd with gold," £25; "a White Sattin
Gown & Pettycoat: Embrm," £7 7s.

STAGE PROPS. Once again the most interesting details concerning
properties appear in the Drury Lane vouchers for 1712–16. During 1715–16,
for example, the property man presented bills for staging more than forty
different plays, with sufficient repetition of some plays to suggest the
pattern for their presentation. The bills primarily concern new materials,
not the basic stock.

The managers apparently gave careful attention to realistic properties.
When *The Cobler of Preston* had its premiere at Drury Lane on 3 February
1716, for example, the theatre hired, for a shilling each night, the "Use
of a Coblers Bench & Tools." The treasurer also paid a shilling nightly
for "The Use of a pr of Fine Holland sheets & Pillowbiers" and another
shilling each evening for "The Use of a Rugg & Blanket." For the first
night there was a charge "For Makeing 12 Whiskers of Hair," and 7s. 6d.
were paid out on 10 February 1716 for "A New Stage Ring."

To old plays the managers gave similar attention. For *The Tender
Husband* 10 February and 23 May 1716 they rented for 2s. 6d. the "Use
of a Painters Eazle, A Pallet with oyle Colours & Pencils" for Wilks, who
presumably played Captain Clerimont. For *The Busy Body* 20 February 1716
the property man provided a spinet for 2s. 6d., a sedan for 1s., a tea table

for 1s., "A Great Deal of Broken China" for 9d., and "An Orange" for 2d. Whenever practicable, the theatre secured live animals for some plays: "A Couple of Hounds from Knightsbridge" for *Aesop* on 5 December 1715 and later at 2s. nightly, and "A Setting Dog" for 6d. for Johnson, who played Clodpate in *Epsom Wells* 9 December 1715. In *The Double Gallant* 27 January 1716 there appeared a monkey, rented for 2s. 6d., and for several performances of *The Emperor of the Moon* the theatre hired a "Calais Horse" at 3s. nightly. This kind of realism was not, of course, always feasible. A few years earlier the Queen's, needing a lion for *Hydaspes*, prudently relied upon human impersonation. Even so, Conrad von Uffenbach was greatly impressed by what he saw: "In especial the representation of the lion with which Hidaspes has to fight was incomparably fine. The fellow who played him was not only wrapped in a lion-skin, but, moreover, nothing could be seen of his feet, which usually betray the fact that a man is hidden within. We were filled with surprise at the way in which the fellow could spring about so nimbly on the ground on all fours as well as on his hind legs."[118]

The Drury Lane entries also indicate a close concern for the cleanliness and appearance of the props. In renting the sheets and pillowbiers for *The Cobler of Preston*, the property man on one occasion (10 February 1716) specified that they must be clean each night. For *The Maid's Tragedy* on 16 April 1716 the rented sheets and cases were adorned by a "Flanders Lace for Trimming the Bed" (rented for 1s. 6d.) and a pair of white blankets (1s.). In *Julius Caesar* 22 March 1716 the property man provided a "Silver Bowl & Cover" (rented for 1s.) for Brutus and Cassius and a "Sheet of New Partchment" (bought for 1s.) for Caesar's will. In *Hamlet* 21 April 1716 a "Basket of Flowers for Mrs Santlow" as Ophelia cost 8d.

Similarly the property man took care to make the action vivid. For *Cato* 19 March 1716 and later he bought blood (2d.) and sometimes, as on 13 April 1716, crimson silk to simulate mortal bleeding. Entries for *The Humourous Lieutenant* on 3 December 1715, *Volpone* on 26 January 1716, *Oroonoko* on 1 February 1716, *The Country Wake* on 30 May 1716, and *Julius Caesar* called for blood with which to stain an actor's habits when he received a fatal blow. For spectacular effects *The Tempest* on 6 January 1716 required three shillings worth of materials for "The Shouer of Fire," 6d. for "Lightning," and 3d. for "White Wands." For *King Lear* on 1 June 1716 "Lightning" cost 6d., and for *The Comical Revenge* on 9 April 1716 the "Use of a Belmans Bell" also cost 6d.

---

[118] *London in 1710. From the Travels of Zacharias Conrad von Uffenbach*, ed. W. H. Quarrell and Margaret Mare (London, 1934), p. 18.

Other entries indicate a wide range of properties secured for particular plays. In the staging of *Apollo and Daphne* on 24 January 1716 boards, nails, cloth, screws, and carpenters' wages came to £3 1s. 6d. In addition, the treasurer paid £7 for painting Apollo's chariot "in Gold, Four Horses," with "a Glory," "A Bench of Rushes," "A Sea," and "A Dafne Turn'd to a Tree." For its premiere *The Drummer* on 10 March 1716 required "half a Quire of Black Edged Paper," 6d.; "Box Quill Pens," 1d.; a "Fountain Pen" for Johnson, who acted Vellum; "A Box to put ye Thimble in," 1d.; a glass, 6d.; "An Earthern Pitcher," 6d.; "Silk Patches & Gum," 6d.; and "Fullum Strong Beer Two Nights by Order," 1s. Occasionally *The Drummer* required a pint of hock at 2s.

Many entries involve purchases of food and drink, some for consumption in the offices and on stage; but it is not really clear what was consumed at rehearsals and what in meals on stage. A bill for *Love's Last Shift* 1 December 1715 lists two chickens, 3s.; four tarts, 1s.; a bottle of red wine, 2s.; two French rolls, 2d.; a lemon, 3d.; and dressing, 6d. For *The Tempest* 6 January 1716 a bottle of white wine, a pint of sack, and a pint of white wine may well have been downed by Trincalo and Stephano as they realistically as well as imaginatively staged their drunken orgies. The charges for *Love Makes a Man* 5 April 1716 on a bill headed "Food for ye Stage" called for three pints of red wine, French rolls, a half pint of sack, "Stale beer Sugar & Toast," tobacco, two chickens and dressing, for a total of 10s. 6d. The two chickens recall Penkethman's exploit (according to tradition) of eating two chickens in three seconds on stage in this play. As Pope remarked,

> *And idle Cibber, how he breaks the laws,*
> *To make poor Pinky eat with vast applause!*

Or, as *Tatler* No. 188 reported, "Penkethman devours a cold chick with great applause; Bullock's talent lies chiefly in asparagus."

The bills suggest that the managers were not niggardly in their use of stage properties. The regular purchase of a "Basket of Garden Mould" at 6d. for the gravediggers' scene in *Hamlet* or the rental of "A Silver Tea Pott, A Lamp and Spoons," "China Cups & Saucers," "A Hand Tea Table," at 5s., and "pd Mrs Smith for Tea" at 1s. 6d. for other plays represent more than a modest attempt to set the stage well. The managers made many other similar expenditures: "Eight Flambeaus" at 8s. for *The Comical Revenge* on 9 April 1716; expendibles like "Sweet Meats" and oranges at 1s. 6d. for Mrs Bicknell in *The Country Wife* 27 March 1716; the regular outlay of 5s. for the "Dressing of a Sham Child" in *The Chances* on 30 March

1716 and later; the repeated expense of 2s. 6d. with 6d. "Porteridge to ye House & Back" for "The Use of a Great Picture" in *The Rover* on 6 March and 21 May 1716.

The managers frequently preferred to rent than to purchase many properties. In fact, many rentals, such as seventeen hirings of Holland sheets and pillowbiers at 1s. or 1s. 6d. nightly raises the question: Why did not the managers, who scrutinized their bills closely to cut expenses, acquire these as permanent properties. One may ask the same questions concerning the repeated rental of a case of pistols. Some items, of course, involved problems of storage: the great picture for *The Rover*, a sedan and "Mr King ye Undertakers Plate" for *Volpone* on 26 January 1716, and "Surgeon's Box" for *The Chances* on 2 February 1716. The rental of blankets, sheets, pillowbiers, etc. presumably represented a borderline between the expense of repeated hirings and the cost of purchase, with subsequent charges for cleaning and depreciation. All of these entries suggest considerable care for realism and propriety on the part of the managers, who sometimes, as on 2 June 1716, made very particular orders to Castelman, the treasurer, including the following: "You are to acquaint all the men actors that after Saturday, the 9th Instant, no gloves will be allowed to any man for the use of the stage, unless such as require trimming upon them."

SCENES AND MACHINES.   Particularly with the development of opera and pantomime machines and scenes loomed larger in the planning and expenses of the theaters. An early example of planning appears on 16 March 1699, when Robert Robinson, a scene painter, entered into an agreement with George Powell, Robert Wilks, John Mills, Will Penkethman, Frances Knight, and Jane Rogers for "Several Sets of Scenes, & Machines" for a new opera by Elkanah Settle.[119] They contracted to pay him £130 in installments of £10 weekly during his work and the remainder during the first run or within fourteen days after he completed his work. The Drury Lane vouchers for 1712–16 offer samples of continuing expenditures of this sort. The managers approved a bill on 19 November 1715 for making "a small flat Scene for the new farce" and for "altering traps" in it, all for 13s. 6d. In April 1716 the managers, having imported Baxter, a pantomimist, spent 1s. 6d. to have a door made "in ye flatt scene for Mr Baxter to leap through" and 1s. for putting together Mercury's chariot. The ledgers for Lincoln's Inn Fields for 1724–25 and 1726–27 show quite large sums paid to John Hervey, a scene painter, and lesser ones to Lambert for similar

[119] Nicoll, *Restoration Drama*, p. 382.

work, and at Drury Lane Tilleman, Eberlin, Devoto, Dominic, and Hayman received mention in the bills for the scenes they created.

In fact, some contemporary references half jokingly suggest that scenes and machines had almost displaced interest in acting and dramatic art. As the Prologue to Steele's *The Funeral* (December 1701) put it:

> *Nature's Deserted and Dramatick Art,*
> *To Dazle now the Eye, has left the Heart;*
> *Gay Lights, and Dresses, long extended Scenes,*
> *Daemons and Angels moving in Machines,*
> *All that can now or please or fright the Fair*
> *May be perform'd without a writer's Care,*
> *And is the Skill of Carpenter, not Player:*

And in the Epilogue to Charles Johnson's *The Victim* (5 January 1714) Mrs Oldfield complained of the problems of the actress in relation to the mechanics of the stage, when she pointed out that the trapdoor was but two feet wide, whereas she had "nine wide Whale Yards of Petticoat."

The growing emphasis on spectacle, especially in scenery, appears in the stage notes for Elkanah Settle's *The Virgin Prophetess* (12 May 1701). In Act I the curtain draws to disclose a scene of Troy, with a chariot twenty feet high drawn by two white elephants; on the "two front Entryes" on each side of the stage are four more white elephants, each of these paintings being twenty-two feet high. In Act II within a "large Dome, are erected five Pyramids" in a semi-circle, each twenty-two feet high. In Act III "a painted Curtain" thirteen by thirteen feet, and a small set of scenes, twelve by twelve, and in IV a scene of Heaven which is converted into "a Transparent Scene of Hell" titillated the audience.

Conrad von Uffenbach, witnessing *Hyadpes* in 1710, reported that the "scenery and properties had all been made expressly for the opera and were very fine, though not so costly as those in Italy."[120] Some of the scenes were lavish. On 22 March 1707 the Queen's used a scene depicting "particularly the intire front prospect of Blenheim Castle," and the opera house on 15 May 1716 for *Pyrrhus and Demetrius* advertised "one in Perfection of a Royal Palace, which exceeds any that has been seen in England, containing about One Thousand Yards of Painting by Sig Roberto Clerici." It was used again on 30 March 1717 for *Cleartes*, to which was added one of a "Room adorn'd with Tapestry, representing the famous Battle of Alexander by Mons le Brun." On 17 November 1729 the *Daily Journal* reported that the

120 *London in 1710*, p. 18.

King's had "Seven Sets of Scenes entirely New" for the forthcoming season.

At the playhouses the scene painters were equally important. Devoto served Drury Lane for some years as a principal designer and created new scenes for *Julius Caesar*, including a prospect of ancient Rome, for a performance on 24 September 1723. He also devised scenes for *Perseus and Andromeda*, a pantomime, on 15 November 1728, which caused the *Daily Post* to comment on the "grandeur of the Scenery." This was part of a movement to use newly designed scenes depicting specific places. For example, when *Harlequin Shepard* was produced at Drury Lane on 26 December 1724 to capitalize on the exploits of Jack Shepard, a criminal with a reputation for breaking out of prisons, the managers advertised the scenes as "being painted from the real Place of Action." For a revival of *Masseniello* at Lincoln's Inn Fields on 29 March 1725 the advance publicity in the *Daily Journal* on 25 March 1725 reported that it would have "a Piece of Scenery, entirely new, part of which will be the Statue and Inscription of Masseniello." These efforts did not always work out successfully. The background and props for Cibber's *Caesar in Egypt* (Drury Lane 9 December 1724) shared in the ridicule bestowed on the tragedy, for Benjamin Victor remembered that "we *then* laught at his *quavering Tragedy Tones*, as much as we did at his Pasteboard Swans which the Carpenters pulled along the *Nile*."[121]

It was, however, with pantomime that the inventors of machines and illusion principally occupied themselves. More and more pantomimes were advertised with stress on machines, transformations, risings and sinkings of characters, witches, and chariots, and many other eye-catching events, some real, some illusionary. Typical of the publicity was that for *Harlequin a Sorcerer* at Lincoln's Inn Fields on 21 January 1725, which was announced as having "the boldest Piece of Machinery that ever yet was seen upon the Stage,"[122] a reference presumably to "A Machine descends with Pluto and Proserpine, and fixes upon the Stage" (edition of 1725).

The effect of this ingenuity in combining scenes, machines, and spectacle appears most strikingly in comments by individuals who saw some of the more popular entertainments. In the *Weekly Journal or Saturday's Post* for 6 April 1723 a correspondent who had seen *Jupiter and Europa*, a new pantomime at Lincoln's Inn Fields, reported that he found dexterity of performers combined with the products of "the finest workmen, and most curious artists" in England. "Here we behold the Power of Machinery

---

121 *The History of the Theatres of London and Dublin* (London, 1761), II, 164.
122 *Weekly Journal or Saturday's Post*, 23 January 1725.

when we see a Heathen God in an erect Posture shot from an Eminence of sixty or seventy Foot upon the Stage; and, when he has finished his Part, he takes the same Flight, from below." This spectator also admired an incident in which the "Transformation of *Jupiter* into a Bull, is done in Sight of the Audience; the Contrivance and Deception is so excellent, that we cannot account for it." A similar dexterity was present in *The Necromancer* at Lincoln's Inn Fields on 20 December 1723, when Doctor Faustus in a wood sees "a monstrous Dragon" appear, which "from each claw drops a Daemon, representing diverse grotesque figures." After Doctor Faustus is seized by spirits, he is "devour'd by the monster, which immediately takes flight." In the *Universal Journal* for 4 March 1723 "Bickerstaff's Ghost" reported on a performance of this pantomime: "You will see strange alterations, Cloaks flying upon Men's shoulders, *Harlequin*, *Scaramouch*, *Punch*, and *Pierrot* riding upon Spirits in the Air; Dancing Wheat Sheaves, flaming Barns, barking Dogs, flying Flasks and Oranges, and Fellows, to escape a Scouring, venture their Necks down a Chimney." The climax came with the "Horror and the Sight of a Fiery Dragon," and one news account, at least partially satiric, reported that "the terrible fiery Dragon . . . took Fire a few nights ago at the Conclusion of the Performance by its extraordinary Emission of Fire . . . but it seems their Dragon Maker has provided them with another which is so well lined and cased, as to be proof against the like Casuality for the future.[123]

The long runs of many pantomimes and spectacles testify to the popularity of pieces in which ingenious scenes, decorations, contrivances, and machines played a large part. Many writers lamented the public devotion to spectacle which enthralled the eye but which did not enrich the mind (so they said), but their objections made no perceptible change in the attitudes of those spectators who loved a good show. Each major spectacle created a taste for a new and greater one, and the theatres spent more money to engage more carpenters, painters, and machinists to enthrall the audience with transformations, colorful displays, and intricate machinery producing marvelous changes before the eyes of spectators.

[123] *London Journal*, 14 March 1724.

The Repertory: General View

THROUGHOUT the opening decades of the century, the repertory—in the broad sense of the total offerings of the playhouse—enlarged steadily and rapidly; it came to include, more often than not, a play and afterpiece, prologue and epilogue, music, dance, singing, and specialties. In fact, a cursory glance at a lengthy bill might suggest a submersion of the play in song and dance; nevertheless, the play remained the center of the program. Except under extraordinary circumstances, the managers built the evening's offerings around it, without, however, any genuine intent to create a single mood, for the manager might schedule a Scotch Dance between Acts I and II of *Othello*, an Italian song at the next interval, a sonata by Corelli between Acts III and IV. Instead, the producer's aim gradually came to be a fully rounded program of drama, music, dance, and specialties that would attract and please the whole range of taste in London.

Relying each season upon a cycle of plays, some old, some new, some repeated twice or more a month, some presented only once during the year, others in runs, the theatres sought constantly to give repetition an air of freshness. At times the managers were criticized for presenting "the same dull circle of plays," only to be praised the next day for giving London "the best of our dramatic heritage." To please everyone, the theatres offered variety, even though not every type of production—pantomime, for example—satisfied all tastes.

Even though each season's repertory was not rigidly organized, certain principles influenced the sequence of plays to be offered. Opening in September, each house acted twice or thrice weekly the best stock plays— *Hamlet, Othello, The Recruiting Officer, The Stratagem, Love for Love.* That these dramas, familiar to actor and spectator, provided a means of getting the company together before undertaking the new or less familiar plays is suggested by an announcement early in the century of a play being given in order "to complete the company." These plays required little immediate study, for the same actors had often performed their roles year after year. In addition, the light performing schedule allowed time for preparing revivals and new plays. After each major piece had been given once in the early autumn, the managers usually repeated the cycle, but not in precisely the same order, until a revival or premiere chan ged the pattern. On the other hand, the managers rarely offered a new play before November. The opera house, opening later, could give the early weeks to preparing a new opera for November or December. By December the season of old and new plays had assumed form and ran uninterruptedly until the benefits altered the cycle.

With no effective copyright to govern the staging of plays, the managers had few compelling restrictions upon their offerings. Except for the most recent ones, they could choose from the whole range of English drama. As a result, each manager watched carefully the offerings of his competitors and sometimes kept a record of all the London programs. In *Rich's Register* (Folger Shakespeare Library) a record kept at Lincoln's Inn Fields from 1714 to 1723, Rich entered not only the plays he offered (with the receipts) but also in a parallel column what Drury Lane staged on the same night. (Unfortunately he did not preserve Drury Lane's receipts as well.) Observing the popularity of plays, no manager long hesitated to put on one which had done well elsewhere. Although Cibber assisted in managing Drury Lane, his plays appeared in all the theatres *if* they had popularity, for after the first season a drama became part of the public domain. For example, Rich offered *The Beggar's Opera* without competition during its first run; thereafter, it appeared all over London. Occasionally cutthroat competition occurred. When Drury Lane put Charles Johnson's *The Cobler of Preston* in rehearsal for a premiere on 3 February 1716, Christopher Bullock (so he says) took a week end in which to write his own *Cobler of Preston* and staged it at Lincoln's Inn Fields on 24 January 1716, more than a week before Drury Lane produced its version. On the other hand, some plays remained active in only one playhouse. For example, although both Drury Lane and Lincoln's Inn Fields gave *I Henry IV* before 1730, only Drury Lane acted *II Henry IV* between 1714 and 1730. In contrast, spectators could see *The Merry Wives of Windsor* during these years only at Lincoln's Inn Fields.

For a variety of reasons, the planning of future programs was somewhat uncertain, and as a rule, although a manager mapped his offerings a month in advance, he avoided advertising what he might offer two or three weeks later, except in the benefit season. His arrangements, therefore, could be easily altered or abandoned, because of a request for another play, the illness of a principal actor, a royal command, or the nature of competitive offerings. It is difficult to know how powerfully some of these influences affected the repertory, but sufficient changes occur in announced bills in every season to show that these factors had more than a casual effect.

A very great number of theatrical advertisements bore such headings as "By Desire," "By Request of several Persons of Quality," or "By the Desire of several Ladies of Quality." Obviously some of these appeared merely to give the illusion of demand, but some represented authentic requests. Lady Cowper, writing in her diary for 15 February 1715, mentioned *The Wanton Wife* and remarked, "It used to be a favourite Play, and often bespoke by the Ladies."[124] William Byrd, attending Lincoln's Inn Fields on 18 January 1718, saw a play which, he remarks, was spoken for by Kitty Sambrooke.[125] The bill that night bore the heading "At the particular Desire of several Ladies of Quality" and advertised *The Busy Body* followed by *Pan and Syrinx*. The afterpiece might also appear by request. On 13 and 16 August 1717 *Titus Andronicus* was followed by *The Stage Coach*; on both evenings the bill stated that the farce was acted "At the Desire of some Persons of Quality."[126] Occasionally a group, such as the Free and Accepted Masons, bespoke a special night, and in 1737 and 1738 a group of patrons known as "Shakespeare's Ladies" so encouraged Rich to revive more of Shakespeare's plays that his dramas dominated those seasons.

Royal commands, of course, were promptly honored, and the bills show many pieces given by command, even some changed at a very late moment. For example, at Drury Lane for 22 November 1718 *The Orphan* had been announced, but, "by special Command," *Love Makes a Man* was played before the King. In Lincoln's Inn Fields *The Provoked Wife* had been announced for Quin's benefit on 17 March 1726, but the King commanded *The Country Wife*, and Quin had to put his benefit off until 19 March 1726. Unhappy relations between the King and the Prince of Wales put the playhouses in an occasional awkward situation. Edward Harley, writing to Abigail Harley, 6 May 1718, stated that the Prince had "bespoke . . . the Indian Emperor" at Drury Lane, but the King told the players that if the Prince came and they acted it, he would turn them out of the house.[127]

---

[124] *The Diary of Mary Countess Cowper* (London, 1864), p. 46.

[125] *The London Diary (1717–1721) and Other Writings*, ed. Louis B. Wright and Marion Tinling (New York, 1958), p. 68. On 4 February 1718 Byrd attended a theatre (unnamed) and mentioned that he had bespoke the play. Of the two dramas acted that evening, the one at Lincoln's Inn Fields, *A Bold Stroke for a Wife*, would not normally be subject to request, as this was the second night of its initial run. At Drury Lane that evening *The Orphan* appeared "at the particular Desire of several Ladies of Quality," but Byrd might have requested it for ladies of his acquaintance.

[126] At Drury Lane on 30 May 1716 the management announced that "at the Desire of several Ladies of Quality" it was "oblig'd" to act *The Country Wake* instead of *The What D'Ye Call It*, which had been scheduled as the afterpiece.

[127] See *Portland Manuscripts*, Historical Manuscripts Commission (London, 1899), V, 560.

The Prince, however, did see it by command at Drury Lane on 6 November 1718 without serious consequences.

Another important element in the selection of plays for the seasonal repertory was the talent available in a theatre or, to state it differently, the kinds of drama which a company could most successfully stage. The talent for sophisticated comedy at Drury Lane, especially evident in the acting of Wilks, Cibber, and Mrs Oldfield, enabled it to offer more comedies of manners and, more important, to present them with style and distinction; Rich's company, on the other hand, had less success with wit and high comedy. Similarly, Drury Lane offered *The Constant Couple* very frequently because Wilks had a fine reputation as Sir Harry Wildair. John Rich was influenced toward pantomime and spectacle, partly because he made a good Harlequin and partly, of course, because of the large sums which these interludes brought to his treasury.

The theatres were subject to other, less tangible, types of influences. If ballad opera or pantomime or Shakespeare drew spectators to one house, a competing manager reconsidered his program to avoid playing to small audiences or possibly having to dismiss the exceedingly small number who appeared before curtain time. If one house did well with Shakespeare, should another offer the same plays which have been successful at it or try to revive some neglected ones. Rich occasionally found his clientele divided in their responses. Pantomime, for example, often filled the galleries at Lincoln's Inn Fields in the 1720's, but did not equally appeal to the boxes or pit. On the other hand, when Rich offered operas in English, the galleries remained half empty but the pit and boxes filled. How should he remedy this situation? Offer an English opera followed on the same bill by a pantomime? Or if the opera house drew vast throngs with a Senesino or a Mrs Cuzzoni, should not the manager of a playhouse counter by offering operas in English or by advertising Italian songs between the acts of *Hamlet* or *The Way of the World*? Perhaps a comprehensive three-hour program of varied entertainments would turn the trick. And so the managers became concerned with afterpieces, prologues, epilogues, skits, songs, dances, imitation, burlesques, processions, instrumental music, even animal acts.

The Repertory: The Afterpiece

THE DEVELOPMENT of a long program presenting a variety of entertainments occurred principally in the first twenty years of the eighteenth century. Before 1700 the characteristic bill offered a five-act play, with prologue and epilogue and possibly *entr'acte* diversities. By 1720 the typical program, more often than not, added an afterpiece as well as giving a greater concentration of song, music, and dance between the acts. During these twenty years the managers tried a variety of programs; out of their experimentation came the practices of the mid-century.

On some evenings, of course, only a play was given (*The Alchymist* at Lincoln's Inn Fields on 9 October 1702, for example), although miscellaneous entertainments, even though not specified in the bill, accompanied it. On many occasions, however, the managers offered a combination of entertainments; the principal ones in the first decade fall into these patterns.

1. A regular full-length play followed by a pantomimic interlude (see 12 and 29 October 1703). This combination might also include *entr'acte* entertainments, as on 19 February 1704.

2. A full-length play followed by a farce (such as *The Spanish Fryar* and *The Wit of a Woman* on 24 June 1704). This pattern might also include other entertainments.

3. A play with a vocal and instrumental concert, a pantomimic interlude, and other entertainments (as on 20 October 1702).

4. A play with vaudeville (animal imitations, tumbling, acrobatics), as on 22 August 1702 or 27 April 1705.

5. A play shortened to make room for other entertainments (as on 8 June 1703).

6. No full-length play but a *commedia dell'arte* farce supplemented by scenes from other plays or operas (as on 5 February 1704).

7. Two short plays with scenes from other dramas (as on 28 March 1704) or followed by rope dancing and acrobatics (as on 30 April 1703, 16 February 1704, 16 June 1705).

8. A vocal and instrumental concert, with a farce and entertainments between the acts (as on 23 January 1703) or episodes from familiar plays (as on 1 February 1703).

9. A short play supplemented by music or musical interlude (as on 12 February 1704).

10. An opera with an act from a farce or songs and dances.

This experimentation did not immediately create a pattern, but it explored most of the possible variations. Throughout the first decade the afterpiece proper (farce or pantomime) was an occasional means of rounding out a program, but supplemental songs and dances for a single play predominated. For example, in 1704–5 out of some 225 programs, only about 10 can properly be called double bills (i.e., play with farce or pantomimic sketch), although many a program included songs, dances, vaulting, and posturing. In 1707–8, during part of which two theatres competed, the houses advertised very few afterpieces; and in 1710–11, with one playhouse offering drama and the other opera, double bills occasionally appeared but not regularly enough to form a traditional pattern.

With the opening of Lincoln's Inn Fields in 1714–15, a renewal of competition gradually wrought a change. Even in that year an acute observer could have sensed a trend. During the autumn months before Lincoln's Inn Fields opened on 18 December 1714, Drury Lane acted some 75 times, with only 2 programs containing an afterpiece. From mid-December onward, Drury Lane performed about 130 times, adding a farce, musical interlude, or pantomimic skit on some 35 evenings. At the new theatre Rich, also open on 130 evenings, added an afterpiece of some kind on some 40 nights. Rich also occasionally offered a bill comprising three short pieces, usually farces, with no comedy or tragedy to dominate the program.

There was really no turning backward after this season, for Rich's enthusiasm for interludes and pantomime stimulated more multiple programs. Yet the frequency of afterpieces varied greatly. By 1717–18, when the two houses had three years of competition behind them, Drury Lane acted about 200 times, with some 45 programs containing afterpieces, whereas Lincoln's Inn Fields, open only some 170 nights, offered double or triple bills nearly 80 times. At Drury Lane farces and pantomimic interludes comprised the afterpieces, with farces less frequently offered. At Lincoln's Inn Fields the second pieces included musical interludes (some of them new), farces (offered more frequently than musical pieces), and pantomimic interludes of "grotesque dancing" (the most popular of all). Lincoln's Inn Fields also took advantage of topical events by offering as an afterpiece *The Perjuror* soon after the political success of Cibber's *The Nonjuror*, a full-length play.

Lincoln's Inn Fields' greater emphasis on double or triple bills continued. In 1721–22, Drury Lane, acting about 200 times, had only 15 double bills, divided nearly evenly between farce and pantomime. Lincoln's Inn Fields, with some 170 performances, had more than 60 multiple bills and staged nearly four times as many pantomimes as farces. In 1723–24, however, an important increase in dual bills occurred, occasioned principally by the success of *Harlequin Doctor Faustus* at Drury Lane and *The Necromancer or Harlequin Doctor Faustus* at Lincoln's Inn Fields, two pantomimes which established the vogue of elaborate spectacles. Drury Lane, acting about 180 nights, had almost 70 double bills, more than twice the number of the previous season; Lincoln's Inn Fields, open on some 190 evenings, had nearly 95 multiple bills, averaging one every other night. At both houses pantomime dominated the second half of the bill.

This season established the afterpiece as a common, though not obligatory, part of the program. Even when the practice had become comfortably settled, however, the theatres usually eliminated afterpieces when new plays, revivals of long-neglected dramas, or benefits were the attraction. Frequently, of course, a host of songs and dances so filled the intervals that adding an afterpiece would have prolonged the program beyond even the enormous capacity of an early eighteenth-century audience. The season of 1723–24 also inaugurated another trend in the history of afterpieces: a fairly long run of the second piece with a change of the main play almost nightly. For example, at Drury Lane *Harlequin Doctor Faustus* ran eight nights consecutively until interrupted by the premiere of a new play; in that run it was preceded by eight different full-length plays, a momentary shift of the play to the position of curtain raiser for the main attraction.

The principal types of afterpieces for the first thirty years of the century fall into the following classifications.

FARCICAL PIECES. When a double bill of farces only was offered, the first was usually a three-act, the second a two-act. When three comprised the program, there was, usually, a mixture of two-act and one-act pieces. An example of the longer followed by a shorter one is *The Emperor of the Moon* with *The Cobler of Preston* at Lincoln's Inn Fields on 31 January 1716. The triple or quadruple bill might be all farcical or a mixture of farce, musical, and pantomime: at Lincoln's Inn Fields on 10 February 1715 *The Country House* (two acts), *The Slip* (one act), *The Beau Demolished* (one-act musical interlude), and *Hob* (one act). The rapid development of double bills after the opening of Lincoln's Inn Fields stimulated many playwrights, some of them actors, to turn their hands to this type, such as *The What D'Ye Call It*, *The Cobler of Preston*, *The Humours of the Counter*, *The Perjuror*, *The Petticoat Plotter*, and *The Hypochondriack*, all produced within a few years.

MUSICAL ENTERTAINMENTS. This type of afterpiece was less popular than farcical pieces or pantomime. This was due, possibly, not so much to a prejudice against music, which actually had a great deal of popularity, as to the greater usefulness of short musical pieces for *entr'acte* entertainment. Early in the century the playhouses offered several musical entertainments based on classical themes: *Venus and Adonis* (in two interludes, often presented independently), *Acis and Galatea*, and *Dido and Aeneas*. In time new ones, some in the same vein, others of quite different character, appeared: *The Professor of Folly*, *Pan and Syrinx*, *Love and a Bumper*, and *The Beau Demolished*. The success of *The Beggar's Opera* stimulated a host of short imitations. Some of these two-act ballad operas received first place on the bill at their premieres but soon became afterpieces.

PROCESSIONS. This uncommon type of afterpiece grew from a series of performances of *Henry VIII* beginning on 26 October 1727 at Drury Lane, when the managers added an interlude depicting the coronation of Anna Bullen. The advance publicity (*Daily Journal*, 24 October 1727) aroused public curiosity by announcing that it would be "performed with greater Order and Magnificence, by the Richest and Largest Figures that have ever been seen on the English Stage." The scene lived up to its billing, and by 22 November 1727 Drury Lane announced "an additional and different View of that Solemnity, by shewing the whole Magnificence at once, with the Ceremony of the Champion in Westminster Hall." In a short while, because "several Persons of Quality being unwilling to lose their usual variety of Plays" (*Daily Post*, 27 November 1727), the Ceremony was offered as an afterpiece to other plays, with some of which (*Wit Without Money* or *The Relapse*) it had no historical or thematic relationship. This practice soon occasioned a burlesque at Lincoln's Inn Fields titled *Harlequin Anna Bullen*, which also became an afterpiece.

PANTOMIME. In the 1720's pantomime became the most popular of afterpieces, a dominance it retained for a long time. Early in the century the theatres produced interludes and "Night Scenes," which, utilizing *commedia dell'arte* characters and themes, told uncomplicated stories in motion. In the next decade the theatres continued to bill some of them as "Night Scenes" or "Entertainments of Grotesque Dancing" or "Entertainments of Dancing in Grotesque Characters," but gradually they acquired titles, such as *Harlequin Executed*. As they gained popularity, they acquired more elaborate plots. Often a classical theme became interlarded with grotesquery and trickery: *Mars and Venus or The Mouse Trap* or *Amadis or The Loves of Harlequin and Colombine* or *Perseus and Andromeda or The Spaniard Outwitted*. Others developed a single situation: *The Cheats or The Tavern Bilkers* or *Harlequin Turned Judge*. Only the opera companies resisted the demand for pantomime, and in the playhouses the most popular ones, possibly with a cast of fifteen to thirty performers, sometimes overshadowed the preceding comedy or tragedy, especially in brilliance of production.

Because the afterpiece was usually of a different order of entertainment from the main play, it contributed to the diversity of enjoyment which more and more dominated the aims of the managers; but this type of programming had its detractors. Charles Johnson, in the Preface to *The Force of Friendship* and *Love in a Chest*, the latter a farcical afterpiece of his own devising, declaimed against the critical degeneracy of the age.

If this can be any Proof of the Licentiousness of the Age we live in, it may be urg'd with some Force, when we see no Audience now can bear the Fatigue of two Hours good Sense tho' Shakespear or Otway endeavour to keep 'em awake, without the promis'd Relief of the Stage-Coach, or some such solid Afterlude, a few Lines indeed are now and then forced down their Throats by the Help of this Gewgaw, 'tis Tack'd to the Tragedy or rather the Tragedy to that, for 'tis the Money Bill; the Actors may design it as a Desert, but they generally find the Palates of their Guests so vitiated that they make a Meal of Whipt Cream, and neglect the most substantive Food which was design'd for their Nourishment.

A wigg for mr Cibber in
othello ———— 0 – 22 – 6
a wigg for young mr.
norrie in ye orphan – 2. 6

———— 0 – 5 – 0

Mr. Cibber is to pay for the Wig-himself

Barton Bord
Rob Wilks
B. Booth
Cibber

CONTROVERSY OVER RENTAL OF WIGS [*ca.* 1715].   Reproduced from *MS. Collection of Wardrobe and Property Bills, Drury Lane* now in the *Folger Shakespeare Library.*

Promptets Bill

3	Grace	}	
2	Bevil	}	
1	Lettice	} love in a tub	0 . 1 . 7½
1	Clark	}	
2	Coachman Bully & Servant	}	
1	Mourner	}	
3	Grahana		0 - 0 . 3
2	Gazet & Trincket		0 - 1 . 4½
11	Fikpow		0 - 0 - 7½
6	Holdup		0 - 0 - 10½
7	Narcisa		0 - 1 - 0
8	Alcmena		0 - 0 - 7½
5	Bromia		0 - 0 - 4½
3	Flora County Wake		

total --- 0 - 6 - 6

Six Shill: Six pence:

Rob: Wilks.

B. Booth

Cibber.

A RECORD OF PAYMENTS [*ca.* 1716] for the writing out of parts from several plays for use by different actors, reproduced from *MS Collection of Wardrobe and Property Bills, Drury Lane* now in the *Folger Shakespeare Library.*

Neither; he'll out-do me at my own Weapon.
~~An Evidence, a Devil; he'll out-swear me, in~~
~~And~~ ~~Blow upon me left.~~ An Impudent Devil?
That can out-face a Judge upon the Bench.
He may hang others, then he may hang me.
~~A holy~~ *dangerous;*
He'll broach some new Religion, and we are
Already over-stockt, with seeming Saints;
Or over zealous Mad men, that are as bad,
A Devil that can speak all Languages:
To entertain Embassadors in their own Tongues,
Or else some pleasant Airie, Dancing Devils,
To treat the Ladies with, who visit me.
Those would do well.
   Del. It shall be done.
Sit there; and if you love your own Life, stir not.
I'll give you a taste of my Art immediately.
You see those Antick Figures in the Hangings.
   Get. Yes, very well
   Del. They are all Spirits; all at my command,
My Servants all, and they shall entertain you;
Come forth, and Dance before this mighty *Edile.*
Come forth, and leave your Shadows in your places.

The Figures come out of the Hangings, and Dance: And Figures
exactly the same appear in their places: When they have
danc'd a while, they go to sit on the Chairs, they slip from
'em, and after joyn in the Dance with 'em.

   Get. Shall these Devils be at my command?
   Del. They shall be more obedient than your Slaves.
You shall have other Spirits if you please,
Shall take you up, and bear you thro' the Air;
Hurricanio, appear; and take him up.
   Get. O deliver me! deliver me!
             [*Get. runs off, the Lictors follow him.*
   Del. So; I have frighted him sufficiently,
He'll trouble us no more. Come my *Drusilla,*
Th' Embassadors of *Persia* are now
With th' Emperor *Charinus* and *Aurelia,*
Demanding freedom for their Master's Sister,

[Handwritten annotations in right margin:]
out
Ready to
Ring for a
Mifick
Ring
Carinus
Aurelia
Caffana
The
Ambassador

FROM AN EARLY EIGHTEENTH-CENTURY ACTING COPY and prompter's version
of Beaumont and Fletcher's *The Prophetess* now in the *Folger Shakespeare Library.*

Ham. 'Tis well, I'll have thee speak out the rest of this soon. Good my Lord will you see the Players well bestowed, do you hear, let them be well used, for they are the abstract and brief Chronicles of the time; after your death you were better have a bad Epitaph, than their ill report while you live.

Pol. My ~~Lord~~, I will use them according to their desert.

Ham. Much better, use every man after his desert, and who shall scape whipping? use them after your own honour and dignity, the less they deserve the more merit is in your bounty: Take them in.

Pol. Come sirs.

Ham. Follow him, friends; ~~we'll hear a Play to morrow~~; do'st thou hear me, old friend, can you Play the murder of *Gonzago*?

Play. I, my Lord.

Ham. We'll have it to morrow-night: you could for need study a speech of some dozen lines, which I would set down and insert in't, could you not?

Play. I, my Lord.

Ham. Very well: follow that Lord, and look you mock him not. ~~My good friends, I'll leave you till night, you are welcome to Elsonour.~~

[Exeunt ~~Pol. and~~ Players.

~~Ros. Good my Lord.~~

[Exit

Ham. I so, ~~God buy to you;~~ now am I alone,
O what a ~~rouge~~ and pesant slave am I!
Is it not monsterous that this Player here
But in a fiction, in a dream of Passion,
Could force his Soul to his own conceit,
That ~~for~~ her working all the visage wand,
Tars in his Eyes, distraction in's Aspect,
A broken voice, and his whole function suiting
With forms to his conceit, and all for nothing,
For *Hecuba*?
What's *Hecuba* to him, or he to her,
That he should weep for her? what would he do
Had he the motive, ~~and that~~ for passion
That I have? he would "drown the stage with tears,
~~And cleave the general Ear with horrid speech,~~
Make mad the guilty, and appeal the free,
'Confound the ignorant, and amaze indeed
'The very faculties of Eyes and Ears; yet I,
'A dull and muddy metted raskal, peak
'Like *John* a dreams, unpregnant of my cause,
'And can say nothing, no not for a King,
'Upon whose property and most dear life
'A damn'd defeat was made: am I a coward?
'Who calls me villain, breaks my pate across,
'Plucks off my beard, and blows it in my face,

F

'Twekes

OWEN McSWINY, Esq., Manager of the Opera 1711–1712
Reproduced from an engraving by J. Faber (1752) from a portrait by Vantoo.
The engravings were sold for 2*s.* each at the Golden Head near the Church,
Bloomsbury Square in 1752.

AMLET, Act II, scene II, reproduced from a 1703 quarto prepared as an
acting copy. *The Folger Shakespeare Library.*

SHEET MUSIC FOR SONGS by Mrs. Anne Bracegirdle

Reproduced from *A Collection of the Choisest Songs and Dialogues by the Most Eminent Masters of the Age*, London [*ca.* 1703–04], printed for and sold by John Walsh now in the *Folger Shakespeare Library*.

GEORGE FREDERICK HANDEL, 1685–1759

Reproduced from an engraving by T. Hudson from the picture belonging to
Earl Howe.

SIR JOHN VANBRUGH, 1664–1726, Playwright and Architect
Reproduced from the engraving by J. Faber (1733) from the portrait by
Godfrey Kneller.

Actors and Acting

ALTHOUGH the profession of acting did not rank very high socially or legally,[128] London liked to gossip about players, both men and women. The *Tatler* and *Spectator* catered to public curiosity about acting, and later the daily and weekly journals published innumerable notes about the quarrels, loves, crimes, and political activities of performers. The death of a major one usually prompted a *Life*, often a collection of anecdotes, testimonials to his character, gossip, his will, amours, perhaps even details concerning his career or talents. Individually so honored were Betterton, Mrs Oldfield, Wilks, Booth, Spiller, Keene, and others; in mid-century W. R. Chetwood published thumbnail sketches of major and minor performers whom he had known. The first third of the century had, in fact, many interesting stage personalities: the dignified Betterton, clownish Penkethman, foppish Cibber, exact and prudent Wilks, quarrelsome Dogget, jesting Spiller, versatile John Mills. An actor for every taste trod the boards.

Generally speaking, the theatres at this time required about twice as many actors as actresses. A document outlining the organization of a company in the first decade lists twenty men and eleven women.[129] At Lincoln's Inn Fields in 1724–25 the account books bear the names of twenty-eight men and sixteen women, and although the proportion of women gradually rose, this was the pattern. As song and dance became more important in the repertory, many of these performers, especially the women, such as Hester Booth and Elizabeth Younger, sang or danced as well as acted. The growth of pantomime and ballad opera called for a wider range of talents, and many individuals whose talents at acting had won them a place in the theatre soon found that versatility won them more applause and money.

---

[128] Early in the century, when Jeremy Collier's attack upon the stage made everyone conscious of his claims of immorality in the theatres, actors occasionally were hailed into court, sometimes fined, for their part in acting presumably licentious roles, and their legal status as actors was perilously close to the standing of a vagabond. In the summer of 1717, when some London actors played in the Fairs, they could hardly have escaped noting an article in the *Post Man*, 2 July 1717, pointing to a statute of the reign of Queen Anne, which provided that "all Common Players of Interludes should be adjudged Rogues and Vagrants," subject to arrest by constables, who should bring them before a Justice of the Peace to be examined and "publickly whipt, or sent to the House of Correction."

[129] Nicoll, *Early Eighteenth Century Drama*, pp. 276–77.

An actor could look forward to some perquisites and potentially good pay. Some supplemented their income by becoming managers: Cibber, Wilks, Booth, Dogget, Betterton. Others assisted in training young actors. In the first decade Betterton was allotted £50 yearly as an instructor in histrionics; in 1724–25 Lacy Ryan received from Rich an additional 3s. 4d. nightly for assisting with the rehearsals and training of performers. A performer who was popular and in demand might try to secure some additional favors. In 1708–9 Mrs Oldfield received a grant of ten guineas with which to purchase costumes for herself. At the Queen's during the negotiations on behalf of Mrs Tofts on 28 January 1706 she demanded payment for each performance before the curtain rose, possession of the practice room as her dressing chamber, two bottles of wine daily to give to the gentlemen who practiced with her, and other bounties.[130] Generally speaking, the major performers made good money. After a dispute in 1708–9, Zachary Baggs, treasurer of Drury Lane, published a pamphlet to prove that the principals had had a prosperous season: Wilks, with salary and benefit, had received £259 1s. 5d.; Betterton, £188 14s. 5d., with an estimated £450 in gifts at his benefit; Mrs Oldfield, salary and benefit, £56 13s. 4d. for only fourteen weeks of acting, since she left off playing after her benefit, supplemented by gifts of £120.

Balanced against these profitable incomes were the uncertainties of the profession. As already indicated, an actor received pay only for the days the theatre remained open; six weeks' mourning in the midst of a season could impoverish the players by an enforced vacation. When only one theatre operated or even two competed, an actor had little opportunity to improve his position by an outside offer, and he had little recourse, except an appeal to the public, against discharge. In the spring of 1733, for example, Benjamin Griffin published a "Humble Appeal to the Publick," after a quarrel between the players and patentees of Drury Lane, in which he reviewed his career as an employee. He reported that in 1724 he had been persuaded to leave Lincoln's Inn Fields for Drury Lane by attractive proposals, but once he had changed his affiliation, he thought himself improperly treated in his new post. In addition, the two companies had agreed thereafter not to let an actor change houses without a written discharge, and his power of negotiation had diminished. Finally, he had received on 4 June 1733, without previous notice, a discharge. In addition, a player always stood, at least technically, in an uneasy legal position. On 12 September 1717, for example, Bullock and Leigh were taken out

130 *Ibid.*, p. 290.

of their booth at Southwark Fair on an information filed against them; Penkethman was also arrested, even though he emphasized that he was a "Sworn Servant to His Majesty." Fortunately for the players, these arrests did not have serious consequences, but the threat remained ever present.

The profession was also characterized by closely knit groups of performers. Family relationships abounded: the Bettertons, husband and wife; the Bullocks (William Sr, William Jr, Jane, Hildebrand, Christopher); the Cibbers; the Mills (John, William, and their wives); the Thurmonds; the three Norrises; Penkethman Sr and Jr; Aston, wife, and son; Barton and Hester Booth; the Spillers. Performers frequently married within the profession. Barton Booth married Hester Santlow, who began as a dancer and became an actress. Anthony Boheme chose for his wife a promising actress, Mrs Seymour, who died shortly after their marriage. Dancers frequently became a husband-wife team. Some families dominated a particular theatre: the Bullocks at Lincoln's Inn Fields, the Cibbers and Booths at Drury Lane. Many families stayed with a theatre much of their collective careers: Bullocks, Spillers, Penkethmans, Cibbers, Booths, Mills, Thurmonds. As has already been suggested, many children followed their parents' bent, and although a fine acting family did not always produce talented children, some did.

The managers also gave special attention to child actors, sometimes from theatrical families, sometimes not. These played the juvenile roles in plays, of course, but spectators had a genuine affection for children with all types of talents. An advertisement nearly always stressed the age: at Lincoln's Inn Fields on 24 July 1704, Miss Willis, age five, danced an *Irish Trot*; at Drury Lane on 6 December 1704, a girl, ten, played Cupid in a Purcell masque, and on 27 March 1706 a child appeared as Princess Elizabeth and spoke the epilogue to *Virtue Betrayed*. In the spring of 1712 the sons and daughters of prominent actors staged a series of plays at the St. Martin's Theatre: Young Boman, William Mills, Henry Norris Jr, Miss Young, Miss Porter. On 17 June 1715 at Drury Lane the "Young Persons," chiefly sons and daughters of actors, had a special benefit at *Don Carlos*. But the most handsomely applauded performances by children occurred at Lincoln's Inn Fields on 1 January 1729 when Rich offered *The Beggar's Opera* with "All the Parts to be perform'd by LILLIPUTIANS." The *Universal Spectator*, 4 January 1729, reported that the Prince of Wales, in attendance, was greatly pleased and that Peachum, Mrs Peachum, Macheath, Lucy and Mrs Dye "were performed to Admiration, and the rest very well." Eight consecutive performances brought good receipts. The playhouses also billed many youthful performers with other talents. At Drury Lane on 13 May 1718 John Weaver introduced his "little Sons" in a dance routine. At Lincoln's Inn Fields on 18 October 1718 de la Garde's two sons made their first appearance as dancers. At Lincoln's Inn Fields on 13 April 1724, Master Clegg, nine years old, played two concertos on the stage, and Matthew Dubourg played the violin year after year, the advertisements carefully noting his age as he performed from thirteen to maturity. In 1716–17 Rich imported young Salle and his sister Marie, who had such a warm reception that Rich extended their engagement.

In the first decade, but rarely thereafter, the theatres occasionally produced plays acted wholly by women. Oddly enough, seven performances between 1704 and 1711 concerned only two dramas: four offerings of *Love for Love* in 1705 and 1706, and two of *Pastor Fido* in 1706–7 followed by another at Greenwich on 21 May 1711. Unfortunately no casts and no commentary exist to shed further light upon them. Occasionally, women took men's roles as a special attraction (Mrs Hunt once acted Ben in *Love for Love* for her benefit) and men often took the more boisterous and vulgar female roles in comedy.

With versatile and brilliant performers, both old and young, playing night after night, audiences became engrossed in an actor and his talent. In part, this interest developed naturally from the repertory and benefit system, for in the eternal round of familiar plays individuality of acting sustained the roles. The long benefit season, when an actor carefully chose a play to display his special talent, made the spring a succession of fine roles. Mrs Oldfield, for example, frequently chose Millamant; Wilks selected Sir Harry Wildair; Estcourt, Sergeant Kite; Cibber, Sir Fopling Flutter or Lord Foppington; Booth, Hamlet or Othello. Occasionally an actor became so identified with a role that his relinquishing it was news, such as Wilks' announcement in the 1720's that he would perform Sir Harry Wildair only one more time. Players made their reputations by a single role: Thomas Walker as Macheath and Lavinia Fenton as Polly in *The Beggar's Opera*. Others dominated specific roles: John Harper as Falstaff, Hester Booth as Ophelia, Barton Booth as Othello, Cibber as Tattle, Wilks as Antony in *Julius Caesar*.

By tradition and seniority an actor might become typed. Cibber, for example, played many fops and, despite his detractors, possessed a creative touch in that type. Booth, on the other hand, was best in tragedy, many considering Othello or Lear his finest delineation. When spectators thought of farcical or low parts, Penkethman, Will Bullock, or Spiller came to mind. Stylization occurred, sometimes because a player learned a role by imitating his predecessors; Cibber acknowledged that he had modelled himself in some parts upon Dogget. In tragedy nearly everyone acted in a heavy and solemn style; it is uncertain whether tragedians chanted, but watching *Tamerlane* at Drury Lane on 6 November 1716, Dudley Ryder observed "in the general that the manner of speaking in our Theatres in tragedy is not natural. There is something that would be very shocking and disagreeable and very unnatural in real life. Persons would call it theatrical, meaning by that something stiff and affected."[131] On the following day, after talking with Signor Castilio, Ryder added: "He thinks we have not enough of action and gesture, our players say their parts as if they were reading a book and have nothing of that expressive force of looks and voice and gesture which gives life and spirit and nature to their action."[132]

Yet individuality persisted, though possibly kept within a narrow range. A comedian could and did improvise and *ad lib*. Will Penkethman, notorious for his jesting freedom with his lines, was "in such full possession of the galleries, that he would hold discourse with them for several minutes. To fine him for this fault was in vain; he could not forsake it, and the managers were too generous to curtail him of his income. At length . . . he and Wilks came to this whimsical agreement: Pinkey consented, That, whenever he was guilty of corresponding with the gods, he should receive on the back, three smart strokes of Bob Wilks's cane."[133] As the *Female Tatler*, 1 August 1709, pointed out, "'*Tis very rare that a* Comedy *succeeds from* Mr Wilks's *inimitable bright Air, without a little of* Pinkethman's Alackaday *and* Bullock's O Lamentable." The same journal for 3 November 1709 commented: "There is nothing . . . more ridiculous, than for an Actor to insert words of his own in the Part he is to act, so that it is impossible to see the Poet for the Player: You'll have *Penkethman* and *Bullock* helping out *Beaumont* and *Fletcher*." But Penkethman could not be restrained. Writing in the *Weekly Journal or Saturday's Post*, 20 January 1722, a correspondent reported that he had seen *The Tender Husband* at Drury Lane on 8 January 1722 and protested "that filthy Brute, Mr Penkethman, who by his Part was obliged to dance, taken in the Galleries with an idle Jest, by pretending that his Activity shuffled down his Breeches." On the other hand, Cibber emphasized that Will Mountfort's theory of acting

---

131 *The Diary of Dudley Ryder, 1715–1716*, ed. William Matthews (London, 1939), p. 360.
132 *Ibid.*
133 Davies, *Dramatic Miscellanies*, III, 51.

humorous roles kept him from laughing "at his own Jest, unless the Point of his Raillery upon another requir'd it."[134]

In this atmosphere of the unnatural in tragedy, genteel in high comedy, vulgarity in low, ad libbing by some and restraint by others, the best actors, nevertheless, set themselves high standards. Robert Wilks, for example, set great store on being perfect in his lines. Cibber pointed out that in a new comedy Wilks once complained of a "crabbed Speech" in his part—phrases which had given him more trouble than all the remaining lines—and asked the author to soften or shorten the passage. But when Wilks returned home from rehearsal, he thought it beneath his dignity to let a part prove too difficult for him and so he made himself "perfect in that Speech, though he knew it was never to be made use of."[135] With similar zeal, Dogget, to fit himself for Ben in *Love for Love*, took lodgings in Wapping to learn how sailors acted and talked.[136] The theory that "the show must go on" forced Christopher Bullock, advertised to play Sir Davy Dunce in *The Soldier's Fortune* at Lincoln's Inn Fields on 9 January 1722, to rise from a sickbed and play until the last act when, too ill to speak, he was forced to let another actor play his part. Similarly, during the later nights of the initial run of *Cato* Drury Lane kept a midwife behind scenes in momentary expectation that Mrs Oldfield, who played Cato's daughter, might give birth to her expected child.[137]

The best actors also excelled in controlling their audiences, especially when the atmosphere in the theatre was difficult. This talent was exemplified at the premiere of *The Provoked Husband* early in 1728.

In all the tumults and disturbances of the theatre on the first night of a new play ... Mrs Oldfield was entirely mistress of herself; she thought it her duty, amidst the most violent opposition and uproar, to exert the utmost of her abilities to serve the author. In the comedy of the Provoked Husband, Cibber's enemies tried all their power to get the play condemned. The reconciliation-scene wrought

[134] *Apology*, I, 128.

[135] *Ibid.*, I, 242. Theophilus Cibber (*Lives and Characters*, p. 48) made a point of how Booth "exerted himself in a particular Manner, and played [Hotspur] with such Fire, and Energy of Spirit" as to bring bursts of applause from the audience; Booth was stimulated that night to an extraordinary zeal by the presence in the cast of Giffard, who had seen Thomas Elrington play Hotspur and whom Booth wanted to impress with his ability to surpass Elrington.

[136] *An Essay on Acting* (London, 1744), p. 10.

[137] Similarly, Booth rehearsed Julio in *The Double Falsehood* (acted first on 13 December 1727), but because of illness gave the role to Charles Williams. Nevertheless, because Theobald, the author, and many gentlemen and ladies begged him to assume the role, Booth, though plagued with "an intermitting Fever," disregarded his condition, acted the role from the fifth to twelfth night, and had not the strength ever to appear on the stage again.— See Theophilus Cibber, *Lives and Characters*, pp. 82–83.

so effectually upon the sensible and generous part of the audience, that the conclusion was greatly and generously approved. Amidst a thousand applauses, Mrs Oldfield came forward to speak the epilogue; but when she had pronounced the first line,— Methinks I hear some powder'd critic say—a man, of no distinguished appearance, from the seat next to the orchestra, saluted her with a hiss. She fixed her eye upon him immediately, made a very short pause, and spoke the words *poor creature!* loud enough to be heard by the audience, with such a look of mingled scorn, pity, and contempt, that the most uncommon applause justified her conduct in this particular, and the poor reptile sunk down with fear and trembling.[138]

Players obviously needed extremely versatile talents. The repertory system demanded, day in and day out, a knowledge of an enormous number of roles, sometimes two in the same play, often parts in different plays in the same evening. An actor had to be quick to learn parts, retentive of lines, and skilful in playing tragedy one night, comedy the next, or even a tragic role in the main play followed by a comic one in the afterpiece. The ranking performers faced a nightly change of bill which obligated them to retain innumerable stock parts, learn their lines in forthcoming new or revived plays, rehearse in the morning the play for that night as well as a forthcoming drama. Although an actor was not troubled by matinees, he could easily have a full and tiring day.

Let the season of 1721–22 serve as an example of the demands placed upon performers. From September to June, Drury Lane played 70 different plays (afterpieces not included) on 192 nights; Lincoln's Inn Fields staged 46 dramas on 163 nights. (Incidentally, 21 of the plays appeared on both stages.) In addition, Drury Lane gave 4 afterpieces, Lincoln's Inn Fields 10 (only one offered in both theaters). Lincoln's Inn Fields had afterpieces on 62 nights, Drury Lane on 15, although the majority of the performers did not appear in both main and afterpiece. At Drury Lane John Mills was the shining example of a talented actor who could play nearly any role with competence and applause. Advertised for 50 roles out of 70 plays acted, he probably appeared in 10 others for which the cast was not named. He had a very wide range: Macbeth, Horatio, Ventidius (*All for Love*), Bajazet (*Tamerlane*), Bellmour (*Jane Shore*), Emperor in *Aurengzebe*, Chamont (*The Orphan*), Edmund (*Lear*), Southampton (*The Unhappy Favourite*), and the King in *The Mourning Bride*, to name only a few. In comedy he played Falstaff in both parts of *Henry IV*, Colonel Standard in *The Constant Couple*, several Worthys (*The Relapse, The Recruiting Officer, Love's Last Shift*), Morelove (*The Careless Husband*), Volpone, and Blunt (*The Committee*).

---

[138] Davies, *Dramatic Miscellanies*, III, 260–61.

Drury Lane's reliance upon Mills showed most clearly in the autumn. In the first two weeks of October he played twelve nights consecutively (except Sunday) in as many roles: Aimwell (*The Stratagem*), Cassius, Cunningham (*The Amorous Widow*), Villeroy (*The Fatal Marriage*), Amphitryon, Edmund, Blunt, Apemantus (*Timon of Athens*), Leontius (*The Humorous Lieutenant*), Sharper (*The Old Batchelor*), Frederick (*The Chances*), and Chamont. In the next twelve nights he played eleven roles, nine of which he had also not performed since the previous spring. In October alone he acted 23 times in 21 roles. Although this was a particularly demanding month, it was typical of Mills' schedule. Of the 192 nights on which Drury Lane was open, he probably played 160 times. Because he rarely acted a role more than three nights consecutively, he constantly had to refresh his memory and his conception of a role. It is no wonder that Victor referred to Mills as "the *most useful Actor* that ever served a Theatre"; Victor added that around 1734 Mills, though nearly sixty, acted some 170 out of 180 nights as his age advanced.

Mills was exceptional only in the consistently large number of roles he assumed. Robert Wilks, a portrayer of the "fine gentleman," not only acted at least 140 times in 1721-22 but also participated in the management. He possibly exceeded Mills in emotional range: Hamlet, Marc Antony, Castalio (*The Orphan*), Aurengzebe, Essex (*The Unhappy Favourite*), Dorimant (*The Man of Mode*), Valentine (*Love for Love*), Horner (*The Country Wife*), and Mosca (*Volpone*).

Although Mills and Wilks had the greatest variety of roles, many others appeared in fifteen or more parts. Barton Booth, a manager also, acted thirty-five advertised parts, mostly serious; he not only played Oroonoko, Othello, Cato Marc Antony, Tamerlane, and Lear, but also those requiring princely dignity, Banquo, Brutus, or the Ghost in *Hamlet*. Among the actresses at Drury Lane, Mrs Oldfield sustained the principal roles, especially in comedy. Enjoying the privilege of starting late in the autumn and quitting in April, she appeared in only twenty-six announced roles. Often playing against Wilks, she was the sophisticated heroine, but she took many tragic roles. In number of roles, however, Mary Porter, with twenty-eight, exceeded her.

In nearly every season at each theatre, this situation existed. Occasionally, a long run, like that of *The Beggar's Opera* in 1728, changed the emphasis to consecutive playing of a single piece, but when a run ceased, repertory returned. Sometimes the exigencies of casting required an actor to play two roles in different plays in the same evening. In 1721-22 James Spiller on 25 October 1721 played Harlequin in *The Emperor of the Moon* followed by Hob in *The Country Wake* and on 13 January 1722 Setter in *The Old Batchelor* and Harlequin in *The Magician*. At Drury Lane on 7 May 1729 Cibber Jr, Harper, Bridgwater, Corey, Oates, Griffin, and Miller played roles in both *II Henry IV* and *The Strollers*. Occasionally in September players appeared in a booth at Southwark Fair during the morning and afternoon and hurried back to their theatres for an evening role.

Acting in the early eighteenth century attracted a rather large number of men and women who began in minor roles in London or in strolling companies or who came over from Dublin. Most of them devoted their lives to the theatre, performing in the winter in London, perhaps joining a summer company, even going to Dublin occasionally. An occasional actor owned a tavern on the side, but a talented player could make good money and did not really need other employment.[139] The frugal ones kept it, and some, like Cibber, Wilks, and Booth, turned their talents into management, invested their earnings in the theatre, and became men of substance, at least in their small world. Beset by many difficulties and insecurity, they faced their hardships and few left the profession willingly for another way of life, although a beautiful young actress could look forward to becoming the mistress, perhaps even the wife, of a young man of good birth and better substance.

---

[139] There are some indications that the managers occasionally tried a system of rewards for fine acting. In a document in the Folger Shakespeare Library, Cibber, Wilks, and Booth, under date of 14 September 1727, ordered Castelman, the treasurer, to put aside 13*s*. 6*d*. each acting day toward a fund to reward actors at the end of the season for "extraordinary service." To whom any of these rewards may have been given is not clear, but possibly the present of fifty guineas to Mrs Oldfield after her memorable performance in *The Provoked Husband* in 1728 came from this fund.

Dancers and Dancing

OF ALL the forms of *entr'acte* entertainment, none exceeded in popularity the dance—solo, duet, or ensemble. From the opening years of the century the theatres advertised "With Entertainments of Dancing" as part of the bill, with the phrasing often including "serious," "comic," or "grotesque." As the bills grew longer, the managers named the dancers and specified in what interval they would appear. In addition, many plays had dances as embellishment to the action—not only the genteel comedies which concluded a scene with a sprightly dance but also spectacles like *The Lancashire Witches* and *The Island Princess* or the operatic versions of *The Tempest* and *Macbeth*, which elaborately mingled dance with song and dialogue. The most phenomenal development of dancing routines came, however, in pantomime; by the 1720's many Londoners felt that theatrical talent resided in the heels rather than in the head. Every theatre—the patent houses, the opera, the amateur groups, the foreign comedians—catered to the apparently unquenchable thirst for the dance.

Exemplifying the dominance of the dance is a benefit bill for Lincoln's Inn Fields (22 April 1728) for the popular dancers Poitier and Salle.

At the End of Act I, the Scottish Dance, by Mrs Bullock. . . . At the End of Act III, a new Grand Dance of French Sailors, by Mr Poitier, Mr Pelling, Mr Newhouse, Mr Dupre, the Pagod, Mrs Bullock, Miss Latour, Mrs Anderson, and Mrs Ogden. . . . At the End of Act V, A New Grand Dance of Moors, by Mr Glover, Mr Pelling, Mr Newhouse, Mr Lanyon, Miss Latour, Mrs Anderson, and Mrs Ogden, in which, at the Desire of several Persons of Quality, Mr Poictier will beat the Kettle Drums. . . . Concluded with a New Grand Dance, called Lads and Lasses, by Mr Poictier, Mr Pelling, Mr Newhouse, Mr Lanyon, Mr Dupre Jr, Mrs Bullock, Mrs Anderson, Miss Latour, and Mrs Ogden.

As an inevitable result of this enthusiasm, the theatres steadily increased the number of dancers on their rosters. Whereas in the early years of the century some actresses doubled as dancers—Hester Santlow, Mrs Bicknell, Mrs Younger—the popularity of dancing and, especially, of pantomime led to the engagement of many performers, especially foreigners, who confined their activities to the dance. The drawing power of foreign dancers demonstrated itself in 1716–17 when Rich engaged for Lincoln's Inn Fields young Salle and his sister Marie. Whenever they danced, the receipts improved, and Rich, consequently, extended their engagement and cautioned the public to see them before it was too late by advertising that they were to appear but five, then four . . . more times before leaving England. By the 1720's the managers had realized that their patrons' liking for the dance was nearly an irresistible force.

THE THEORY OF THE DANCE. One of the principal theorists was John Weaver, who early in the century produced "Night Scenes" at Drury Lane and who created dances and pantomimes for many years. Performing in them, he had a practical as well as theoretical knowledge of the art. In 1712 he published *An Essay Towards an History of Dancing*, in which he outlined the history, theory, and beauties of the dance. Most important theatrically was his analysis of "Stage Dancing" (in which he included "Theatrical or Opera Dancing"). This he divided into three types: "Serious, Grotesque, and Scenical."[140] Originally, "Stage Dancing" was "design'd for *Imitation*: to explain Things conceiv'd in the Mind, by the *Gestures* and *Motions* of the Body, and plainly and intelligibly representing *Actions*, *Manners*, and *Passions*; so that the Spectator might perfectly understand the *Performer* by these his *Motions*, tho' he say not a Word."[141] In his own times, however, this art had become more devoted to "diversion than Instruction; more how to please, than what is natural, fit, or proper."

Outlining the three types, he considered the serious dance to be somewhat like the "Common-Dancing usually taught in School" in that the steps for both were much the same but on the stage the serious should appear "soft, tender and delightful" though having a "rough and ridiculous Air" in an ordinary room. In serious dancing he saw two forms: brisk and grave, in which the French were the best. He cited the Chacone or Passacaille as examples of the "*grave* Movement." The brisk required vigor, lightness, agility, and quick springs, whereas the grave needed softness, "easie *Bendings* and *Risings*, and *Address*."[142]

Grotesque Dancing, the second of his types, was, he pointed out, "wholly calculated for the Stage, and takes in the greatest Part of Opera-Dancing." It was thought to be more difficult than the serious; to be a master, one should be skilled in music, particularly that related to time, well read in ancient and modern history, and possessing a taste for painting and poetry. In essence, it involved historical dancing, "which consist[s]

[140] John Weaver, *An Essay Towards an History of Dancing* (London, 1712), p. 169.
[141] *Ibid.*, p. 159.   [142] *Ibid.*, pp. 163–64.

most in figure, and represent[s] by *Action* what was before sung or express'd in Words."¹⁴³ Whether the dancer was concerned with ancient or modern themes, he should conform his steps, actions, and humor to the characters, sentiments, and passions which he wished to convey, with proper regard to habits, properties, and tunes. Weaver objected to the "mean performances" by some of "the *French* Masters who have been in *England*" and mentioned as an absurdity a dance composed by a Frenchman which was designed to be an Entry for Four Furies but which a week later was performed to represented Four Winds, the only alteration being that the Master injected himself into the middle as a fifth. Weaver saw the same mistake made in a dance of Four Seasons.

The third kind, Scenical Dancing, he considered a "faint Imitation of the *Roman Pantomimes*" and it differed from the Grotesque in that the latter represented only persons, passions, and manners, whereas the Scenical explained "whole *Stories* by Action,"¹⁴⁴ as in the ancient pantomimes. Similarly, Weaver thought that the French had degenerated the pantomime by introducing too much trickery and grimace, tumbling and "odd and unnatural Actions."

CHOREOGRAPHERS. Weaver was only one of many dancing masters, performers, and artists who planned and supervised dances and pantomimes. In the early years of the century these choreographers were generally anonymous, at least so far as the bills were concerned, but the enormous vogue of the dance brought them public recognition. For example, at Drury Lane in the 1720's Monsieur Roger was a principal dancer, often playing Pierrot in pantomimes; more and more frequently a spectacle was announced as being composed by him: *Le Badinage Champetre* (19 November 1725), *Perseus and Andromeda* (15 November 1728), *The English Medley* (4 April 1730). At much the same time Drury Lane also employed John Thurmond Jr, who created *Apollo and Daphne* (11 February 1726), *The Miser or Wagner and Abericock* (30 December 1726), and *Harlequin's Triumph* (27 February 1727). In 1728 Drury Lane announced that he was preparing *The Rise of Venice*, given on 30 November 1728. Later Drury Lane engaged Monsieur Desnoyer. At Lincoln's Inn Fields Rich had Monsieur Poitier, who created *A Jalousie of 3 Pierrots* for 21 April 1727, Francis Nivelon, and one Jones. As a rule, each took a principal part in his composition, and at his benefit he was likely to emphasize his latest works.

THE DANCES. It was not long before the practice of the theatres outgrew the theory which Weaver outlined early in the century. A great

¹⁴³ *Ibid.*, p. 165.   ¹⁴⁴ *Ibid.*, p. 168.

many types of dances evolved, and the practice of the playhouse became varied and loose. Imitations abounded. A "Night Scene" appeared in many forms, with slight variations in the characters. A national-occupational dance (French Sailors, for example) was capable of being adapted to every nation which had a navy. As a result, any classification is tentative and inconclusive, but the principal types fall into these groupings:

I. *Figure Dances, traditional and classical:*

Chacone, including such variations as a "Flute Chacone"
Cotillion, with such variations as "Les Cotillions"
Entry, with national variations such as French Entry, Spanish Entry, etc.
Louvre
Minuet
Passacaille
Piourette

II. *National Dances.*

These usually depicted a characteristic dance of a nation or province, sometimes realistically, sometimes satirically:

Bonny Highlander
Dutch Skipper
Folie d'Espaigne
Highland Lilt
Indian Tambour
Irish Jig
Irish Trot
Irish Dance
Quaker's Delight
Highland Laird and his Attendants
Sultan and Sultaness
The Swedes
The Whip of Dunboyn (an "Irish Humour")
Turkish Dance
The Muzette
Newmarket's Delight

III. *Narrative Dances.*

These pieces, which might be satiric, serious, light, or romantic, often unfolded a slight story or developed a situation:

A. Ancient mythology

Cyclops Dance (from the Opera *Psyche*)
Fury's Dance

B. Occupation, perhaps combined with nationality, and usually satiric or light

Foresters Dance
French Sailor
French Clown
Miller's Dance
Milk Pail Dance
Running Footman's Dance
Dance of Eight Linkmen
North Country Maggot
The Country Revels (Colin, Phoebe, Yeomen, Yeomen's Wives and Peasants)

C. Couple Dances (romantic, farcical, comic)

Boor Left in the Lurch
Burgomaster and his Frou
Country Frenchman and his Wife
Country Lad and Lass
Fisherman and his Wife
Miller and his Wife
Sailor and his Lass
French Sailor and his Wife

D. *Commedia dell'arte* themes

Dame Ragonde and her Eight Children
Dame Ragonde and her Two Sons
Entertainment in a Tavern between Scaramouch, Harlequin, and Punchanello
Scene between Scaramouch, Harlequin, Country Farmer, and his Wife

E. Stunt, Game and Grotesque Dances

Blind Man's Buff
Card Dance
Dance of Court Cards (King and Queen of Spades, Knave of Spades, King of
    Hearts, Queen of Diamonds, Knave of Clubs)
Chest Dance
The Echo
Flag Dance
The Humours of Bedlam (in *The Pilgrim*, but also separately)
Mad Man's Dance
Mademoiselle and her Dancing Dogs (Miss, Serviteur, Beau, Peasant, Scaramouch,
    Harlequin)
Stripping Dance
Three Children on Ice
Tub Dance

F. Serious Dances, single and ensemble

Grand Dance
Grand Wedding Dance
Grand Dance from *Rinaldo and Armida*
Pastoral Dance of Myrtillo
Union of Two Nations
Wood Nymph
The Faithful Shepherd
The Nassau
Les Caracteres de la Danse
Le Badinage Champetre
La Jeunesse
Les Amants Constants
Les Plaisirs
La Follette s'est Ravizee

G. Atmosphere Dances within Plays

Indian Dance in *Mongara* (later performed separately)
The Four Winds (*The Tempest*)
The Six Watermen (*The Tempest*)
Grand Dance of Spirits (The *Tempest*)
Moorish Dance (*Oroonoko*)
Pyrrhic Dance After the Manner of the Antients (*The Rival Queens*)

A brief examination of this sampling of dances suggests the high degree of similarity among the hundreds of routines, which could be altered to suit many nationalities, occupations, or moods. There were, for example, hosts of peasant dances: French, Swedish, Swiss, etc. The sailor dances could be varied to suit every seafaring land, with variations in costume and details. A couple dance had endless possibilities, by nationality, occupation, or combination of nationality and occupation, or mood. The lazy or unimaginative choreographer simply worked out variations methodically.

Repetitious or not, unimaginatively or creatively inspired, the dance enthralled thousands of spectators. Out of some dances came ballets; out of the grotesque grew combinations of incidents which became pantomimes. Whereas the play often changed nightly, sometimes a single dance occurred night after night, only to be readapted by another performer a few years later. A French sailor's dance at one theatre became in the hands of another dancer at an opposing house a new delight. Perhaps the pleasure which Zacharias von Uffenbach found in a performance at the Queen's on 2 June 1710 will suggest the appeal of the *entr'acte* dance.

Between every act they introduced several dances for variety. . . . [Mrs Santlow] danced charmingly as Harlequin, which suits her excellently and much pleases the English. . . . After her a man appeared as Scaramouch, but he was far from being as elegant a dancer, though he excels in droll attitudes, leaping and contortions of the body, in which I never saw his equal. The most amazing of all was that he danced a "chique" with great agility on the tips of his toes with his feet turned intirely inwards, so that one cannot conceive how he was able to bend his feet thus backwards, stand on tip-toes, and spring about without straining his feet or breaking them at the ankle-joints. He jumped so high in the air and with such frequency, alighting each time on his toes, that, when he suddenly collapsed, his feet were not to be seen; then he immediately sprang up again without putting his hand to the ground to help himself. That he further set one foot exactly before the other backwards, and, placing himself flat on the ground, sprang up immediately with great nimbleness, is not so much out of the ordinary, and I have seen it done often.[145]

[145] *London in 1710*, pp. 30–31.

Theatrical Music

LIKE the other forms of entertainment, music played an increasingly large part in the programs of the early eighteenth-century theatres. Perhaps the increase in vocal and instrumental music was not so spectacular as the development of dancing, but the introduction of Italian opera, the enormous popularity of concerts (both within and outside the theatres), the introduction of ballad opera, as well as the continued presence of the playhouse orchestra and individual soloists, both instrumental and vocal, created a greater diversity of musical entertainments. For *entr'acte* diversion vocal solos and dialogues proved more popular than instrumental solos, but the latter had its own diversity in a rather large range of instruments by which a musician proved his virtuosity. Instrumental music was much more properly the province of the playhouse orchestra, which had long been in existence and which continued to have an important, though less publicized, function.

THE ORCHESTRA. The variety which typified one duty of the playhouse orchestra was neatly stated in a short poem, *The Green Room* (1742).

> *In former Times no Orchestra was known*
> *But thrice before the Play a Horn was blown.*
>
> . . . .
>
> *But since the Æra of the Restoration,*
> *The Playhouses grew politer with the Nation;*
> *Drums, Kettle-Drums and Trumpets, Hautboys, Flutes,*
> *Violoncellos, Violins and Lutes*
> *Concerts, Concertos, Overtures, and Airs,*
> *Are now all us'd to introduce the Players.*

As the poem indicates, the orchestra entertained the assembling spectators before the curtain rose. Early in the century the bills usually mentioned simply "Select Pieces of Music" as part of the program, but later, in keeping with the tradition of the blowing of the horn three times, these instrumental pieces became known as the First, Second, and Third Music. Generally these were not announced by name, although the broadened interest in music led to an occasional announcement that a particular overture would be played. This custom also spread to include introductory music before the afterpiece began.

The size or composition of the playhouse orchestra is not exactly
known. In the document establishing a company around 1707[146] the proposals
call for a Master of the Music and twenty musicians under him, each to be
paid £1 weekly through a season of forty weeks. In another document
(probably 1710) the list of musicians for the Queen's contains twenty-
eight names.[147] It was at this time that Zacharias von Uffenbach, seeing
Hydaspes at the Queen's on 30 May 1710, thought that the "orchestra is so
well composed that it could not be better. They are all foreigners, mostly
Germans and then French, for the English are not much better musicians
that the Dutch, and they are fairly bad. The conductor is Pepusch from
Brandenburg, who is known every where for his amazingly elegant compositions."[148] He did not indicate the size of the orchestra, but on 14 June
1710 he attended a concert which Pepusch directed: the "orchestra was
not very strong, consisting of no more than sixty persons";[149] in spite of
his phrase "not very strong," it seems unlikely that a playhouse (perhaps
even the opera) orchestra was normally that large. As late as 1724–25 the
nightly charge for the orchestra at Lincoln's Inn Fields was £3 14s. 2d.,
and if the 1710 rate still held—£1 weekly for each musician—it would
have had a complement of about twenty instrumentalists. This figure
seems the most likely one for a playhouse orchestra. An individual might
receive from 3s. 4d. upward for a solo performance. A note from the Drury
Lane managers to the treasurer (2 June 1716) instructed him to pay Paisable
5s. per diem, with a guinea every time he performs any piece on the stage.[150]

In addition to playing overtures, the orchestra also assisted in the
presentations of masques and vocal music accompanying many plays. In
the first decade of the century, for example, *Bonduca*, *King Arthur*, *The
Tempest*, and *The Indian Queen*, with the music composed by Henry Purcell,
were frequently played.[151] The orchestra also greatly assisted *The Island
Princess* and *The Prophetess* to a high degree of popularity. For the revival
of *Massaniello* at Lincoln's Inn Fields on 29 March 1725 the orchestra
performed "a Composition of solemn Musick, Vocal and Instrumental, on
the Confirmation of the Neapolitan Charter, admirably set." In *Perseus and
Andromeda*, a pantomime given at Drury Lane on 15 November 1726, "the
Overture that leads to the Scene of Andromeda's being chain'd to a Rock,

[146] Nicoll, *Early Eighteenth Century Drama*, p. 277.   [147] *Ibid.*, pp. 278–79.
[148] *London in 1710*, pp. 17–18.   [149] *Ibid.*, p. 66.
[150] Fitzgerald, *New History of the English Stage*, I, 419.
[151] For the vogue of Purcell in the early eighteenth-century theatres, see Eric Walter
White, "Early Theatrical Performances of Purcell's Operas," *Theatre Notebook*, XIII (Winter,
1958–59), 43–65.

is so charmingly diversify'd, and interspers'd with such a graceful Confusion of Harmony, that it steals into the very Soul of an Audience, and works up the different Passions of Joy and Grief, Pity and Hatred, Hope and Despair, to Admiration."[152]

INSTRUMENTALISTS. Soloists from the orchestra and from outside the ranks of the theatres often appeared on the program. For such appearances from its own staff a playhouse generally paid extra: in 1726–27 Lincoln's Inn Fields paid £2 14s. to "Mr Gillier of the Musick for a Hand Organ used in Proserpine." It frequently allowed 2s. nightly for kettle drums, more for trumpets, in addition to the orchestra proper. The bills show also a considerable range of numbers and instruments, with emphasis at times on novelty. Drury Lane on 20 May 1720, for example, offered a piece of music "in Imitation of the Tattoo." At the King's on 12 June 1716 Atilio played "upon a New Instrument, call'd, Viola D'Amour" in a rendition of his own "New Symphony." A solo on the German Harp, at Lincoln's Inn Fields on 27 February 1720, marked Signor Angel's first appearance on the stage. At Lincoln's Inn Fields on 4 April 1704 (and later) Godfrede Pepusch and seven young Germans gave a concert composed by John Christopher Pepusch for hautboys, flutes, and German horns.

In addition, a great variety of instruments appeared in solo or ensemble numbers: trumpet, violin, hautboy, double cortell, little flute, flagelot, harpsichord, flute alleman, arch-lute, great theorbo, mandelitta ("an Instrument hitherto unknown"), viol di gambe, to use the designations of that day. Sometimes the pieces were named: Handel's *Water Musick* at Lincoln's Inn Fields on 4 April 1722; Corelli's 1st and 8th concertos (very popular); Clayton's *The Passions of Sappho* at Lincoln's Inn Fields on 15 September 1718. Many were described, but not named: "a New Concerto for the Flagelot, compos'd by Dr Pepusch" at Lincoln's Inn Fields 3 July 1717; "a Piece of Musick for the Violin and Flute by Signior Gasperini and Mr Paisible, it being the most Masterly perform'd of any Musick that was ever heard upon the English Stage" at Drury Lane 19 November 1703; "a New Solo on the Violin compos'd and perform'd by Signor Bitte on the Stage" at Drury Lane 25 May 1717. Well-known performers occasionally did novelties: "A Piece of Music accompanied by Mr Joachim Frederic Creta, who will blow the First and Second Treble on Two French Horns in the same Manner as if Two Persons" at Lincoln's Inn Fields on 16 January 1729.

VOCALISTS. Each theatre required a corps of singers for plays which had choruses or solos as part of their traditional presentation; in

[152] *London Evening Post*, 23 November 1728.

addition, some plays proved more popular when music supplemented the action. In the operatic version of *The Tempest*, for example, performed at Drury Lane on 22 May 1727 the masque of *Neptune and Amphitrite* was sung by Boman, Rainton, Ray, Miss Raftor, Mrs Willis, and Mrs Boman. For the operatic *Macbeth*, *The Island Princess*, or *The Prophetess*, Lincoln's Inn Fields usually featured four to six vocalists; it also had on its roster three to five singers of sufficient fame to be advertised for many masques and interludes: Mrs Barbier, Rochetti, and Leveridge for *Venus and Adonis* on 2 April 1725 or Leveridge, Salway, and Mrs Chambers for *The Fickle Fair One* on 21 March 1726.

More important for *entr'acte* entertainments, however, were solos and dialogues, and these required a number of singers capable of pleasing the audience in a variety of musical offerings. Many a performer—Richard Leveridge is a major example—sang his way to the hearts of his countrymen season after season. These vocal numbers, like the dances, can be grouped in a few general classes which are not free from overlapping: *1*] Italian songs, *2*] songs from English plays, *3*] topical and patriotic songs, and *4*] popular and romantic themes.

After Italian opera had won applause, the playhouses found it advantageous to offer singing in Italian. As a result, each theatre engaged a few vocalists who could present attractively the most popular airs from the operas. During the years from 1705 to 1710 the managers often advertised Katherine Tofts, Margarita de l'Epine, or Maria Gallia to sing in Italian and English, sometimes specifying that the songs came from recent Italian operas. In later years, as audiences grew more familiar with foreign music, the announcements became more precise. On 5 April 1727 at Lincoln's Inn Fields, for example, Mrs Isabella Chambers at her benefit sang a new cantata composed by Signor Bononcini. In May of that year Mrs Warren was occasionally advertised to sing "De mi Cara" between the acts of an English drama. At Lincoln's Inn Fields Mrs Barbier, who had had experience in Italian opera, attracted a following as well as one of the highest salaries among singers.

Early in the century many *entr'acte* songs had originally appeared in plays: "Britons, strike home" from *Bonduca;* "The Dame of Honour" from *Wonders in the Sun;* "The Enthusiastick Song" from *The Island Princess;* "Drunken Officer and Town Miss" from *The Mad Lover;* "I burn, I burn" from *Don Quixote*, Part II. Many of these were separately advertised when the play to which they belonged was offered, but many also appeared as solos or dialogues when another play occupied the bill. For example,

Leveridge made "The Enthusiastick Song" a favorite both for himself and for his followers.

The topical song, of course, capitalized upon a recent incident and frequently died with the event. For example, two songs inspired by the South Sea Bubble had a short life: "Four and Twenty Stock Jobbers" and "South Sea Bubble." From mercantile affairs came in 1719 "The Weavers Complaint against the Calico Madams." As a result of an order banning the wearing of masks in the playhouses, "The Misses Lamentation for want of their Vizard Masks in the Playhouse" had momentary appeal in 1704. Songs with patriotic or national themes had a longer stage life, such as "Oh, London is a Fine Town" or "Hyde Park Grenadier." A topically patriotic one with a shorter life was "A Dialogue between English and Paris Gazetteers on the Victory at Ramilly" in 1707.

The great mass of songs, naturally, dealt with universal themes, particularly love and romance. Some were nostalgic, some satiric, some conventionally moving. Sometimes the title implied a mocking mood: "A Mock Song of the Country Life" or "A Widdow in Tears for the Loss of her Husband and a Town Rake making Love to Her." Others could be sung wistfully, sorrowfully, or maliciously: "Fair Iris," "Go, Perjured Man," "John, ere you leave me," "No Kissing at All," "The May Morning's Adventure," "The Bath Teazer," "'Tis Joy to Wound a Lover," or a "Rural Dialogue between a little Boy and Girl."

In addition, many songs, like the dances, dealt with incident, mode of living, professions, situations: "Sailor's Song," "A Chimney Sweeper's Dialogue," "A Dialogue representing a vain promising Courtier and a Sycophant," "Satyr upon all Trades," "In Praise of Fishing," "The Enter'd Prentice's Song," "Song in the Character of a Butcher's Wife," "Ballad on my Lady's Twitcher," "The Ballad of Sally," "Smugg Upon Tuesday," or "Turkey Cock Song."

Hundreds of songs came upon the stage, echoed briefly, and were soon forgotten, but many survived countless repetitions. Some came from earlier composers whose names added luster to the song: "Written by the famous Henry Purcell." Among contemporaries, Richard Leveridge wrote, sang, and published many popular pieces. As Henry Carey gained fame, his name appeared in the bills. Many songs became identified with individuals: "In Praise of Love and Wine" was almost a trademark of Leveridge and Legar. Mrs Willis returned time and again to sing "The Mock Song of a Country Life" or "Smugg Upon Tuesday." Pack and Boman frequently sang a duet, one impersonating a girl. Nearly every vocalist had a song or two which he inevitably offered at his own benefit.

CONCERTS. Only a reading of the daily newspapers in the first thirty years of the century can fully demonstrate the enormous appetite of the public for concerts and musical programs, both within the theatres and in taverns, halls, dancing rooms, academies, and private rooms.[153] Generally speaking, concerts flourished in mid-winter (January through May), partly because instrumentalists from the opera house were available for other engagements and partly because the ban on plays on Wednesday and Friday in Lent did not extend to concerts. Many concerts were performed, rather vaguely, by the "best Masters"; others were promoted by vocalists or musicians who for their own benefit solicited their friends to hear them and other artists perform. Admission for a concert was usually set at from 3s. to 5s., and these benefits were comparable to those for actors. An example of an elaborate program is a concert given at Drury Lane on 26 March 1729 as a benefit for Mrs Turner Robinson.

[153] Occasionally an individual proposed an ambitious program of monthly concerts. On 9 January 1717 an announcement called for subscriptions to a "Monthly Concert of Vocal and Instrumental Musick" for the first Wednesday in each month. The proposals promised never fewer than three of the finest singers and nineteen musicians. Each subscriber would pay a guinea for a year, and the concerts would begin when there were three hundred subscribers. The series began on 27 February 1717 at Stationer's Hall. The author of *Letters Describing the Character and Customs of the English* (London, 1726) stated, "The People of Quality of both Sexes never fail to be at these Concerts" (p. 33).

The Specialties

NOTING the popularity of song, dance, and instrumental music, the managers found themselves tempted to supplement these with specialties of a more exotic nature. Sometimes they seemed to yield against their better judgment, especially in the early years of the century when acrobatics and rope dancing slipped into the programs. During at least two early seasons, the managers made an effort to restrict the widening range of specialties and return to pure drama. Early in 1707–8 the Queen's announced categorically that it would offer plays "Without Singing or Dancing," and in the following season, with a monopoly of plays, Drury Lane made a similarly virtuous promise. But these attempts to halt the flood of *entr'acte* entertainments had no permanent effect, unless the gradual decline of tumbling, rope dancing, and vaulting in the first decade resulted from this movement. There remained, however, a range of specialties, some not thematically appropriate to a theatre, others a traditional part of dramatic offerings.

ACROBATICS AND ODDITIES. The close relationship between the fairs and theatres early in the century fostered entertainments of this sort within the playhouses. What Penkethman presented to enthusiastic audiences at the booths he sometimes brought into the theatres in the winter. In the first decade a fairly long parade of acrobats, rope-dancers, and posturers, seemed intent, in Cibber's much ridiculed phrase, to "out-do their usual out-doings" before pit and boxes. They performed on the sloping rope and the "manag'd Horse," vaulted over bars and poles, and turned themselves into grotesque postures. At Lincoln's Inn Fields on 11 October 1705 "The Two famous French Maidens [performed] so wonderfully on the Rope, the eldest . . . Dancing without a Pole and turning herself round, which never could be done by any yet before her" that, according to the bills, everyone who saw her could never forget her. On the same bill "the famous Mr Evans" vaulted on the "manag'd Horse," doing several "surprizing Entertainments, especially his Body lying extended on one Arm, and drinking 9 Glasses of Wine from the other." At the Queen's on 7 December 1709 appeared "the famous Mr Higgins, who turns himself into such variety of Amazing Shapes and Figures, that the particulars wou'd be incredible to all Persons who have not seen him." None of these, however, excelled the young gentlewoman whom Penkethman brought to his theatre in Greenwich on 17 August 1710: she "turns round upon one Foot 300 times, and as she is turning fixes 12 Swords points about her, 2 to her Eyes, 2 to her Eye-lashes, 2 to her Eye-brows, 2 to her Nose, 2 to her Lips, and 2 to her Breasts, &c."

As song and dance gained in popularity, however, acrobatics and posturing lost ground within the theatres. They continued in the bills at the fairs, and when foreign companies came to London in the 1720's they stressed vaulting and gymnastics as *entr'acte* diversion. The managers of the English theatres could not, of course, resist an occasional display of this kind. They also introduced some human oddities. *Pasquin*, 28 January 1724, commented upon a diversion at Lincoln's Inn Fields: "There is to be seen a Giant of an erect and lofty Stature, a graceful Mien and Motion, and an Arm often stretch'd forth in Conquest. He comes upon the Stage, attended by an Enchanter, by whose Assistance he performs the most surprizing Exploits to the Delight and Terror of the Audience." *Applebee's*, 30 November 1728, reported that the "Wild Boy . . . from Hertfordshire" had been seen at the same house. In mid-December 1726 Rich had introduced into *Harlequin a Sorcerer* a new "Rabbit Scene" as a result of the publicity given to a woman of Guilford, known as the "Rabbit Woman," who, reportedly, had given birth to nine rabbits. But pantomime, with its floating chariots, posturing by Harlequin and Scaramouch, transformations, and magical illusion, sufficiently compensated the audience for the loss of incidental oddity.

IMITATIONS AND BURLESQUES. In a vein more closely related to drama were the specialties which burlesqued the familiar or imitated something not customary in man. Representing the first type is the burlesque of a scene in the French *Andromache* staged by M and Mlle Salle at Lincoln's Inn Fields on 11 December 1716 and later. He played Orestes, she Andromache; calls for encores brought the skit onto the stage several times. Of more questionable taste was a burlesque of *Cato* given at Penkethman's theatre in Richmond on 6 July 1719. W. R. Chetwood reported, in effect, that Penkethman, Norris, and other comedians "defil'd those noble Sentiments of Liberty," and Lady Bristol stated that she "had no patience to see [Addison's] play burlesqued" in this crude way.[154]

154 See W. R. Chetwood, *A General History of the Stage* (London, 1749), p. 198; *The Letter Books of John Hervey* (Wells, 1894) under 7 July 1719; and Rosenfeld, *Strolling Players*, pp. 280–81.

THE LONDON STAGE, 1700–1729   cxliv

In another imitative vein Clench, from Barnet, proved a sensation at Drury Lane in 1701–2 with his vocal novelties: "Mr Clench of Barnet will perform an Organ with 3 Voices, the double Curtell, the Flute, and the Bells with the Mouth; the Huntsman, the Hounds, and the Pack of Dogs." His popularity secured him new engagements in later years, and in 1709–10 Layfield, announcing himself as an imitator of Clench, created the "Horn, Huntsman, and Pack of Hounds, all perform'd by his natural Voice." This specialty never wholly died out; at the Haymarket on 4 June 1733, for example, a gentleman performed on stage "The Crowing of the Cock." In a similar imitative vein, though nearer to the dance, was the ever-popular "Drunken Man," a novelty performed by John Harper and John Hippisley as well as others. And Rich brought to Lincoln's Inn Fields on 7 December 1720 "Two Germans . . . who imitate the French Horn and Trumpet with their Natural Voices, in all their different Parts."

RECITALS AND ORATIONS. Because the traditional prologue and epilogue provided the actor with opportunities to show his declamatory powers, other types of recitals and orations were relatively rare. If Cibber could make a popular skit out of his epilogue "Upon Nobody" or Penkethman one out of his epilogues spoken with an ass by his side, the player had little need to step outside this framework. Nevertheless, an occasional specialty of this type appeared, such as Thomas D'Urfey's frequent orations, usually at his benefit or at a performance of one of his plays. For example, at Drury Lane on 3 June 1715 he addressed an oration to "his Majesty, and their Royal Highnesses the Prince and Princess of Wales, on the glorious Advantages of Unity and Amity among us," a perennially popular theme; and on 29 May 1716 he gave his more entertaining oratory, "On several famous Heads." But D'Urfey had few rivals in this form of entertainment.

PROLOGUES AND EPILOGUES. The eighteenth century inherited the custom of opening the play with a prologue and concluding it with an epilogue. Although the managers did not necessarily list these in each night's bill, they may have formed a normal part of each night's offerings. Certainly, every new play of any potential importance had its prologue and epilogue spoken on each night of the initial run and printed with the text of the play. Exceptions were rare; in fact, Susanna Centlivre, in the preface to *The Perplex'd Lovers* (19 January 1712) felt impelled to mention that on the first night the play appeared without an epilogue because the managers feared to have spoken the one written for it "without I cou'd get it Licens'd." With similar implication, the prologue to Jane Wiseman's *Antiochus the Great* (November 1701) stated:

> 'Tis a hard Tax upon the Stage we know,
> That without Prologue, you'll no Play allow.

Sometime later, at Lincoln's Inn Fields, 27 February 1727, when *The Savage* and *The Rape of Proserpine* comprised the double bill, the manager inserted a special note to explain that the program "for Brevity, will be presented without Prologue or Epilogue."

The prologue served, in part, to gain the attention of the audience and, further, to persuade it, by humor, topical comment, a note of solemnity, an appeal, or with wit to give the play a warm reception. The prologue to Mrs Centlivre's *The Perjured Husband* refers to Mrs Oldfield, who spoke it, as entering the lists or tournament where the audience cannot fight her "(with honour safe) for she's a fair Inviter." That to Mary Pix's *The Czar of Muscovy* (March 1701) argued

> And I, a Sacrifice, before am sent,
> Your Vengeance on the Poet to prevent.

As a variation, the prologue to Cibber's *Love Makes a Man* compared a play to a feast to which the purchase of a ticket makes one a welcome guest and, instead of having grace spoken, a prologue prepares the spectator's palate for the bill of fare. The prologue to *Hibernia Freed*, 13 February 1722, outlined various theories of its method.

> Some usher in their Plays with keenest Satyr
> And by Invective wou'd Incite Good Nature.
> . . . .
> Others by mean Submission plead their Cause,
> And by insidious Flattery win Applause.
> . . . .
> And some by Faction, and in Party, strong,
> Through five dull Acts their Politicks prolong.

To vary the approach, the prologue to Farquhar's *The Inconstant* (November 1702) stated: "Plays are like Supper: Poets are the Cooks." Other poets likened the audience to a jury (Epilogue to *The Successful Pyrate*, 7 November 1712; Prologue to *Love the Leveller*, 26 January 1704).

Nevertheless, the frequent repetition of prologues, for a play acted several times in a season was preceded by its original prologue, and the difficulty of providing witty new ones sometimes made the custom a bore rather than a delight. As the prologue to John Gay's *The Captives*, 15 January 1724, put it:

> *I wish some author, careless of renown,*
> *Would without formal prologue risque the town,*
> *For what is told you by this useless ditty?*
> *Only that tragedy should move your pity:*
> *That when you see theatric heroes shown,*
> *Their virtues you should strive to make your own.*

The epilogue, according to that for *Three Hours After Marriage*, 16 January 1717, originally had a simple function.

> *The ancient Epilogue, as Criticks write,*
> *Was, clap your Hands, excuse us, and good-night.*

That for *Irene*, 9 February 1708, developed this theme:

> *Our Epilogues at first were an Excuse,*
> *To pardon Faults of unperforming Muse:*
> *But much improv'd of late, our Modern way is,*
> *To part in Mirth, however sad the Play is.*

And the same objections to the ever-present prologue applied to the epilogue; that for Theobald's *The Persian Princess*, 31 May 1708, bluntly put it:

> *Curse on the Custom, that demands your Stay*
> *For Epilogues, when tir'd with damn'd dull Play!*

Satirically, the epilogue to *The Rival Modes*, 27 January 1727, outlined the poet's methods.

> *The Arts that now conduct a Poet's Aim,*
> *To raise an Epilogue to certain Fame,*
> *Are these: If bad the Play, you must cry down*
> *All other Follies that divert the Town.*
> *A Pantomime once nam'd gives Mirth its Trap,*
> *And the Word Eunuch proves a Thundering Clap:*
> *Or in some Wanton Play of Words be shewn*
> *Two Meanings, to conceal the Want of One.*

The managers also turned to a topical or special circumstance to give a fresh basis for an appeal. For example, a revival of *Tamerlane* on 5 November 1716 included a "Royal Prologue," and the custom of reviving this play on 4 and 5 November prompted many royal or loyal prologues. At the close of 1701–2 Drury Lane offered a topical "New Vacation Epilogue." The wars of the first decade produced such prologues as that on 8 December 1702 "All in Honour of the Officers of the Army and Fleet, and to Welcome them Home from Flanders and Vigo."

Another means of diversifying the appeal was to develop a humorous theme, whether or not it had relevance to the play of the evening. The most lively and enduring of this type were the epilogues in which the speaker either rode or stood by an ass on stage. Joe Haines popularized this type; in fact, according to Chetwood, "The Epilogue in particular that he spoke riding an Ass, created such a Laughter, and reiterated Applause, that it was near Half an Hour in the speaking."155 His most successful imitator was Will Penkethman, who spoke many a "Comical Joking Epilogue upon an Ass"; he also stimulated imitators, of whom the most entertaining were James Spiller and the inimitable Tony Aston.

Writers and actors produced many variations. Drury Lane on 26 December 1707, for example, advertised "An Equi-Vocal Epilogue, after the English manner, compiled and spoken by the most famous Signior Pinkethmano, upon an Ass that never appear'd but twice on either Stage." This, in turn, inspired another at the Queen's on the same day: "The last new Vocal Epilogue, Compos'd and Perform'd by the famous Signior Cibberini, after the newest English, French, Dutch, and Italian Manner." When Penkethman in 1719 opened his summer season at Richmond, his theatre had been converted from a stable for asses, a situation very apt for his specialty.156

There was, obviously, almost no limit to the types of situations which could be developed for prologues and epilogues. Drury Lane welcomed George I to England in 1714 with a fitting prologue. In 1715–16 a display of the aurora borealis gave rise to another. At a performance of *The Debauchees* on 4 August 1708 Norris, acting Tom Saleware, spoke an epilogue "To His Brother Salewares of the City." On 5 March 1716 Mrs Oldfield gave one "Recommending the Cause of Liberty to the Beauties of Great Britain"; its political implications called for repetition. Among others were an epilogue on "The Hoop'd Petticoat" (18 March 1717); Cibber's skit on "The Person of Nobody" (28 January 1710), which he frequently repeated; Pack's "In a Riding-Habit, upon a Pad-Nagg, Traveling to Tunbridge." A moment of importance to the theatre might bring on a new "Prologue to the Town," which would exhort, plead, or inform. Many of these had sufficient appeal to be printed in newspapers or periodicals; even the prologues and epilogues to new plays might appear in the journals before publication in the printed version of the drama. They also offer exceedingly interesting insights to the tastes of the audiences as well as the practices of the playhouse.

155 W. R. Chetwood, ed., *The British Theatre* (Dublin, 1750), p. 120.
156 The prologue is reprinted in Rosenfeld, *Strolling Players*, pp. 278–79.

The Production

ALTHOUGH the presence of song, dance, pantomime, prologues, epilogues, and even acrobatics might suggest otherwise, the theatres existed to produce a play. All of their complex organization, financial operations, and human relationships formed the background from which a good production should come. The process of getting up a play, whether old or new, was essentially the same, yet the production of a new one involved more complex steps. A play had to be obtained, read, and cast; scenes and costumes had to be designed and made or altered from old stock; rehearsals had to be set in motion. Eventually came that most critical moment of all (especially for a new play), the first night. Tracing some phases of the production of plays as the steps appear in the bills, correspondence, prefaces, and critical notices will clarify the problems of management in the early years of the century.

SECURING A PLAY. The playhouses had two main sources for dramatic materials: the ever-increasing reservoir, in the public domain, of old plays; and those in manuscript, as yet unproduced. Every year the store of old plays in prompt copies and printed versions grew larger, and although no theatre could hope or even desire to act all of them in a single season, every playhouse examined the copies of plays not acted recently in search of revivals. Some plays dropped out of the active repertory, and others, long absent from the stage, were tried out again. Survival of the fittest operated to thin the list of eligible choices, with both managers and spectators constantly redetermining which were the fittest. The managers understood, also, the limits to indiscriminate competition; neither theatre saw wisdom in preparing for its own repertory *each* drama the opposition staged. Rich's company, for example, tended to give *The Double Dealer* without competition and Drury Lane usually had *The Way of the World* to itself, whereas both played *The Old Batchelor* and *Love for Love* competitively.

The securing of new dramas was a different and more difficult matter. Generally speaking, little evidence exists of genuine commissioning of plays, although dramatists refer occasionally to more than casual suggestions from managers or actors. For example, Elkanah Settle, in the preface to *The City Ramble*, 17 August 1711, suggests that it was due to Barton Booth's "Recommendation . . . of Two of the Plays of Beaumount and Fletcher" as source materials that he fashioned his play. Charles Shadwell, in the preface to his highly successful comedy, *The Fair Quaker of Deal*, 25 February 1710, mentions that Booth gave him assistance in the preparation of the play.

Without commissioning, each theatre, nevertheless, received abundant offerings of manuscripts, and each involved not only a decision to be made but a potential argument, in private or public, with a touchy author, whether his play was rejected or, possibly, accepted and then, in his eyes, imperfectly staged. Each manuscript might bring the managers at least one new enemy, for Vanbrugh, writing on 18 June 1722, told Tonson, "Cibber tells me, 'tis not to be conceiv'd, how many and how bad Plays, are brought to them."[157] A new production also cost time and effort and had to meet the great hazard of the premiere. In fact, Barton Booth "often declared in public company, that he and his partners lost money by new plays; and that, if he were not obliged to it, he would seldom give his consent to perform one of them."[158] Yet, as Booth stated, the managers had to read new plays, accept some, and stage them. Printed prefaces and the columns of many papers are strewn with the bitter remarks of authors and their friends at the treatment accorded them. The managers of Drury Lane, for example, never lived down their refusal of Fenton's *Mariamne*, which Rich eventually turned into a solid success. Samuel Madden, in the preface to *Themistocles*, which had a successful run of nine nights at Lincoln's Inn Fields in 1729, complained that it had been "peremptorily refused, after the most earnest and early Sollicitations, at the Old House [Drury Lane] for two Winters together." In 1709 Susanna Centlivre's *The Busy Body*, probably her most successful play, just barely survived the process of selection and rehearsal; in fact, Mrs Centlivre had the unhappy experience of witnessing "Sir *Harry Wild-Air* [acted by Wilks] in great dudgeon [fling] his *Part* into the *Pitt* for damn'd Stuff" at a rehearsal.[159] Although the lot of an aspiring dramatist was not an easy one, no dearth of dramatic manuscripts occurred.

READING A PLAY. Many a manuscript was read by a manager (or the prompter) and got no further, being quickly rejected. Cibber had a reputation for being unskilful in accomplishing this disagreeable task; as

---

[157] *Works*, IV, 146.
[158] Davies, *Memoirs of the Life of David Garrick, Esq.*, I, 208.
[159] *Female Tatler*, 10 October 1709.

Davies remarked, "His denial of a new piece was not attended with that delicacy and politeness which is so necessary upon an unwelcome repulse,"[160] and many prefaces complain of Cibber's brusque dismissals of an author's hopes. If a play passed this first reading, it was ready to be read aloud; possibly, for the more important prospects, a reading, with the author and managers present, became the first step in the process of selection. In the Restoration authors had occasionally read their own plays to the managers and actors; Cibber referred to the cold manner in which Dryden read his *Amphitryon* and the dramatic tones with which Lee spoke the lines of his dramas.[161] That this practice continued is indicated by a letter from John Dennis to Steele reporting on his meeting with Cibber and Booth on 28 February 1718 over *Coriolanus*, which Dennis had submitted to the managers: "the Play with the Alterations was approv'd of, nay and warmly approv'd of, by your self, Mr *Cibber*, and Mr *Booth* (the other Manager was not there)."[162] In addition, Victor, discussing the procedure for handling a new play, stated that the author read it aloud to the actors three times to familiarize them with his conception of the tone and action.[163] Not every author, however, felt able to do this; when the group met to hear *Cato* read, Addison was so bashful that he asked Cibber to read the tragedy aloud.

SECURING A PERMIT.   Although this problem has already been examined in the section on the playhouses, above, it should again be emphasized that possibly any prospective play might be found unsuitable by the Lord Chamberlain. It is difficult to know, however, whether before the Licensing Act of 1737 every play was submitted for his judgment. Certainly he banned some: Baker's *An Act at Oxford* (1704) and Swiney's *The Quacks*, both later acted; Gildon's revision of *Lucius Junius Brutus;* and, of course, Gay's *Polly*. Certainly the managers of Drury Lane for years resisted efforts to control the content of plays, prologues, epilogues, and skits; but before the procedure was codified in 1737, the evidence is meager and contradictory.

[160] *Memoirs of the Life of David Garrick, Esq.*, I, 209.

[161] *Apology*, I, 113–14.

[162] *The Works of John Dennis*, II, 162. By this time—see Thaler, *Shakespeare to Sheridan*, facing page 64—the Drury Lane managers had issued an order to the effect that no play should be received into the house or the parts of any drama ordered to be written out except by a written statement over the hands of the three managers.

[163] *The History of the Theatres of London and Dublin*, II, 4–5. Apparently individuals not connected with the theatres met and read together the manuscripts of plays in advance of the performance. The Earl of Egmont and others read *Themistocles* on 29 January 1729 before it was acted at Lincoln's Inn Fields, 10 February 1729.—See *The Diary of the First Earl of Egmont*, Historical Manuscripts Commission (London, 1920–23), III, 336.

WRITING PARTS. A necessary step in the production of a play, this task seems generally to have been assigned to the prompter. For example, when the masque *Apollo and Daphne* was being readied for performance at Drury Lane on 24 January 1716, the prompter wrote it into parts, had the score bound, and put the units into covers (Egerton 2159). For this type of work, he frequently received extra pay; at Lincoln's Inn Fields during 1726–27 Stede, the prompter, received his salary and also £10 15s. 11d. for writing out lines. If the play being prepared was an old one but newly cast, he often wrote out the lines afresh or, if a single role was to be newly assigned, he made a new draft of it. For example, an undated voucher (probably 1716) in Egerton 2159 specified the parts written out: two, Bonario for Ryan at 3d.; two, Martha in *The Scornful Lady* for Mrs Bradshaw at 3d.; three and one-half, Captain in *The Scornful Lady* for Leigh 5d.; six, Smugler in *Jubilee* for Johnson 9d.; two and one-half, Mustacho in *The Tempest* for Leigh 4d.

CASTING. This duty, quite naturally, lay in the hands of the managers, who might well take parts for themselves, as often happened at Drury Lane during the rule of the triumvirate. For example, when Cibber read *Cato* at the first examination of the tragedy, Addison, according to Victor, was so pleased with Cibber's rendition of it that he wanted Cibber to play Cato[164]. When the managers cast the roles, however, Cibber selected Syphax for himself and Wilks took Juba. For Cato the managers thought Booth best suited, yet Wilks feared Booth might think himself "injured, by being compelled to appear in so venerable a Character." To make certain that Booth would see the value of his playing Cato, Wilks took the part to Booth's lodgings in order to persuade the actor, if persuasion was needed. Booth "seemed to accept it entirely at the Manager's Desire and Recommendation."[165] The assignment of parts turned out to be eminently satisfactory.

Sometimes a playwright wrote his drama with specific actors in mind and hoped to see it cast according to his desires. For example, in writing *Jane Shore*, Rowe envisioned Wilks as Hastings; but Wilks took Dumont at Mrs Oldfield's insistence.[166] A more fully documented case occurred slightly outside the limits of this period, but it shows the practices of the late 1720's. Aaron Hill had a long correspondence with Wilks in the autumn of 1731 concerning *Athelwold*, which Hill hoped to see produced at Drury Lane. On 17 September 1731 Hill rather coyly referred to a tragedy written

---

[164] *The History of the Theatres of London and Dublin*, II, 29–30.   [165] *Ibid.*, II, 30.
[166] *The Life of that Eminent Comedian Robert Wilks Esq.* (London, 1733), p. 30.

by "a Friend" with a character (running to about five hundred lines) written with "Mr *Wilks* in his eye."[167] Five days later Hill confessed to Wilks that the tragedy was his own; on 25 September Hill acknowledged his pleasure at the approval of Wilks and Cibber but expressed concern that Wilks might not take the role of Athelwold. Further, he intended Edgar for Booth, Oswald for Cibber, Leolyn for Mills, Elfrid for Mrs Oldfield, and Ethelinda for Mrs Porter.[168] But the death of Mrs Oldfield, the unavailability of Mrs Porter, and the possibility that Booth would be too ill to act forced Hill to change his original conception.[169] The matter was still unsettled on 4 November, when Hill reiterated his desire that Wilks play Athelwold.[170] Eventually the play got cast and staged, although Hill did not get to see Wilks in the title role.

The casting of old plays was not always any easier than assigning the roles for new ones. At Drury Lane on 22 February 1718 the managers decided to present *Cato* without any indication in the bills that the parts customarily played by Wilks and other major performers would be acted by young, inexperienced persons. The result was disastrous. As a correspondent to *Applebee's Original Weekly Journal* for 1 March 1718 put it, "I found Cato Disrob'd of several of his principal Parts: a new Juba; a Monster for a beautiful Maria; and a Hoiden for Lucia." A riot ensued, in which oranges, lemons, apples, and lighted candles dropped on the stage and the tragedy unceremoniously stopped in the middle of Act IV. Some years later, on 4 January 1722, the Drury Lane management revived *The Rival Fools*, not seen for ten years, and cast it with younger actors, again without advertising the roles. The novices once more faced hisses, catcalls, and the usual barrage of fruit, whereupon Cibber stepped out to explain that he and his fellow managers, having been upbraided by the town for not "pushing forward their young Actors," had decided to give them an opportunity; he begged the audience to let the play go on.[171] Briefly appeased, the spectators quieted. On the next evening the managers tried the play again, this time announcing the cast in the *Daily Journal;* but there was an even greater disturbance and the actors were pelted off with oranges and the play stopped at the end of Act III. Cibber mentioned in his *Apology* other kinds of difficulty which rose from rivalry among the managers or among the friends of performers over who should play a new role or inherit an old one. Casting could often be a delicate matter.

[167] *The Works of Aaron Hill*, 2nd ed. (London, 1753-54), I, 123.
[168] *Ibid.*, I, 126-28.   [169] *Ibid.*, I, 138-39.   [170] *Ibid.*, I, 149-52.
[171] *Daily Journal*, 5 January 1722.

REHEARSALS. At Drury Lane rehearsals, in theory at least, had a careful schedule. According to Victor, a series of readings followed the decision to put on a play. As already pointed out, the author was invited to appear, and on three days read the manuscript to the cast. If the drama was an old one, whichever manager was a "principal Performer" in it read the play aloud. Apparently the three managers took weekly turns at presiding over general rehearsals. When the readings had been concluded, there followed a "limited Number of Rehearsals," at which each actor had his part in his hands.[172] A date was then set on which "every Person in the Play [was] to appear Perfect, because the Rehearsals only then begin to be of Use to the Actor: When he is quite perfect in the Words and Cues, he can then be instructed, and practise his proper Entrances, Emphasis, Attitudes, and Exits." The practice then proceeded under the "Eye of a Person who had Ability to instruct, and Power to encourage and advance those of Industry and Merit; and to forfeit and discharge the negligent and worthless."[173] The managers, Victor concluded, soon found that "*Regularity* was the first Step to Success." In outlining the duties of managers, Cibber similarly emphasized that one needed to be present "or else every Rehearsal would be but a rude Meeting of Mirth and Jollity."[174]

Rehearsals generally began in mid-morning, lasted two or three hours ordinarily but often much longer. (Presumably some of the heavy expenditures for food in the Drury Lane vouchers for 1712–16 represent meat and drink consumed during long rehearsals.) These hours were not always so well regulated or efficient as Victor or Cibber hoped. At times the players did not take their duties seriously, and preparations for a new play had moments of hilarity and festivity. An extreme example occurred in the autumn of 1717 when Lincoln's Inn Fields accepted Thomas Moore's *Mangora, King of the Timbusians.* According to Victor, the players thought the tragedy a foolish one, but, having had small encouragement from the public, they hoped this play might divert the town. At the rehearsals Moore "gave them many good Dinners and Suppers" and the actors hid from the author their mirth at the play's absurdities but repeated among themselves such choice lines as

> By all the ancient Gods of Rome and Greece
> I love my Daughter better than my Niece:
> If any one shou'd ask the Reason why—
> I'd tell 'em—Nature makes the strongest Tye.

[172] Victor, *History of the Theatres of London and Dublin*, II, 4–5.
[173] *Ibid.*, II, 5.   [174] *Apology*, II, 203–4.

The tragedy reached a third day and a benefit, had to be supplemented on the fourth by a farce, and then died.

On the other hand, many a preface lauds one manager or another for his devoted efforts to bring on a new play with propriety and success. Charles Johnson, in the preface to *The Masquerade*, which appeared on 16 January 1719, complimented Wilks for his deligence in forwarding the comedy. Outsiders occasionally gave praise to the conduct of a rehearsal; a correspondent to the *London Journal*, 29 January 1726, reported: "We were now at the House; and found the Rehearsal just beginning. We sat with Attention till it was ended; not without a particular Admiration of the Skill and Justice with which Mrs Porter entered into the Distress of Hecuba," the principal character in a tragedy of that name by Richard West."175

Nevertheless, complaints of inadequate preparation were numerous and loud. Lincoln's Inn Fields, preparing Theobald's *Richard II* for a premiere on 10 December 1719, had to omit acting (an unusual postponement) on the preceding day because the company was "oblig'd to lie still to Day for a Practice of the Tragedy." The author of *The Impertinent Lovers*, performed in the summer of 1723, prefaced his edition of the play with an indignant account of inadequate rehearsals: "The Play follows, but how imperfect? How awkward? How absurd is all? The 1st, and 2d, Act, though ill express'd, was yet somewhat perfect, but the 3d, and 4th, so confus'd, irregular, and unlike, as will with Difficulty be believ'd. They Playing about half of the 3d, and of the 4th, not above the 7th Part of it, and so injudicious and ill-chosen, as made the whole together Monstrous and Incoherent."

Some of the difficulties occurred because of short periods for rehearsal. Normally about three or four weeks elapsed between casting and premiere. For example, in the summer of 1700 Crauford's *Courtship à la mode* took twenty days from casting to opening. In rehearsal on 23 January 1721, Cibber's *The Refusal* appeared on 14 February 1721. Rehearsals of *The Artifice* began on 20 September 1722 and it appeared on 2 October 1722. Many plays progressed much more rapidly, though not with complete success. In the preface to *The Half Pay Officers*, 11 January 1720, Molloy states that "This farce was ... finished in Fourteen Days; it was got up with so much Hurry, that some of the Comedians ... had not time to make themselves Masters of their Parts." A farce might be speeded along

175 The preface to *Wit Without Money*, dated 4 January 1707, gave similar praise to the prompter: "I cou'd be lavish in your Praise with relation to your Business in the Play-House, make large Enconiums on the Vigilance you always show in your Station, for keeping the Order and Decorum of the Stage."

even more. Christopher Bullock stated that he began writing *The Cobler of Preston* on Friday 20 January 1716, finished the copy the next day, rehearsed it promptly, and had it acted on Tuesday 24 January 1716, five days from pen to premiere. He does not, however, say how perfectly the actors knew their parts. Similarly, *A Tutor for the Beaus*, read on a Tuesday, had its premiere the next Monday. Because the town usually expected an actor to know his lines perfectly, such speed placed the performers in greater danger of hisses and catcalls at the premiere.

The most colorful account of the problems of rehearsal was written by Aaron Hill in 1735 as a result of his long association with the theatres. In the *Prompter*, 6 May 1735, he stated:

The Want of Order and Propriety in Rehearsals, is very often the Occasion of Confusion, when the Play comes to be acted.—If an Actor does not know precisely the minute Circumstances that relate to his *Roll*, as to Entrances, Exits, the Part of the Stage he is to fill up, and the Action he is to be in, when he has nothing to say, he may be very perfect in the Sense and Meaning of the Author, and yet commit most egregious Blunders in the Representation. *This* is what Actors generally trust to their Memory, instead of performing in *Rehearsals*, on which Account it seldom happens that a Play is well acted the first Night, which, as I observed before, ought to be the most exact of all.

He returned to the problem on 23 May 1735 in a more elaborate discussion of the relation of a rehearsal to a good performance.

A *Rehearsal* should, to answer the Purpose It was intended for, be a PLAY *compleatly acted*, so as to want only *Dresses*, and *Spectators*.—The WORDS of a Play shou'd be perfect on the Memory, *before;* and the Business of *Rehearsing* serve, in general, to *shew* how Every Actors' Character *relates to*, shou'd be *influenc'd by*, Another's:—Whence the *Passions* ARISE:—In what *Changes*, of VOICE, LOOK, and MOVEMENT, they ought to be express'd:—By what *Attitudes*, the very *Silence* of Those who have nothing to *say*, may *concur*, to impress the Imagination of the Audience with the *Attention* which wou'd be due, and be given, to the REALITY, of such *acted* Distresses.

INSTEAD of all THIS, the *Pride* and *Conceitedness*, of these vain Men and Women, who are *slow* to *believe* they have Any thing to *learn*, tho' they find they have something to *remember*, have reduc'd a *Rehearsal* to a mere *muttering over* the Lines, with seldom as much as *Articulation* of *Voice;* so far are they from supposing it necessary to *practice* any of the *more considerable* Duties.—The *Prompter* dispatches his Boy to the *Green Room*, to give Notice when the *Lady*, or the *Gentleman*, is waited for, in the *Scene:* Then, in rush they, one after another, *rumbling their Parts, as they run* [like the Bullets (their *Brother Actors*) when they roll down the *Thunder-Pipe*] Hurrying, with a ridiculous Impatience, till they have catch'd, and beat back, the CUES: and, then, immediately, forsaking the Stage, as if they had nothing to do, in the Play, but to *parrot* a Sound, without *Consequence*.

As has already been pointed out, the opera companies used a public rehearsal as a trial run for a new production, the public practice occurring (usually before a paying audience) two or three days before the premiere. For example, *King Richard I*, scheduled for 11 November 1727, had a rehearsal on 8 November 1727 before "a prodigious Concourse of Nobility."[176] To rehearsals of a play the managers sometimes invited the author and his friends, but the practice of a drama before a paying audience seems rare. The *Weekly Medley*, 3 January, mentions, however, that *The Humours of Oxford* "has been rehearsed with great Applause, to a very small Audience" in advance of its premiere on 9 January 1730.

TIME OF PREMIERE. As noted earlier, managers and authors considered the period from November through February as most suitable for a premiere, although the summer companies tried an occasional new play (usually a minor piece) in July or August. During the winter no single night of the week seems to have been considered most fortuitous for a premiere, but a good many fell on Saturdays. In mid-season of 1718-19 three new plays appeared first on that day, thus allowing an extra day for revisions and rehearsals before the second performance on Monday. John Dennis, on one occasion, however, mentioned that "*Friday* is . . . the worst Day of the Week for an Audience" (preface to *The Invader of his Country*), particularly for a premiere or author's benefit.

A good many imponderables entered into the selection of the best time for a premiere. Sometimes an author felt that the season chosen for his play simply had no taste for drama; the preface to William Taverner's *The Maid the Mistress* (5 May 1708) stated that his comedy appeared "in a Season in which another *Dryden* might have talk'd to bare Benches." Elkanah Settle, complaining of the necessity of bringing out *The City Ramble* (17 August 1711) "in the long Vacation," thought the cold attitude of the town toward him prevented its appearing in the regular season.

The major obstacles to a successful premiere came, however, from competitive attractions. Dennis, chronically unhappy over the treatment accorded his plays, gave a long account of the difficulties attendant upon *The Invader of his Country*. After being rehearsed for five weeks, the tragedy was set for 10 November 1719. He asked for a week's delay, as the King

176 *Weekly Journal or British Gazetteer*, 11 November 1727.

was momentarily expected to return to London and the town awaited
its duty in welcoming George I; but the Drury Lane managers demurred.
Then, suddenly, they decided to postpone it, because 10 November would
be the night of an author's benefit at the opposing playhouse. To Dennis'
dismay, the postponement was for a single day only, which would place
the first benefit on a Friday, not only a normally poor night but particularly
unfavorable this time because "a Hundred Persons who design'd to be
there" had either gone to meet the King or had prepared to do so.

George Sewell, in the preface to *Sir Walter Raleigh*, 16 January 1719,
alluded to the problem of competition, as he felt that the Drury Lane
managers unfairly brought on *The Masquerade* by Charles Johnson, "a veteran
Poet strong in a Multitude of applauded Plays," for a first viewing on the
same night of his own premiere. In the preface to *The Recruiting Officer*,
8 April 1706, Farquhar acknowledged that his comedy first appeared on
the third night of D'Urfey's *The Wonders in the Sun*, an event which made
D'Urfey quite unhappy. Farquhar pointed out, however, that his play had
been set before D'Urfey's. Fielding, in discussing the fate of *Love in several
Masques*, 16 February 1728, alluded to another competitive difficulty; his
comedy had to follow the exceptionally successful run of *The Provoked
Husband* and appear simultaneously with the even more spectacular success
of *The Beggar's Opera*.

Playwrights faced still other kinds of difficulties. Mrs Manley, in
commenting upon the fate of *Almyna*, 16 December 1706, believed that
both Betterton and Swiny might be "justly condemn'd for playing it, at
so ill-fated a Time, *viz.* The immediate Week before *Christmas* between
Devotion and *Camilla*." Shadwell's *The Fair Quaker of Deal* had to compete
with the "Tryal in Westminster Hall, and the Rehearsal of the New Opera."
The illness or indisposition of a principal performer might alter unexpectedly
the best laid plans of manager and author. The premiere of Charles Johnson's
Love in a Forest, intended for 2 January 1723, had to be postponed a week
"by Reason of Mrs Younger's Indisposition," and there was the unfortunate
case, presumably a not unforeseen crisis, of a new play cast, rehearsed,
and set for 31 January 1721 at Lincoln's Inn Fields, only to be put aside
because pregnant Mrs Bullock was too near her time to risk opening the
play on schedule.

THE PREMIERE. At long last the tensely awaited moment arrived:
the most fateful time for the author, a difficult one for the actors, and
often a lively one for the spectators. The severity of an audience, the presence
of parties for or against an author, the studied disturbance of Templars

or young men about town, all created an atmosphere inimicable to good acting, impartial criticism, and, especially, a calm attention by the author. As the prologue to Joseph Trapp's *Abra Mule*, 13 November 1704, put it,

> *What various Thoughts a Poet's Breast divide,*
> *When brought before an Audience, to be try'd!*
> *Guilty of Scribling, with beseeching Hands,*
> *Before your Bar the Malefactor stands.*
> *Now hopes 'twill please, no doubts 'twill prove but dull;*
> *Mourns a thin Pit, yet dreads it when 'tis full.*
> *These are at best the anxious Writers cares:*
> *But he, who now your fatal Censure fears,*
> *Has no great Man to Countenance his Muse,*
> *And shield him from the Arts which Rival Factions use.*
> *No necessary Friends to start Applause,*
> *T'o'erpower Ill-nature, and support his Cause.*

As the *Prompter*, much later on 27 February 1736, remarked, actors could not perform well in an atmosphere electric with partisanship: "When the *Watch word* of Inhumanity had once been given, from the Pit, and in affected *Groan*, at the End of an Act, (like the imaginary Tollings of their *Brother Spirits*, from Infernal Theatres) Then, *Prejudice* and *Folly*, and Presumptuous *Ignorance* and *Barbarism* broke through all Bounds, of Decency or Reason." When disturbances arose, actors became more nervous; they forgot their lines, and the proper tone became fatally lost.

Even under the best circumstances, a premiere was a suspenseful moment. The well-known accounts of the uncertainty prevailing on the first night of *The Beggar's Opera* record the tense waiting which, on that occasion, turned into a happy ending: "The first Act was received with silent Attention, not a Hand moved; at the End of which they rose, and every Man seemed to compare Notes with his Neighbour, and the general Opinion was in its Favour. In the second Act they broke their Silence by Marks of their Approbation, to the great Joy of the frighted Performers, as well as the Author; and the last Act was received with universal Applause."[177] It could easily go the other way. When Southerne's *Money's the Mistress* came on at Lincoln's Inn Fields on 19 February 1726, the dramatist stood watching, and "when they were hissing dreadfully in the fifth Act, Mr *Rich*, who was standing by Mr *Southern*, asked him, if he heard what the Audience were doing? His Answer was, '*No, Sir, I am very deaf.*'"[178]

---

[177] Victor, *History of the Theatres of London and Dublin*, II, 154.
[178] *Ibid.*, II, 152.

Factions could destroy decorum. When *The Distrest Mother* was in progress, the managers designed Mrs Rogers for Andromache, but the author and his friends hoped to place Mrs Oldfield in the role. When it was finally given to Mrs Oldfield, "Mrs *Rogers* raised a Posse of Profligates, fond of Tumult and Riot, who made such a Commotion in the House, that the Court hearing of it sent four of the Royal Messengers, and a strong Guard, to suppress all Disorders."[179]

On the other hand, many a play suffered indignities at the premiere and yet survived to become a moderate success. The general tenor of the town was to wait skeptically upon a new play; if a party had not formed against it and made a fair hearing impossible, it might have a moderately judicious appraisal. On 26 March 1730 the *Grub Street Journal* took a long look at the probable course of a new drama; its view, though cynical, could be substantiated from other sources.

When a Play is to appear upon the Stage, the Town is generally prepared for it by some particular account of its excellency, printed in some of the news Papers, either by the Author himself, or by some particular Friend. While it is in action, the Audience is magnified from time to time, in the like accounts; and whatever it is in the Playhouse, it is always *represented* in the Coffee house to a numerous Audience. When it comes to be printed, if by the good management of a party it has been kept upon the Stage, with indifferent success for several nights, the Author is so grateful, as publickly to *thank the Town for their great Indulgence*, and to make his acknowledgments to some of the principal Actors, for their *extream civility, care, and excellent Performance*. If it have but just escaped being damned and hissed off the Stage, the Patron is then assured by the Author, that the *approbation of the rational and unprejudiced part of the Town* has *stamped some kind of value upon it*. Soon after this it dies, lamented chiefly by the Bookseller; and none of those Friends who were so kind as to celebrate its birth, shew any signs of grief at its death, or bewail its untimely fate, either in an Elegy, or an Epitaph.

---

[179] William Egerton, *Faithful Memoirs . . . of Mrs Anne Oldfield* (London, 1731), pp. 31–32.

The Audience

AFTER the orchestra had played the First, Second, and Third Music, the hour of six signalled the beginning of the evening's entertainment. If a prologue was scheduled, a player stepped forth to wait for the hum of conversation to subside. If the theatre was crowded, he stood very close to many of the spectators: individuals sitting or standing on the stage, in the boxes to right and left. Before him, at a slightly greater distance, spectators massed in the pit and, above, in the galleries. In a thinly populated house, perhaps no one sat on the stage, a few looked on from the boxes, and in the pit and galleries spectators sat less closely and warmly together.

The composition of the audience in the first third of the century gradually broadened to include a greater diversity of classes and tastes than had frequented the theatres in the years immediately following the accession of Charles II to the throne. By the early 1700's the population of London had increased considerably, and although the theatre remained a fashionable place, the middle classes, citizens, gentlemen, and ladies, the apprentices, and even servants formed a larger proportion of the audience. Although John Macky's description of a London audience, noted in the section on the playhouses, above, was probably a simplification of the variety, prologues and epilogues constantly allude to the diversity: "a Knight . . . a Burgess . . . Lawyer" (Epilogue to *The Old Mode and the New*, 11 February 1703) in the pit, "the good Husbands . . . a Non Con Person" in the middle gallery, a "Side-box Molly" (in a mask) and "a Captain" in the side boxes. The epilogue to *The Wonders in the Sun* (5 April 1706) pointed to "Beaus, Citts, Ladies, Knights, and Lords." The prologue to *Sir Harry Wildair* (April 1701) commented upon the footmen who "judge, and lodge, three Stories high," and the *Censor*, 13 April 1717, gave an amusing glimpse into this part of the theatre in the instructions to a servant to "keep his Seat in the Upper-Gallery without Noise, and never to point at his *Master*."[180]

180 A prejudiced but sharply etched glimpse of the theatres at the beginning of the century appeared in Richard Burridge's *A Scourge for the Play-Houses* (London, 1702): "I went with [my Friends]; but going thro *Play-House-Yard* (where the Females were Flocking along as thick as *Seaman's* Wives) . . . one Saucy Impudent Slut or another would, in a manner, be

Among these classes of patrons, royalty during the first fifteen years of the century paid less attention to the theatres than was true in the reign of Charles II. Queen Anne much preferred to have a play or opera performed at court, usually on her birthday, rather than attend the play-house. Not until the accession of George I did royalty again have much importance as a theatrical patron. Within three days after George I landed at Greenwich, Robert Wilks spoke (21 September 1714) a prologue at Drury Lane on its opening night in honor of the King. The royal family appeared principally at Drury Lane and the King's, with His Majesty attending occasionally, the Prince and Princess of Wales much more often. Not until 10 March 1715, four months after the opening of Lincoln's Inn Fields, did any member of the royal family appear there, and for many years Drury Lane, often thought to be more loyal to the Crown than Rich's company, had more patronage from royalty than did Lincoln's Inn Fields.

The attendance of royalty, as has already been indicated, added to the receipts of the theatres, not only from the money paid for the royal box but also from admission charges from spectators who attended to see both a play and royalty. In addition, one member or another of the royal family lent his name to benefits. In 1716–17, for example, at least one member attended the benefits for Mills, Mrs Oldfield, Mrs Porter, Dupre, Mrs Santlow, Booth, and Mrs Bicknell. At Drury Lane during that season command performances totalled at least twenty-three. In the next fifteen years, however, the patronage of royalty fluctuated a good deal. In 1718–19, with plays commanded at Hampton Court in September, patronage remained high throughout the season: the royal family supported liberally the French comedians at the King's and Lincoln's Inn Fields, saw at least seventeen

forcing their *Oranges* on us . . . Now taking out *Tickets* for the *Pit*, into which I no sooner enter'd, but I thought it was very properly so called; for no Place could more represent the Pit of Hell than that, there being no Light but by Fire. . . .

"Looking upwards, I saw the Upper Galleries was taken up by such Rubbish as *Butlers*, *Chamber-Maids*, quacking *Apothecaries*, and *Apprentices*. . . .

"In the middle *Gallery* sat the middling sort of People, such as Merchants Wives, and Shop-keepers Froes . . . among whom creep Ladies Waiting-women, *Lawyers Clerks*, and *Valet de Chambres*, as likewise some Inferior sort of Town-Misses . . .

"In the side Boxes (I saw) were got upstart Officers, younger Brothers . . . and other pragmatical Beaux, Complimenting and Courting a parcel of Strumpets. . . .

"In the front Boxes sat Persons of Quality. . . .

"Some of our Scolasticks were got on the Stage, though 'tis desired to the Contrary in their Bills. . . .

"Sometimes the Fops would be attentively listening to the Maggots which *Purcel's* Train play'd on several sorts of Instruments. . . .

"But at last, the Fellow that play'd at Bo-peep behind the Curtain, having made Report to the Patentees, there were Fools enough to bear the Charges of the House . . . it was drawn up, and the gawdy Scenes are exposed to open View." (pp. 2–10).

performances at Drury Lane and two at Richmond. The formation of the Royal Academy of Music in 1719-20, however, diverted royalty from Drury Lane and Lincoln's Inn Fields to the opera. And in 1726-27 the King again often showed a preference for the foreign comedians and neglected the legitimate houses. On the other hand, as the young princesses came of age to attend the theatres, their presence in the late 1720's gave new support to Drury Lane and Lincoln's Inn Fields.[181]

No other social or occupational class within the theatres offered quite the prestige lent by the presence of royal patrons. As already indicated, however, citizens, apprentices, ladies of fashion, beaux, soldiers, and even the clergy attended the playhouses, but although newspaper accounts suggest that young men about town might be very noisy or critical or outspoken and the ladies kind and courteous, the patrons, with a few exceptions, distinguished themselves less by social or occupational grouping than by their behavior. A few special groups, however, made themselves known to all, sometimes vividly and vehemently. For example, early in the century the Mohocks disturbed the calm of the theatre; as the *Grumbler*, 13 May 1715, pointed out, in the "Memorable Reign of the Mohocks, these merry Gentlemen were the great Improvers of the *Cat-Call*." Within a few years the young men of the temples of law supplanted the Mohocks as an actor's or dramatist's severest critic. As Pope, writing to Caryll on 3 March 1716 concerning *The What D'Ye Call It*, said, "Several Templars and others of the more vociferous kind of critics, went with a resolution to hiss."[182] In addition, some Gentlemen of the Temple published a letter (addressed to Steele) in the *Weekly Journal or Saturday's Post*, 13 January 1722, offering him firm advice on the government of the company at Drury Lane. By the 1730's the Templars had so increased their power and reputation that the mere prospect of Templars in the pit on a first night frightened many a timid dramatist. On the other hand, the Free Masons became a peaceful group within the playhouses. On 30 December 1728, for example, "the Grand Master and Wardens and most of the Gentlemen . . . took Tickets to appear in White Gloves" at *II Henry IV* in Drury Lane, "and it is said, a Prologue and Epilogue will be spoken suitable to the Occasion, and in Honour of that Society" (*Daily Journal*, 30 December 1728). In the

---

181 The anticipated presence of royalty sometimes created problems for the theatres in keeping decorum and managing the crowds. For example, with Their Majesties expected for *Henry VIII* on 11 December 1728, "several disorderly People forced themselves into the House pretending to keep Places, broke and did a good deal of Damage before they could be dislodg'd."—*Universal Spectator*, 14 December 1728.

182 *The Correspondence of Alexander Pope*, ed. George Sherburn (Oxford, 1956), I, 282-83.

1730's the Free Masons made still more frequent appearances as a body to hear prologue and epilogues spoken in their honor at special performances.

Of much greater importance, at least in the first third of the century, was the presence of partisanship in the theatre. After the accession of George I party politics, similar in some respects to that which had greeted *Cato* not long before, caused the anonymous author of *The Lucky Prodigal*, 24 October 1715, to point out that the Rebellion had instigated "the too popular Outcry, that the *Theatres* are *Party-House*," Drury Lane being thought more loyal than Lincoln's Inn Fields. During the next decade, many authors felt that political partisanship had hindered or helped their productions. When Dudley Ryder heard Mrs Oldfield deliver an "Epilogue recommending the Cause of Liberty to the Beauties of Great Britain" at Drury Lane on 13 March 1716, he was "pleased to hear it clapped by a full house and a general approbation of the sentiments."[183] Attending *The Spanish Fryar*, 13 February 1716, he observed that "most of the clappings were upon party accounts," the Whigs applauding vigorously some reflections in it upon priests, the Tories hissing faintly.[184]

As a result of party feeling, *Tamerlane* had a revival on 5 November 1716, "With a New Prologue, written by the Author of the Play," which Ryder heard on 6 November 1716 and which received wide circulation in the *Weekly Journal or British Gazetteer*, 24 November 1716. For many years the theatres played the drama on 4 and 5 November, frequently with new prologues extolling loyalty to the government and honor to William III. Cibber took advantage of the temper of the times to bring out his *Nonjuror*, 6 December 1717, which the King attended and which the *Weekly Journal or British Gazetteer* cited for its portrait of the "most stupid and unparellell'd Bigotry of an old rich Jacobite." On the other hand, as indicated earlier, Mrs Knight in the spring of 1716 felt impelled to print an epilogue spoken by her at her benefit on 5 April 1716 because of prevailing rumors that it was "not fit to be spoken." The accompanying comment stressed her "Zeal to the Government." At times Lincoln's Inn Fields needed to assert its loyalty, for on 26 November 1722, John Ogden, one of its actors, was committed to Newgate for "Treasonable Words," and on 1 August 1724, the anniversary of the Hanoverian succession, William Marshall, another of its company, "rode triumphantly in a Turnip-Cart, with a Crown and Pair of Horns on his Head" until officers committed him to Bridewell.[185]

---

[183] *The Diary of Dudley Ryder*, p. 195.   [184] *Ibid.*, p. 181.
[185] *British Journal*, 8 August 1724.

The repercussions of party politics produced a variety of comment concerning partisanship by dramatists, actors, and audience. The author of *Palaemon to Caelia* (1717) stated:

> Seldom I visit our declining Stage,
> The Scene of Noise, and sunk to Party-Rage.

The anonymous author of *The Younger Brother*, 7 February 1719, accused the Hugenot faction of hurting his play. The *Freeholder's Journal*, 21 February 1722, criticized Ambrose Phillips' new play, *The Briton*, acted at Drury Lane, 19 February 1722, because the author was "so hard put to it, as to have recourse to Politicks for the Entertainment of the Stage. The Words *Liberty, Invasion, Romans*, could not but force a Clap from a *British* Audience." The commentator also expressed surprise at the warm reception of *Hibernia Freed*, remarking, "I never knew a Play so Clapped . . . till a Friend put me in Mind that half the Audience were *Wild Irish*." And the *Craftsman*, 29 March 1729, insinuated that Cibber ingratiated himself at court by "suppressing obnoxious Passages in all Plays." He cited as an example Cibber's cutting from *Love for Love*

> FORESIGHT. Pray what will be done at Court?
> VALENTINE. Scandal will tell you; I am Truth, I never come there.

At times a partisan attitude affected the players as well. The most violent of these divisions occurred in 1726–27 over the merits of Signora Cuzzoni and Signora Faustina in the opera. The claques created a noisy disturbance at a performance of *Astyanax* on 6 June 1727, the contention at first being "carried on by Hissing on one Side, and Clapping on the other; but proceeded at length to catcalls, and other great Indecencies."[186] The feud extended itself into the social affairs of London,[187] and helped to bring about a temporary downfall of the Royal Academy of Music. A similar conflict, though of smaller dimensions, occurred in the spring of 1725 when Mrs Younger left Drury Lane and Mrs Horton succeeded her as Phillis in *The Conscious Lovers*. Mrs Younger had been so popular in the role that Mrs Horton met with unpleasant treatment from the audience "who so far forgot what was due to merit and the handsomest woman on the stage that they endeavoured to discourage her by frequent hissing." Mrs Horton bore the treatment patiently for awhile and finally made an appeal to the audience: "What displeases you; my acting or my

---

[186] *Ibid.*, 10 June 1727.
[187] See *Lord Hervey and his Friends*, pp. 18–19.

person?" This show of spirit won over the partisans of Mrs Younger and the audience told her, "Go on, go on."[188]

Of still greater importance to the dramatist especially was the critical temper of the audience, the way in which spectators as critics approached a play. Many a prologue or epilogue referred to that ill-defined class of spectators termed "The Critics": "To you tremendous Criticks in the Pit" (Epilogue to *Love in Several Masques*), "To you, the Tyrant Criticks of the Age / To you, who make such Havock on the Stage" (Epilogue to *The Platonick Lady*), "Our Bard the Critick dreads" (Prologue to *Cinna's Conspiracy*), or "a snarling Sect o'th'Town / That do condemn all Wit, except their own" (Epilogue to *The Stage Coach*). Prefaces, prologues, and epilogues did not define sharply the composition of this group of lively critics, although they often mentioned the Templars, side-box beaux, and wits; nevertheless, the dramatists and newspapers make quite clear how the alert and articulate critics made their opinions known and how strongly they influenced the fate of plays. In fact, the preface to *Wit at a Pinch*, 24 October 1715, addressed "To the Peaceable Patrons of the Stage," lamented the scarcity of this type of critic: "But, alas . . . You, Peaceable Gentlemen, who make but a narrow Class of Worthies; and your Visits alone are not enough to support the Stage."

Many dramatists pointed out the vagaries and unpredictability of the critical part of the audience. The preface to Farquhar's *The Inconstant*, February 1702, reported: "There were some Gentlemen in the Pit the first Night, that took the Hint from the Prologue to damn the Play." Mary Davys, whose *Northern Heiress* came out on 27 April 1716, thought herself fortunate because the "first Night, in which lay all the Danger, was attended with only two single Hisses: . . . The one was a Boy, and not worth taking Notice of; the other a Man who came prejudic'd." Charles Molloy, in appraising the fate of *The Perplexed Couple*, 16 February 1715, spoke of its being so roundly attacked that after the first night its enemies gave out that the play had failed; fortunately, it had a recovery of prestige on successive evenings and survived. Cibber could nearly always predict the reaction to one of his new plays; at *The Refusal*, 14 February 1721, "Mr *Cibber*'s Enemies . . . began to hiss it before they had heard it, and I remember very well, began their Uproar, on the first Night, as soon as he appeared to speak the Prologue."[189] Earlier in the century, Catherine Trotter, in the preface to *The Revolution of Sweden*, 11 February 1706, expressed views which many later dramatists echoed.

[188] See Davies, *Dramatic Miscellanies*, I, 103-4.
[189] *A Compleat List* (London, 1747), p. 197.

I shall be allow'd to appeal, at least, from two sorts of Judges who have pass'd their Censure on it; those who have never seen any part of it, and those who, tho' present at it, minded very little of it. . . .

'Tis confess'd, it would be very unreasonable to desire, that every one who comes to a Play, shou'd be attentive at it; those who find in the Audience a better Entertainment, must be allow'd to turn their Eyes and Thoughts from the Stage; but then 'tis no more equitable to expect, that they shou'd not judge at all, of what they have no leisure to mind.

An occasional dramatist, reviewing not only the reception of his own work but also the general practice of the town, gave a vivid, though possibly exaggerated view of the reaction of the "critics." Typical of these glimpses into the behavior of the audience was Charles Johnson's account in the preface to *Medea* (1731) of the behavior of those who damned his play.

. . . a Set of noisy Criticks; who have, for two or three Years past, taken upon themselves to condemn, in a very extraordinary Manner, almost all Performances, that have appear'd on the Stage, and to give their Judgment, in a Manner not easily to be opposed; not only in feeble Hisses, but in Hootings, horse Laughs, squalings, Catcalls, and other mechanical Criticisms pointed at any Passages in the Play, that could possibly raise in them any of these riotous Emotions; but to shew the Force of their Wit and their Lungs this Way, to prevent the Attention of the Audience, to disturb the Action, and to condemn the Play, without hearing or suffering others to hear it.

On these important Occasions they cabal together before-hand, they meet over their Coffee, and deliberately resolve to assassinate the future Piece, without having read or seen it, if the Author does not happen to be of their Faction. They form themselves into Committees and regularly take their Seats for the Purpose, arm'd with Catcalls and Clubs. One of these Wags, at a proper Cue given, breaks into a loud hoarse Laugh, his Brother Criticks ecchoe it round, and while the rest of the Audience resent their ill Manners, and endeavour by their Applause to shew their Opposition, the Scene stands still, the Confusion increases, and these *Gentlemen*, as they call themselves, enjoy the Disturbance. The Players tremble; the Play is condemn'd; and Victory is sounded.

Although the dramatists often exaggerated their plight, they and others could point to numerous examples of disorderly, even riotous, behavior within the playhouses. A disturbance begun at a premiere some-times extended for a long period. At the first night of *The Village Opera* (6 February 1729) the audience produced "such Hissing and Clapping that the like was never known. . . . People got together, and fell a Hissing before the Performers utter'd a Word,"[190] and on the following night "some

190 *Applebee's*, 15 February 1729.

Persons in the Gallery were so clamorous that the Play could not go on"
until guards ejected the disturbers.[191] After a third night, the managers
laid the play aside for three weeks, hoping the spectators would forget
their animosity. The *Flying Post* reported extensively its reception on
27 February 1729.

No sooner did poor Colin appear upon the Stage, but his Arrival was usher'd
in with a Serenade of Cat Calls, Penny-Trumpets, Clubs, Canes, Hoarse Voices,
whistling in Keys, Heels, Fists; and Vollies of whole Oranges; however, the Players
went on with uncommon Intrepidity, and like the truly great Men, seem'd greater
by opposition. The Audience call'd out for any other Play, Farce or Entertainment,
but the *Peasants* seem'd too intent upon what they were about, to give Ear to them.
This so exasperated the Spectators, that they mustered up all the Artillery they
could possibly lay hold and made such an Uproar, during the whole *intended* Entertainment, that it was scarce possible to hear a Word the Actors said. As every Player
came upon the Stage, they call'd upon him by his real, not fictitious Name, and
Swore not a Man of them would come to his Benefit. When Mrs T—— appeared,
they call'd out for a Quartern of Gin, to chear up her Spirits. The Word *Constable*
being first mentioned in the Gallery, it ran round the House like Wild-fire; and
immediately the general Cry was, *No Constable, No Constable*. At the Conclusion
of the Play, a Fellow came upon the Stage, to put out the Lights with his long
Pole, but a Gentleman broke it in two, and another taking a Candle out from one
of the Sockets of the Sconces, his Example was immediately followed by several
others, who soon clear'd them of their Lights, when a new kind of Shower compos'd
of Candles fell thick as Hail on the Stage.

The preface to *Hecuba*, 2 February 1726, referred to a similar disturbance:
"why this *Tragedy* did not succeed . . . It was not heard. A Rout of Vandals
in the Galleries, intimidated the young Actresses, disturb'd the Audience,
and prevented all Attention."

Other kinds of disturbing behavior affected actors and spectators.
Mrs Trotter, in the preface to *The Revolution of Sweden*, emphasized her
dislike of inattention by some of the spectators, some of whom enjoyed
the company about them more than the performance. William Byrd recorded
in his diary several occasions when he went to the playhouse, looked around
briefly but did not stay (31 January 1718, 25 February 1718), and once
admitted that he left because there "was no company at either" (5 November
1719). Perhaps still worse, on two occasions (1 February and 27 March
1718) he frankly recorded the fact that he slept. Both sleeping patrons

[191] *Daily Post*, 8 February 1729.

and those bobbing in and out in restless search of diversion disturbed the even tenor of the house.[192]

The theatres also became arenas in which individuals settled differences to the discomfort of more decorous patrons. At Drury Lane on 2 June 1719 a "Quarrel happening . . . betwixt a Gentleman and an Officer, they immediately drew their Swords, and the latter was wounded in the Arm."[193] At the premiere of *Chit Chat*, 14 February 1719, "Disorder happen'd in one of the Side Boxes, occasion'd by a Gentleman Drawing his Sword on a Footman, who was keeping Places."[194] Byrd, attending Lincoln's Inn on 19 December 1718, had a quarrel with some footmen about their wearing their hats. At Lincoln's Inn Fields, 30 April 1718, "A Gentleman sitting in a Side-Box pointed at a young Gentlewoman, which another Gentleman perceiving, and she being one of his Acquaintances, he went to him and challenged him: They made some passes at each other, which put the Play-House in an Uproar."[195]

In spite of so much evidence to the contrary, in all probability the audiences week in and week out behaved with greater care to proper decorum than might seem likely. A play which successfully touched the town had a warm reception. A report in the *Weekly Journal or Saturday's Post*, 16 January 1720, on *The Half Pay Officer* and *Hob's Wedding* at Lincoln's Inn Fields indicated that "they have hit the Humour of the Town, and . . . take exceedingly well." Byrd, at the premiere of *Chit Chat*, 14 February 1719, remarked that it was well liked by nearly everyone. Southerne's Preface to *The Spartan Dame*, 11 December 1719, spoke of its success as being "extraordinary" through the "Favour of the Town, and indulging assistance of Friends." A revival of *The Merry Wives of Windsor* "was so perfectly played in all its parts, that the critics in acting universally celebrated the merit of the performers."[196] Thomas Baker described the reception of *The Fine Lady's Airs*, 14 December 1708, by a highly favorable audience: "as it had the Fortune to be well receiv'd, and by some of the best Judges esteem'd much preferable to any of my former, and as it was highly favour'd the Third Night with as beautiful an Appearance of Nobility, and other fine Ladies, as ever yet Grac'd a Theatre." A prologue or epilogue occasionally suggested a comfortable pleasure within the theatre, as in the Epilogue to *The Fine Lady's Airs*.

[192] One wonders also at the implications of a notice in the *Daily Post*, 6 February 1725: "Lost from out of the Pit at Drury Lane . . . a small black and white Spaniel Dog."
[193] *Original Weekly Journal*, 4 June 1719.   [194] *Ibid.*, 21 February 1719.
[195] *Weekly Journal or Saturday's Post*, 3 May 1718.
[196] Davies, *Dramatic Miscellanies*, I, 139.

And when an Epilogue entirely pleases,
In thund'ring Jests, it takes the House to pieces;
The Pit smiles when the Gallery's misus'd,
The Gallery sniggers when the Pit's abus'd;
Side-Boxes wou'd with Ladies Foibles play,
But they themselves stand Buff to all we say,
For nothing strikes them Dead, but—Please to pay:

The great range of response by an early eighteenth-century audience suggests one of the problems of the spectators. They wished to express their responses freely and clearly; they wished to make their verdict known, not only in general approval or disapproval of a play, but also for its casting, for the acting, and for the details of a production. Charles Johnson, reviewing the disastrous reception of his *Medea*, discussed the problem as follows.

It is difficult to account what Motive there can be for any, who wear the outward Forms of Gentlemen, to behave thus ill in a publick Assembly; it is most certain they might, by Means less noisy and ungrateful to all Ears but their own, shew their Dislike of any Performance; and I think they have a Right so to do in a decent and modest Manner, though it were to be wish'd they would suspend their Judgment without interrupting the Witnesses till the Cause was heard; that they would wait to the Conclusion of the Piece before they approv'd or condemn'd it, and then they ought not to go it with noise; because, tho' some dislike, others may approve, and they must in Consequence be offended and disturbed.

But the town had a long tradition of plain speaking and freedom of speech; Johnson's voice of moderation defined a method of preserving independence of judgment coupled with decorum, but the crucial part of the town did not yet feel ready to accept it.

The Course of Contemporary Criticism

ALTHOUGH the emphasis in this Introduction has been upon the organization of the playhouses and the means by which they provided London with
entertainment, these matters are closely allied with the response of the
public to the offerings of the theatres. Obviously much of this response
is lost to us. Although the bills often indicated that a play had been selected
because of requests, desire, or command, these are an inadequate basis
for evaluating the critical views of the spectators. We may, of course,
examine the reputations of plays as they appeared and re-appeared in the
repertory season after season, and although this method has told us a good
deal about the delicate mechanism by which a repertory system adjusts
itself to changing taste and to the influx of new dramas, these variations
in the popularity of individual plays or types are most revealing over quite
long periods of time. For the short-term view, the most visible and, possibly,
the most substantial judgments appear in the public press, supplemented
and reinforced by the considered opinions of individuals as reflected in their
letters, journals, and published criticism. Since most of these individual
judgments—the comments in journals, diaries, and letters—did not appear
in print during the period covered by this study, the most tangible printed
influences come from the press.

At the opening of the century theatrical criticism in newspapers and
magazines was infrequent and casual. Occasional comments upon plays
appeared in a few periodicals in the late seventeenth century, but no one
really attempted systematically to review the offerings of the theatres.
A Londoner who wished to know the news of the stage and the status
of individual plays sought out his informed friends or sat in the coffeehouses
to hear the arguments over the state of the drama. When the first daily
papers began publication in 1702, neither tradition nor their physical size
made it likely that they could or would devote much space to the theatres.
Their small size—ordinarily a single sheet printed on both sides—and
emphasis upon foreign and domestic news and advertisements left little
room for comment upon any subject. By the 1720's the daily press gave
more space to theatrical news—a puff or two for forthcoming plays, dis-

putes or riots in the theatres, engagements of new singers, dancers, and actors—but these offered little suggestion of a critical view of the stage.

But the early years of the century also saw a constant increase in the number and kinds of periodicals: dailies, twice-a-week, weekly, monthly, those specializing in general news, others in political polemics, some dealing with informal comment, public affairs, or business. In some of those, especially the ones not narrowly specialized, the editors made occasional promises of an intention systematically to comment, criticize, or review new and revived plays, but the journals did not fully develop this intention. Perhaps the greatest stimulus to theatrical criticism came in the *Tatler* and *Spectator*, both of which discussed the stage frequently and might easily have turned to more deliberate reporting of the theatrical world. Although each occasionally offered interesting comment, regularity of penetrating appraisal was not achieved. In the next two decades other journals similarly turned occasionally to the stage as a subject of interest to readers: *The Female Tatler* (1709–10), *The Censor* (1715–17), *The Tea Table* (1724), *Pasquin* (1722–24), *The Plain Dealer* (1724–25), and some weeklies with longer lives: *London Journal, Applebee's, Mist's, Fog's.* Correspondents occasionally submitted letters dealing with a new play, the function of the drama, a defence or criticism of an author; occasionally a writer volunteered to become a regular contributor of theatrical comment without, apparently, ever securing the position he sought. Some plays, especially if they dealt with controversial subjects as did Cibber's *Nonjuror*, received extended though not necessarily careful discussion, and several periodicals kept up a running attack upon Cibber and his fellow managers at Drury Lane or against *The Conscious Lovers* or *Three Hours After Marriage.* Often lively and invigorating, this discussion often led nowhere, however; it frequently descended to tedious quarrels over details, irrelevancies, and personalities.[197]

In spite of the uncertain direction of theatrical comment before 1730, writers tended to emphasize certain ideas which reflected or influenced the views of spectators as they attended the theatres, gossiped in coffee houses, and turned to the periodicals for confirmation or stimulus of their opinions. One dominant theme, especially strong in the first fifteen years of the century, concerned the morality of the theatres, an old problem which had been given new currency in 1698 by Jeremy Collier. Some

---

[197] The path of a particular play can be traced in the discussion of *The Conscious Lovers* (Drury Lane, 7 November 1722) in the works of John Dennis, the daily papers, *Freeholder's Journal, St. James's Journal*, and several pamphlets.

writers—Defoe, the Reverend Arthur Bedford, the propagandists for the Societies for the Reformation of Manners—kept alive an attack upon the stage.[198]

These critics had no genuine interest in the drama as a form of art; their stand emphasized the effect of presumably licentious actions and speeches upon an audience thought to be extremely susceptible to immoral influences. They seized upon isolated passages in plays, any actions by performers which appeared injurious to the public welfare, and behavior of dramatists and spectators which alarmed the clergy and reformers.

The quick response of the moralists to any event which seemed to prove the iniquity of the stage is visible in the complex of events surrounding the Great Storm of 1703, a seemingly unlikely subject for propaganda against the theatres. But it served. Late in 1703 a disastrous storm rolled over England for two weeks with high winds and pelting rains. On the night of its greatest severity the theatre in Drury Lane acted (presumably through normal scheduling of its repertory) *Macbeth*. Jeremy Collier promptly seized upon a detail in the spectators' actions that night.

> What Impression this late Calamity has made upon the *Play-House*, we may guess by their Acting *Macbeth* with all its Thunder and Tempest, the same Day: Where at the mention of the *Chimnies being blown down* . . . the *Audience* were pleas'd to *Clap*, at an unusual Length of Pleasure and Approbation. And is not the meaning of all this too intelligible? Does it not look as if they had a Mind to out-brave the Judgment? . . . Was it possible? Mirth at such a Season! Satisfactory Plaudits on such an Occasion! What can you call This, but another Prodigy of Horrour, to be chronicled with the Storm?[199]

When, a few days later, the theatres staged *The Tempest*, the moralists took the staging of that play as a deliberate flouting of the will of God in punishing England's sins by sending a great storm.

Allied with the views of the moralists was the conviction that the function of the stage was to promote virtue and to teach an abhorrence of vice. As the Prologue to *Injured Virtue* (1714) emphasized:

> *For it was first the sole Intent of Plays,*
> *To punish Vice, and give to Virtue Praise.*

Some writers, especially the moralists, expressed this view with deep conviction; others seemed merely to utter it out of a sense of duty to

---

[198] A comprehensive view of the controversy appears in Joseph Wood Krutch's *Comedy and Conscience after the Restoration* (rev. ed. [New York, 1949]), especially chapters V, VI, and VII.

[199] *Mr Collier's Dissuasive from the Play-House* (London, 1704), pp. 15, 18–19.

tradition or as a useful basic point in any discussion of the beneficial role of the theatre in society. Many asserted, of course, that the theatre ought also to entertain or give pleasure; but nearly everyone implied, sometimes sincerely, sometimes with tongue in cheek, that, of course, virtue is superior to pleasure and must unmistakably have first place. Even though a critic might intend to view a play as a work of art, he nearly always felt the influence of an underlying assumption that the stage, like the pulpit, had a moral duty to perform. Many spectators, in all probability, came to the playhouses giving lip-service to the doctrine of morality as the first aim of drama only to lay it aside to enjoy wholeheartedly the pleasure of a particular performance.

Another common assumption in theatrical comment was that the present age—the 1710's, the 1720's, or whatever moment a writer considered—was inferior to the past. Taste had declined; the quality of writing had lessened. After Congreve and Vanbrugh ceased to write for the stage, the lament arose that true comedy had died or, after Steele left the theatre, that wit ended with Congreve and Steele. In tragedy greatness had departed when Otway and Dryden left the stage. The past always seemed brighter than the present. Shakespeare, Beaumont, Fletcher, and Jonson were the great dramatists of pre-Restoration times; Wycherley, Etherege, Congreve, Dryden, and Otway of pre-1700 days. As the Epilogue to *The Cares of Love* (1 August 1705) stated:

> Old Shakespear's Genius Now is laid aside,
> And Johnson's Artful Scenes in vain are try'd;
> Otway and Wycherley, tho' Bards Divine,
> Whose Nervous Passion, Wit and Humour shine,
> To empty Benches to our Cost we Play:
> To Sense too Faithful, thus We lose our Pay.

Although Rowe, Vanbrugh, Addison, Steele, and Cibber had admirers, the 1720's often felt faint-hearted about the drama of their own century. For example, *Mist's Weekly Journal*, 20 November 1725, asserted:

The tiresome dull Round of the same Plays over and over again, at both the Theatres, would make one readily imagine, that either Wit is at a very low Ebb amongst us, or the Managers are grown insufferably lazy, or the Spectators come with no other Design, than to while away three awkward Hours. . . . Probably it is to a Spice of all these together that the present Calm of Humour is owing. Or has it so spent itself in the last Ages, that it sleeps in ours, and will no longer be able to recover its Spirits again till our Great Grand-daughters sparkle in the Boxes?

Or, as Pope expressed it in the *Epistle to Augustus*:

> *All this may be; the People's Voice is odd,*
> *It is, and it is not, the voice of God.*
> *To Gammer Gurton if it give the bays,*
> *And yet deny the Careless Husband praise,*
> *Or say our Fathers never broke a rule;*
> *Why then, I say, the Public is a fool.*
> *But let them own, that greater Faults than we*
> *They had, and greater Virtues, I'll agree.*

Some of this disdain for the present appeared in a more critical attitude towards new plays. Possibly this mood was more apparent than real, in the sense that more published theatrical comment concentrated attention upon the cold receptions or the hissing and catcallings on many first nights. In addition, the increase in the number of theatres naturally allowed opportunities for more new plays, without, necessarily, an increase in the number of *good* new plays. Hence, a conviction of the weakness of the present age grew. The point might be made as Thomas Rundle stated it in a letter written around March 1720: "in this midnight of dramatic wit, a thing that shines no brighter than a glow worm, will call our eyes to it, and amuses a spectator."[200] In another vein, the *Weekly Journal or Saturday's Post*, 10 February 1722, compared the success of *The Drummer* at its revival on 2 February 1722 with its poor reception at the premiere some years before; the journal laid its earlier cool reception to the fact that it then "was supposed to come from one of no Reputation in Parnassus, therefore the Publick could see nothing in it. . . . This Circumstance should mortifie the Vanity of Writers, who value themselves upon the Vogue of the Town, since it is plain, that . . . the Publick seems to have no Judgment of its own." And sometimes a new play thought worthy of a better reception had a dispiriting first night because of the low taste of the public. For example, writing of the premiere of *Belisarius* on 14 April 1724, the *Weekly Journal or Saturday's Post*, 18 April 1724, stated: "But how contemptible an Opinion must the next Generation have of this Age, if it should be known amongst them, that the first Night this Tragedy appear'd upon the Stage, it did not bring half a House, because it happen'd to be acted upon a Masquerade Night."

In a similar vein writers expressed the belief that the present age had succumbed to the attraction of novelty and foreign importations. A prologue spoken at the Haymarket, 20 February 1724, lamented:

[200] *The Letters of the late Thomas Rundle* (Gloucester, 1789), pp. 11–12.

> *New Artists, new Machines, new Dances rise,*
> *('Tis Pity Novelty can't make ye wise,)*
> *Now shrill Cutzoni reigns, and Harlequin*
> *And Faustus thunders thro' the magick Scene.*
> *His Spells, this mighty Necromancer forms,*
> *How strangely does the subtle Witchcraft spread?*
> *His Windmill turns in ev'ry frantick Head?*[201]

In spite of the great popularity of pantomime, many stalwart defenders of true English taste regarded it as low and barbaric buffoonery, unworthy of the attention so many foolish people gave it. As *Pasquin*, 4 February 1724, expressed it:

> Between the fashionable *Gout* for Opera's on the one Hand, and the more unaccountable Curiosity for I know not what [Pantomime] on the other, all Taste and Relish for the manly and sublime Pleasures of the Stage are as absolutely lost and forgotten, as though such Things had never been. Custom indeed so far prevails, that the Play (in Point of Order only) precedes the Dance; but 'tis visible that the Audience languishes through the whole Representation, and discovers the utmost Impatience till *Harlequin* enters, to relieve them from the Fatigue of Sense, Reason, and Method, by his most incomprehensible Dexterities.

The *Universal Spectator*, 10 April 1731, looked with sorrow upon the contemporary scene.

> In the present Condition of Theatrical Entertainments, the true End of the Stage is almost wholly lost; we go not thither to see Folly exposed, but to see it acted; whence the Paradox is solved, That the most applauded Pieces for some Years past in our Theatres, have not been the Composition of *Poets*, but of *Dancing-Masters*.

This critical attitude implied that spectators no longer genuinely wished to have their minds elevated by the drama. The Prologue to *The Beggar's Wedding*, 29 May 1729, emphasized this point.

> *Fruitless has Nature join'd the Poet's Art,*
> *Vice to suppress, and Virtue to impart;*
> *A good Machine alone can win the Heart.*
> . . . .
> *What, please the Mind! No, rather take the Eye,*
> *On Carpenters, not Poets we rely.*

Mist's Weekly Journal, 14 January 1727, stressed the rage for the "*irrational class*" of entertainments (operas, rope-dancing, Italian farces, and panto-

[201] See *British Journal*, 29 February 1724.

mimes). The writer added: "The *rational* . . . can be only *Tragedy* and *Comedy*. And to what a low Ebb of Success these two Branches are shrunk, the Receipts of the Play-Houses, (when they are ventur'd *nakedly* to the Town), are mournful Evidences."

As is readily apparent, Italian opera and *commedia dell'arte* came in for ridicule from many who saw in it foreign novelty, effeminacy, and luxury, with both opera and foreign performers foolishly and lavishly admired by many Englishmen who should have known better. Almost from the first appearance of Italian opera in London, writers had lightly or caustically lamented the "fashionable Gout" for it; the *Tatler* and *Spectator* are cases in point. As the Prologue to *The Fashionable Lover*, April 1706, emphasized, in the past

> *The Poets Labour, then the Player grac'd,*
> *E're* SHAKESPEAR *was with Mimmickry debas'd.*
> *As Foreign Opera's were so much known,*
> *And squawling Songsters so bewitch'd the Town.*

Because both the operas and foreign plays were uttered in languages which relatively few Englishmen understood well, their popularity seemed faddish, irrational, foolish. Lamenting a proposal to bring a foreign company to London, the *Weekly Journal or Saturday's Post*, 5 October 1717, argued that the "only Plea offered for this Attempt" was the fact that the King was "perfect Master of the French Tongue," an argument of little weight, the writer thought, since few Englishmen had the same facility. Opera never really escaped attack, for many objected to the high salaries paid Italian singers as contrasted with lower ones for English actors; others felt that Italian music displaced native melodies. Occasionally, as in the *British Journal*, 9 January 1731, a writer expressed the belief that the English genuinely loved music and that, since the words of Italian opera were "below Criticism," English operas, if phrased well to fine music, could restore native supremacy in this realm. He cited Addison's *Rosamond* as an example.

Of course, the other side of the coin showed itself. Writers defended many new plays, perhaps over-admiring them as much as others underrated them. Some saw pantomime and spectacle not only as good entertainment but as contributing to the invention of new scenes, machines, decorations, and ingenious designs. Others saw in the love of opera a reflection of English liking for fine music and in ballad opera a resurgence of native popular music. Commentators emphasized also that the broadening of the evening's show brought to the theatre an array of talents and entertainments to please wider segments of the public. As Richard Leveridge pointed out in the preface to *Pyramus and Thisbe*, 11 April 1716: "As Diversion is the Business of the Stage, 'tis Variety best contributes to that Diversion." *Pasquin*, on 4 March 1724, discussing pantomime, made the point that "I would not here be thought to condemn Dancing in general; I know it is an Entertainment very proper for the Stage, and may artfully be made use of to divert the Spectator, when Necessity requires that some considerable Time be spent between the Acts."

On the whole, however, it remained for the 1730's to develop more fully the principle of dramatic criticism as a proper function of a newspaper or journal, and although the following decades did not materially alter some of these undercurrents of taste, many new and vigorous journals made criticism more lively, more systematic, occasionally more sophisticated and penetrating. The first thirty years of the century made a beginning of dramatic criticism in the public press, but it remained for the *British Journal*, *Universal Spectator*, *Grub Street Journal*, and *Prompter* to look at the theatre fully and continuously. In turn, some of the daily newspapers which had begun publication in the 1710's and 1720's devoted more space to dramatic criticism; for example, the *Daily Journal* in the 1730's often reprinted essays from the *Prompter* and had at one time a very illuminating series of its own entitled "The Occasional Prompter." It is to these that one must turn to see the full course of theatrical criticism which the opening years of the century initiated.

INDEX